# The Cristero Counterrevolution

# The
# CRISTERO
# Counterrevolution
## AND THE BATTLE FOR
## THE SOUL OF MEXICO

✳ ✳ ✳

FR. JAVIER P. OLIVERA RAVASI, SE

*Foreword by Alfredo Sáenz, SJ*

Os Justi
Press

First published in Spanish by Katejon Editions, Buenos Aires, 2019;
republished by Parresía Ediciones, Buenos Aires, 2021
English edition © 2025 Javier P. Olivera Ravasi
Translated from the 3rd edition, corrected and augmented

Os Justi Press
P.O. Box 21814
Lincoln, NE 68542
www.osjustipress.com

Send inquiries to
info@osjustipress.com

ISBN 978-1-965303-45-0 (paperback)
ISBN 978-1-965303-46-7 (hardcover)
ISBN 978-1-965303-47-4 (ebook)

Layout by Michael Schrauzer
Cover by Julian Kwasniewski
Cover image: Niño Soldado, Archivo General
de la Nación, Wikimedia Commons

# CONTENTS

# FOREWORD

I T IS A REAL PLEASURE FOR ME TO HAVE THE OPPOR-
tunity to preface this excellent study of the feats of the Cristeros,
heroes of one of the most glorious episodes of Church history
in the twentieth century. I will limit myself here to highlighting the
author's main accomplishments.

First, I appreciate the excellent analysis offered when he discusses
the era's early antecedents. He focuses especially on the ill-fated development of the twentieth century, highlighting the paradigmatic figure
of Agustín de Iturbide. First Emperor of Mexico, Iturbide raised the
flag of Christianity in his fatherland, in continuity with the project
of missionary Spain, as well as proposing to maintain the respect
with which the Indians were treated by the conquerors and first
settlers from the mother country. These aims were embodied by the
great leader in the colors of the flag of independent Mexico. Shortly
after, Benito Juárez came to power, with a consequent "revenge" of
worldliness: the mid-century liberal constitution and the persistent
attempt to secularize the country. Here, already charted, are the
two lines that tragically intersect in Mexico's history: the vertical of
the Hispanic-Catholic tradition, and the horizontal of modernity,
namely, the massive anti-Christian revolution of recent centuries. A
difficult clash, to be sure, but at the same time a brilliant expression
of the deep struggle framing the era of the Cristero war. Without this
background, it is impossible to understand this heroic act.

Going beyond merely economic or political interpretations, Father
Javier Olivera Ravasi outlines this struggle in the context of the great
Augustinian vision of history. "Two loves founded two cities," said
that Father of the Church and great theologian of history. "Love
of God to the point of contempt for self, which is the City of God,
and the exaltation of man to the point of contempt for God, which
is the city of the world."

Historical events, to be fully understood, must be considered
from God's perspective, from that of the divine plan of humanity's
redemption through the blood of Christ. These two worldviews have
clashed over the centuries. In the twentieth century, the faction of
"modernity" acquired a special power. It excludes God, and is inimical
to the Kingship of Christ.

Anacleto González Flores, the great martyr of the Cristero era, was Mexico's best teacher of the true and deepest interpretation of history, of the theology of history. He was able to gather numerous young people around himself, helping them understand that the struggle in which they were engaged was not reducible to an incidental and random fight, but was another chapter in the age-old confrontation of two radically antagonistic worldviews. He explained that Mexico and, more generally, Latin America, was the heiress of imperial Spain. The vocation of Spain, he wrote, had a glorious origin in eight centuries of fighting the Muslim hordes, sword in hand. This continued with Charles V, the vanguard against Luther and the princes who seconded the new and destructive ideas. Philip II personified his ideal of justice. Later in the Ibero-American provinces, this force created nations — always in continuity with that day in 718 when Pelayo of Asturias made the first cry of reconquest sound. González Flores continues:

> Our vocation, traditionally, historically, spiritually, religiously, and politically, is the same as Spain's. And in following the open path of Spain's vocation, lies the secret of our strength, our victories, our prosperity as a people and a race. Together with Spain, the Catholic Church came to our land, blessing the foundations our nationality is built upon. She lit the torch of the Gospel in the dark soul of the Indians. She put on the conquerors' lips the precepts of a new civilization. She was present in schools, colleges, universities, to pronounce her word from the seat of authority. She was present in all the moments of life — birth, study, youth, love, marriage, old age, and the grave.
>
> After the glorious project of Hispanic identity had been achieved, the anti-Catholic, and anti-Hispanic spirit loomed on the horizon. This is the great subversive movement of modernity, embodied in three enemies: the Revolution, Protestantism, and Freemasonry. The first opponent, Revolution, found in modern Mexico a terrifying realization in the 1917 Constitution of Querétaro, a nefarious attempt to dislodge the Church from its proud and longstanding achievements. Confronted with the nuptials between Spain and our virgin land, the Revolution sought to celebrate a new marriage, obviously in the dark and in the mysterious shadows of error and evil. The new and dissolute ideas entered the body of the Mexican fatherland, like an evil potion or an epidemic penetrating even the flesh and bones, creating generations of blind, paralyzed, and mute of spirit.

In Mexico the intention was to overthrow the nation's cultural and religious inheritance. González Flores expresses it brilliantly:

> The revolutionary has no home, neither of stone nor of spirit. His home is a phantom that must be made with the collapse of everything that exists. That is why he has sworn to demolish our home, that home where for three centuries, missionaries, conquerors and teachers sweated and bled to build foundations and roofs. And then they drew up the plan for another home, that of the future. So far, they have not managed to completely demolish the home we have built in these three centuries. If they have not been able to do so, it is because there are still forces that resist, because Ripalda, the old and frayed [catechism of] Ripalda, like the atlas of mythology, maintains the pillars of authority, property, and family. They persist in invading our home, with their political banners: temples, homes, schools, workshops, consciences, language, everything. They are invaders. They are intruders. So far, they have only succeeded in destroying. They seem incapable of building.

Along with the devastating Revolution, González Flores denounced the battering ram of Protestantism, which came to Mexico mainly through the influence of the United States. González Flores recalls what Theodore Roosevelt said when asked if the assimilation of the Spanish-American peoples by the United States would happen soon: "I think it will take a long time, so long as these countries are Catholic." The old clash between Philip II of Spain and Elizabeth II of England was now renewed between traditional Mexico and the forces of Protestantism that tried to penetrate everywhere, thereby reaching the heart of the masses, taking hold of the youth, and overrunning everything.

The third enemy is Freemasonry, which raises the banner of rebellion against God and against His Church. González Flores sees it incarnated especially in the ideology of the French Revolution, mother of liberal democracy. This arrived in Mexico also primarily through the mediation of the United States. Its great lie is *universal suffrage*. Any man taken from the formless mass is believed to be capable of taking into his hands the supreme leadership of the country. He can be a minister, legislator, or president. Simultaneously, it does not promote personal initiative; tenacious and individual labor is not rewarded. "Our democracy," he said, "has been endless Stations of the Cross, the worst part of which has fallen on the so-called sovereign people. First, they were proclaimed king, then they were crowned with thorns, a reed scepter was placed in their hands; they were dressed in rags and, then naked, they were covered with spittle."

Modern democracy, González Flores goes on to explain, is based on a mendacious slogan, that of absolute equality: "They threw themselves into the arms of number, of its rigorously mathematical results, and serenely awaited the reappearance of the Golden Age. Their democracy turned out to be a counting machine." The proponents of this system regard humanity as an immense mass of figures where each man is valued not for what he is, but as part of a whole, as a mere unit. "And if that democracy does not need wise men, or poets, it does not need heroes, or saints either." Why make an effort? Why sacrifice ourselves to improve ourselves if, in the swamp, life is a counting machine, and each man is worth as much as the others? Thus there has been a generalized collapse, a devastating and dizzying decline. We have all gone down, everything has declined. "We crawl under the burden of our terrifying misery, of our overwhelming impoverishment."

In González Flores's opinion, the three great instigators of anti-Christian and anti-Mexican politics were the revolution, Protestantism, and Freemasonry:

> The revolution, which is a faithful ally of both Protestantism
> and Freemasonry, continues its tenacious march towards the
> demolition of Catholicism and defeats the Catholic way of
> thinking in the press, schools, streets, squares, in parliaments,
> in laws; everywhere. We are in the presence of a conspiracy
> against the Church's sacred principles.

Father Javier Olivera Ravasi expands on these topics in this book. Consider the instructive analysis he offers us on Freemasonry in the nineteenth century and the first decades of the twentieth, with special attention to its various groups and currents. To this could also be added, not only the ideology of the French Revolution, but also that of the Soviet Revolution. Its leaders took power in Russia in 1917, shortly before the Cristero uprising, and specifically inspired the trade unions attached to the persecuting government.

The motto of the Catholic uprising was unambiguous: "For God and Country." The struggle was carried out in defense of Catholicism and Mexican nationalism. Both of these were being attacked by an enemy of God and the nation, an enemy who held power with foreign support. It was a matter of two hierarchical loves: love of the violated fatherland, subordinated to the love of God. This is why those who died for the sake of the fatherland can be considered authentic martyrs, according to the teachings of St. Thomas Aquinas. The battle cry of those heroes — "*¡Viva, Cristo Rey!*" (Long live Christ the King!), which earned for them the derisive name of "Cristeros" from their enemies — became not only a slogan or formula of recognition, but a complete interpretation. When St. Augustine wrote of the two Cities, he did not hesitate to point out that each had its own ruler: in the City of God it was Christ, and in the city of the world it was Satan. It is not surprising, therefore, that the two contending armies should exalt their respective Captains. To the question of the "federales," that is, of the soldiers of the antagonistic government, "Who goes there?," the Cristeros always answered, "Long live Christ the King!" Their adversaries, for their part, did not hesitate to shout: "Long live Satan!"

It was, in fact, a religious war, a theological war, as we have repeatedly noted. President Plutarco Elías Calles, the head of the repression, was described by some chroniclers as "a mystical man." Yes, but an inverse mysticism — that of Satan. The persecutor president understood, albeit in his own way, that the war he was waging was not reducible to mere political designs but hid religious roots. An American journalist who interviewed him at the time on the religious question, admitted that he was dismayed at the words he heard him say: "I saw at the bottom of them [viz., the words] not the hatred of one life, but a hatred of many generations." Emilio Portes Gil, who succeeded Calles as president, said something similar at the end of a banquet: "The battle is not beginning. The battle is eternal. The battle began twenty centuries ago." We might say, from our standpoint, that it began even earlier, much earlier, at the beginning of human history; having its turning-point in the personal confrontation between Christ and Satan in the wilderness. An eyewitness tells us that during the Cristero War he attended a banquet in Guanajuato, in enemy-held territory, which degenerated into a true orgy. The general who presided over it, "after damning Christ and the Immaculate Virgin with obscenities, toasted Lucifer to howls of approval." The insults were forceful: "Death to Christ! Down with Christ! Crush Christ! May our god be Lucifer! He is our leader! Up with Lucifer! Long live Lucifer!"

In conclusion, I would like to emphasize the very wise way in which the author has addressed the last and painful chapter of the Cristero era, the so-called "Settlements (*los Arreglos*)," which ended the conflict.[1] Father Olivera Ravasi points out, with due delicacy and respect, the various responsibilities in these "settlements," which many of the signatories knew would not be fulfilled. The Church yielded its previous positions, and the State allowed its places of worship to reopen, without repealing the very laws that had been the cause of the uprising in the first place.

Referring to the saga of the Vendée, which occurred in France two centuries earlier, of which the exploits of the Cristeros are almost a replica, a French author, Reynald Secher, pointed out that the genocide of the Vendéans, carried out by the army of the French Revolution, was followed by a new genocide. However, this was an intellectual one. He called it memoricide. Thanks to this, the Vendéans' heroic feats became a taboo subject which should not be mentioned—a subject deliberately forgotten. According to the official version, it was a group of "bandits" who took up arms and were suppressed. Here, too, we have witnessed a long-term memoricide. In Mexico, until recently, this issue could not even be discussed; the memory of the events had been erased. Javier Olivera Ravasi courageously refuses to comply with this iniquitous decision and, he has done so with deep understanding. I offer him warm congratulations.

Alfredo Sáenz, SJ

---

[1] Note to the reader: the term *los Arreglos* could be rendered with numerous English words: "arrangements," "settlements," "agreements," "accords," even "compromises." However, "settlements" is probably the best of these terms inasmuch as it conveys multiple ideas, and even a hint of disappointment (for the Catholics indeed settled for less than they had hoped and fought for).

# PREFACE

*There were two worlds, two worldviews.*

—Alfredo Sáenz[1]

*Those who preside over the government of the Republic are waging a war against the Catholic religion.*

—Pius XI

TO BE TREATED AS IT DESERVES, THIS LONG-silenced part of Mexican history would require numerous volumes merely to cover the documents and testimonies otherwise inaccessible to the general public. It so happens that the great Cristero drama has been one of the episodes of the history of the Americas almost ignored outside of Mexico. Thirty long years had to pass before scholars began to dedicate the necessary time and attention in the 1960s to the period that will concern us here. What happened? What havoc occurred so that such a deafening silence controlled both the ecclesiastical hierarchy and the Mexican State?

A new phenomenon was unleashed in Mexico: two worldviews[2] confronted each other in the manner of two religions.[3] Indeed, in the middle of the twentieth century, as Alfredo Sáenz writes,

---

[1] *La nave y las tempestades. La gesta de los cristeros* (Gladius, 2012), 408.

[2] It is worth clarifying here that, when we speak in this work of "two conflicting worldviews" we are referring, in all cases, to the Christian worldview against that of the world. The Pope, the bishops, the priests and the faithful advocated a free and Catholic Mexico, while the Mexican government advocated a state secularism according to liberal and Masonic principles, as we will show.

[3] "*It is a clash of two faiths, a war of religions*, and the leaders who pretend to be attentive to the people's feelings despise and want to transform a 'fanatical' people. Moreover, *the religion of unbelief that they want to impose* is no less fanatical than the other that they want to destroy" (Jean Meyer, *La Cristiada* [Siglo veintiuno, México 1974²], 2:211, emphasis ours). Later he would add: "it is a *real war of religion* that begins in August 1926" (ibid., 231). Henceforth, referring to the same edition, we will abbreviate the work and cite only the volume and page. Regarding the well-known historian of the *Cristiada*, Jean Meyer, to whom we refer multiple times, it is worth observing that the use of his famous work as well as the testimonies collected by him are absolutely essential. The fact is that—beyond the judgments that his assessments deserve—the work that he undertook during "official silence" (personal interviews with eyewitnesses, unpublished documents, recordings on magnetic tapes and graphic documentation, etc.) cannot be avoided without detriment to the truth; a book, article or review that is read on the subject will rarely omit his name.

a theological conflict developed between the traditional spirit of Christianity, which came to our lands thanks to the Spain of the Habsburgs, and embodied in Mexico by Agustín de Iturbide. Opposing this was the French spirit, promoted by Freemasonry and the United States of America, and embodied by Benito Juárez in the nineteenth century, and by Plutarco Elías Calles in the twentieth century.[4]

The radicalism of the Mexican government, when it sought to create a society dispensing with God and his Church amongst a fervently Catholic people, caused the seeds planted previously during the conquest and evangelization to germinate suddenly and defend against the looming revolution. A new worldview attempted to implant itself in "Catholic and Guadalupan" Mexico: a revolution that tried to overturn, to shake the foundations of society. This caused the opposite effect in a large part of Mexicans who preferred to defend and assail with a counterrevolution in the classical meaning of the word: seeking the opposite of revolution.[5]

It was a question of doing the reverse, as counterrevolutionaries had done in the uprising of the Vendée region in France against the French Revolution, or in the uprising of "White Russians" against Bolshevism.

A new religion sought to be implanted in Mexico in the name of the Revolution and it encountered a huge barrier formed by simple people in a nation that would have to fight not only against the overwhelming defiance of conscience but also against a part of the ecclesiastical hierarchy that would accuse them of "rebelling" against authority—a two-pronged struggle that would cost them dearly. It was not a rebellion, but a struggle for the survival of the people;[6] not

---

[4] Sáenz, *La nave y las tempestades*, 409.

[5] "What they call counter-revolution will not be a contrary revolution at all, but the opposite of the revolution" ( Joseph de Maistre, *Consideraciones sobre Francia* [Dictio, 1980], 147). When the Cristero leader heard that they were called "revolutionaries," he protested violently, adding that "it is exactly the opposite of a revolution." Meyer, *La Cristiada*, 3:145.

[6] The Archbishop of Durango, Monsignor José María González y Valencia, who was convinced that the uprisings constituted a true act of legitimate defense, wrote to Monsignor Pascual Díaz, secretary of the Episcopal Committee, regarding some statements by the latter in which the legality of the movement was questioned: "We are very surprised that Your Most Illustrious Lordship clearly condemns the movement of legitimate defense; it is neither rebellion nor revolution." José María González y Valencia, *Letter to Mgr. Pascual Díaz*, 16-II-1927, cited by Andrés Barquín y Ruiz, *José María González y Valencia, Arzobispo de Durango* ( JUS, 1967), 50.

a revolution, but a coordinated movement of all the active powers of the country to oppose revolution.

It must also be noted that this was a war of the State against the people. This is worth stressing, since in superficial historical analyses, revolutions are usually presented as popular movements and counterrevolutionary movements as movements directed and manipulated by social elites. The history of the Mexican Cristeros and that of the great modern counterrevolutionary movements show the opposite: they are genuinely "of the people." Most of these movements began without the support of the major powers of their time, whether civil or ecclesial, as we will try to demonstrate. Most of the time, they take up arms against revolution, because their conscience commands it, and against all predictions or political calculations. As Azcué said, it is the "clear image of a Christian people that refuses to die at the hands of modern revolution."[7]

In the present study, we will focus on the most important years of this tragic drama, namely 1926 to 1929, making use of classic and current bibliography, and dividing the book into the context and background, the attitude of the independent Mexican laity, and the consequences of the tragic conflict.

We will enter, thus into an infinite, transcendent and eternal history: a story guided by two loves, as St. Augustine said. Self-love to the point of contempt for God and the love of God to the point of disregard of self.

---

[7] Quoted by Sáenz, *La nave y las tempestades*, 356.

# PART I
# The Background

\* \* \*

## TWO CONFLICTING
## WORLDVIEWS

# I

# A Revolution Against the People

*Poor Mexico: so far from God and so close to the United States.*
— Porfirio Díaz

I T IS NOT EASY TO SUMMARIZE THE HISTORY OF Mexico in one chapter; however, we must give an initial over-view so as to situate ourselves in the political context that lead, like a hurricane, to the phenomenon we are about to discuss.

## INSURGENCY VERSUS INDEPENDENCE

As Enrique Díaz Araujo correctly observes,[1] Mexico's independence, unlike that of other colonies of the Kingdom of the Indies, had two well-marked periods: that of the "insurgency" (1810–1821) and that of the "national war" (1821).[2]

In the first period, coincidentally, two priests have been named for posterity as the leaders of the insurgency against the *"gachupines"* (Spaniards): Miguel Hidalgo and José María Morelos. They opposed the colonial government against King Ferdinand VII, and displayed anti-Spanish hatred. They even went so far as to murder "peninsulars" for the mere fact of being born in Spain, as Carlos Pereyra, the American historian, points out: "Death to the *gachupines!* From the shout (*grito*) he went to deeds. In the silence of the night, shielded by his own mobs, Hidalgo murdered European Spaniards, believing that by imprisoning and exterminating them that the last obstacle to Independence would vanish."[3] As José Vasconcelos rightly said, "with Hidalgo a series of conflicts began in which nothing was achieved but destroying the work of generations for the sake of swapping certain rich people with others, always to the advantage of the foreign capitalist."[4] There were two ways of achieving independence and these churchmen chose the worst. Instead of peaceful autonomy, they opted for an unjustified and savage battle against one class of society,

---

[1]  See Enrique Díaz Araujo, *La Epopeya Cristera* (IVE Press, 2013), 20.
[2]  See José Bravo Ugarte, *Compendio de Historia de México, hasta 1964* (JUS, 1968), 141.
[3]  Carlos Pereyra, *México falsificado* (Folia universitaria, 2003), 1:28.
[4]  José Vasconcelos, *Breve Historia de México* (Cultura Hispánica, 1952), 287.

mixing resentment of everything "old" with racial and social hatred.

This seed of independence did not have the desired effect and, although official historiography continued to extol the clergy's liberating work, it was not until 1820 — with Don Agustín de Iturbide, the great liberator of the north — that Mexican independence was achieved with a different outlook, as Iturbide himself stated:

> The division of North America is inevitable... Then let it be done, Lord, without the cost of blood from the same family. Let the glorious decree come from the center of wisdom and let the fathers of the country (that is, the congressmen) be the ones who sanction the peaceful separation of America. Let a Sovereign of the house of Ferdinand the Great come here to occupy the happy throne which the sensible Americans prepare for him and let the closest of friendships be established between the two august monarchs, in union with the Sovereign Congresses, amazing the whole world with such a sweet division.[5]

The "peaceful and prudent liberator of the north," as Iturbide was called in almost all Central America, established his "tri-guarantor pact" for independence from Spain. It was not a question, in his view, of breaking completely with the founders but of making a harmonious separation. This pact comprised three main points: national independence (avoiding ethical rupture with Spain), the union of all social classes (Spaniards, Creoles, and Indians), and the Catholic religion as the spiritual basis of Mexican life. Beyond the criticism that can be made of Iturbide (Agustín I, as he came to be known), his strategy achieved a temporary peace despite certain blunders he committed in his administration, as Carlos Pereyra notes.[6]

The aforementioned safeguards were initially able to ensure the three fundamental features. However, it was not long before former "insurgents" discovered in caudillista anarchism their natural ally against the only thing they did not fully accept: religion as part of the national identity.[7] This, added to the actions of the U.S. (which wanted a weak bordering country), caused the resentment at the efforts of the great liberator.

---

[5] Pereyra, *México falsificado*, 1:33.

[6] Pereyra, 1:38.

[7] Pereyra (1:35) describes as "irreligious" the followers of Hidalgo and Morelos, who in a strict sense "did not act as freethinkers, nor as philosophers in the French style, but as mere scoundrels."

The work of American ambassador Joel Roberts Poinsett came into play here. His idea was to establish a federal and secular republic in the southern country, casting aside all existing Catholic and Hispanic values. With the collaboration of the Freemasons and Liberals Lorenzo de Zavala, Valentín Gómez Farías, and the constitutionalists José María Luis Mora, Friar Servando Teresa de Mier, Miguel Ramos Arizpe, and others, Poinsett achieved his objectives: the dismissal of Agustín de Iturbide, the installation of the government of General Vicente Guerrero (a collaborator with the U.S.), approval of the Constitution of 1848, Central American separatism, anti-Catholic propaganda, and the Texas War. The latter was badly mishandled by the "traitor Antonio López de Santa Anna,"[8] and concluded in the Treaty of Guadalupe-Hidalgo, of February 2, 1848, by which Mexico would lose Texas, New Mexico, Arizona, and Alta California, forever.

With the execution of Iturbide in 1824, another idea of Mexico was born.[9] It would be left to internal conspiracies and external interests, without a historical and moral framework to support it. It was, perhaps, only during the period of Lucas Alamán as Secretary of Foreign Affairs of Mexico that a national defense policy was conceived; but it did not manage to last. As Vasconcelos said, "Mexican foreign policy was subordinated to the United States."[10]

MEXICAN LIBERALISM

The second important moment in Mexican history in the middle of the nineteenth century, was the "Reform" by Benito Juárez, which eventually led to the Constitution of 1857 and the laws that followed it in 1873 with Sebastián Lerdo de Tejada. If at the time of the insurgency anticlericalism and anti-Hispanic sentiment existed in an incipient way, here the obviously liberal and anti-Hispanic claims began to appear; that Spain was the Church and the Church was Spain for the reformers,

---

[8] Vasconcelos, *Breve Historia*, 362.
[9] Vasconcelos notes rightly that "the peace treaties called Guadalupe, signed by a provisional President, took Texas away from us as far as the Rio Bravo, New Mexico, populated to this day by Mexicans, Arizona, and California. The most shameful thing about the treaties was the form of land purchase that was given to them, from the moment that the compensation of fifteen million pesos was accepted. For fifteen million they sold our brethren in New Mexico and California into slavery, without consulting us. Much more honorable would have been to accept that the victor would take what he wanted, but without staining the fatherland with the gold of a conquest that was accepted and valued. But who could understand honor in a country that had a Santa Anna as its hero?" (*Breve Historia*, 372).
[10] Vasconcelos, 321.

and therefore that Mexico had to be refounded, "Americanized" and even "Protestantized" if it were to progress:

> Mexico's problems...would be solved instantly by the nationalization of Church property and the establishment of secular public schools. Many of the first proponents of progressivism were sincerely Catholic, but not a few longed for the time when Mexico would become Protestantized, imitating the model of the United States. The fabulously wealthy country had only one obstacle to its prosperity. When the ecclesiastical stranglehold disappeared, economic factors would come into play, thus reviving the moribund nation.[11]

In the Constitution of 1857, the Reform Laws of President Juárez (1859–1863), and those promulgated by President Lerdo de Tejada in 1873, violence against the Church would intensify. In the words of Octavio Paz, this was "rupture with Mother Spain, with Mother Church."[12]

But liberalism would go further, even if its measures were to the detriment of national sovereignty itself. This was the case of the famous McLane-Ocampo treaty, which was the frightful granting in perpetuity of right of passage by three different roads to the United States (1859), mainly through the Isthmus of Tehuantepec, in order to link the two oceans. This concession was given by Benito Juárez in exchange for American support for the development of his Jacobin government. Ultimately the U.S. Senate never endorsed the treaty. But the intention of selling out was clear.

The situation became worse and worse and if Mexico lacked anything, it was foreign intervention. Indeed, after the so-called Three Years' War or Reform War (1857–1861), when the liberal and conservative sides bitterly clashed, the country was impoverished. Debts came due and the Juárez government decided to suspend payments on foreign debt, which did not please the foreign powers, mainly France, England and Spain. Seeing their interests threatened, the three powers agreed to carry out an armed expedition that would "support" justice in the country. Thus, Napoleon III's dream of a grand "Latin Empire of the West" would be fulfilled.

Accordingly, with the support of France and having withdrawn from the conflict with England and Spain, the Archduke of Austria, Ferdinand Maximilian was appointed emperor of Mexico (1864) after a few battles. He was in power for only three years. Cultured, but

---

[11] Pereyra, *México falsificado*, 1:46–47.
[12] Quoted by Meyer, *La Cristiada*, 2:27.

without firm character and, moreover, with somewhat utopian and even liberal ideas (for instance, he permitted the sale of ecclesiastical property), Maximilian I was not able to stay in power. His lack of vigor, France's delay in helping in Mexico's economic recovery, and the U.S. pressure left Maximilian in the lurch. Poorly advised and after hesitating about his abdication, he was imprisoned on May 15, 1867, a result of the disastrous campaign by generals Miguel Miramón and Tomás Mejía. A month later he was executed with them.[13]

With the fall of Maximilian, the regime moved rapidly towards the most radical liberalism. The laws with regard to religion were an obvious sign of this, as can be seen in the legislation of the period. Yet it would take a further decade to see in practice what was to be the breeding ground for the issue under consideration. Hence, the famous "Lerdo Law"[14] of 1873 stated in article 3 that holidays "that do not have the exclusive purpose of solemnizing purely civil events" were prohibited. In article 4, religious instruction was prohibited and, in article 5, any act of worship outside the churches as well as the use of ecclesiastical clothing in public was forbidden.[15] These laws went against not only that which was "ancient" and "Catholic"; they went directly against the people. The fact is that when the confiscation of ecclesiastical properties began, the measures harmed civilians, clergy, indigenous people — all social sectors were affected.

It was at this point that certain public figures came into play, after the "Reform" and the laws of Lerdo de Tejada, which are the antecedents of our subject. This was the case of the "*religioneros*," men who rose up especially in the regions of Jalisco, Michoacán, Guanajuato, and Querétaro, between 1873 and 1876 against the government's anti-Catholic policies and excessive pro-Yankeeism. "For God and Country" was their cry. These battles, in the style of "guerrilla warfare," eventually brought about the fall of Lerdo de Tejada and the rise of Don Porfirio Díaz. In fact, when tempers cooled and in the face of constant revolts, the government of Lerdo de Tejada was overthrown by Díaz in 1876. He remained in power until 1911 (with only interruption of the "dauphin," Manuel González Flores, from 1880

---

[13] See Pereyra, *Breve Historia de América* (Zig-Zag, 1946²), 537–41.

[14] The "Lerdo Law" is known as the *Law of Confiscation of Rural and Urban Properties of the Civil and Religious Corporations of Mexico*, issued on June 25, 1856, but regulated with constitutional rank in 1873.

[15] See Luis J. de la Peña, *La legislación mexicana en relación con la Iglesia* (Universidad de Navarra, 1965), 24–25, quoted by Juan González Morfin, *La guerra cristera y su licitud moral* (Porrua-Universidad Panamericana, 2009), 85.

to 1884). Don Porfirio knew how to man the helm and, although a
liberal dictatorship was maintained, his attitude towards the Church
was one of relative tolerance, ignoring, in practice, the anticlerical
legislation in force. He understood, as we will show later, that to
persecute the Church was to persecute Mexico. But not everything
was peaceful in the "Porfiriato"—the era of Díaz.

When U.S. President William Howard Taft became annoyed with
Díaz's refusal to extend the term of the lease of Magdalena Bay to the
United States, he apparently ordered 20,000 U.S. soldiers from San
Antonio, Texas, to lend support to Francisco I. Madero's maneuvers in
Ciudad Juárez to oust Don Porfirio. That was how the Mexican *caudi-
llos* came on the scene, without knowing it served the cause of the U.S.
As President Wilson later said, referring to Mexico as if it were a child,
"I am going to teach the South American republics to elect good men."[16]

## THE REVOLUTION

After the Porfirian dictatorship and after several years of governance,
in 1911, the regime transferred command to a civilian: Francisco I.
Madero, an ally of the United States. He did not last long in office,
and given the social problems that Mexico had been suffering and
his lack of expertise in managing matters, the United States became
convinced of the need for a strong political party that knew how to
maintain order in the country. An anarchic period then began, which
included the assassination of Madero by General Victoriano Huerta
and the uprising of the *caudillos* of Sonora in the north (among them
Francisco "Pancho" Villa and in the south, Emiliano Zapata).

The new ruler, Huerta, had risen to power after multiple alliances
and his stability was weak. After dissolving Congress and effecting
some unpopular measures, he was immersed in the tension that swept
over Mexico due to the assassination of the previous president, who
had been democratically elected. To all this was added the Church's
recommendation that Catholics should not participate in the government because it lacked the legitimacy to rule.[17]

At the same time, General Venustiano Carranza, governor of the
northern state of Coahuila, was one of the first military officers to

---

[16] Ángel Lascuráin y Osio, *La segunda intervención americana* (JUS, 1957), quoted
by Antonio Rius Facius, *La Juventud Católica y la Revolución Mexicana, 1910–1925*
(JUS, 1963), 54.

[17] See ASV [Vatican Secret Archive], *Archivio della Delegazione Apostolica in
Messico*, Fasc. 108, 89, quoted by González Morfin, *La guerra cristera*, 87.

reject Huerta's regime. Little by little, he succeeded in imposing his ideas, dominating the national territory, and taking power. Venustiano Carranza's reign, the great inspirer of the Constitution of Querétaro of 1917, was a model of barbaric illegality: "the new Juárez, enemy of the Church and the landowners, and friend of the Indian...and of the Yankees,"[18] Rius Facius called him. The level of illegality reached such a point that, to this day, the verb *"carrancear"* means in Mexico the insolence of theft accompanied by cruelty against the victims. But the term changed over time and, perhaps to clear Carranza's name, during Calles' presidency this concept began to be known as *la mordida*, "the bite" (bribery), according to Pereyra.[19] A governor of Querétaro surnamed Llaca, according to Meyer, said at that time: "if I don't take the opportunity to steal now when I can, then when am I going to do it...?"[20]

With Carranza's ascent to power, the Church began to be called the "ally of the Huerta government" so that from this point on there was not only the intensification of the government's campaign to discredit the Church, but also the promotion of the looting of churches, convents, and ecclesiastical properties, not to mention the murder of clergy for the simple fact of being clergy. In this period fell the martyrdom of Father David Galván Bermúdez. On January 31, 1915, he was shot merely for confessing the dying on the streets of Guadalajara.[21] The people were so upset that Pope Benedict XV himself wrote a personal letter to Archbishop José Mora y del Río to express his concern about what was happening in Mexico.[22]

Anti-Christian outbursts were already the order of day in 1914:

> Carranza's governor of the state of Mexico, General Arnulfo Gómez, issued a decree prohibiting sermons, fasting, discipline, baptisms, alms-giving, requiem Masses, confession, and kissing the hand of priests.
>
> In Aguascalientes, after the burning of the confessionals and images in churches, Governor Fuentes threatened with death all priests who dared to celebrate Mass (August 4, 1914).

---

[18] Seeing the immense popular opposition that the anti-religion articles had, Carranza tried to modify them without success given the "spirit of closed sectarianism that dominated" in the legislative chambers (Antonio Rius Facius, *México Cristero* [APC, 2002], 1:130–31).

[19] Pereyra, *México falsificado*, 1:278.

[20] Meyer, *La Cristiada*, 2:186–87.

[21] Father David Galván. He was canonized on May 21, 2000, by John Paul II.

[22] Benedicto XV, Epist., *De gravi mexicanae Ecclesiae statu*, 25-X-1914, AAS [*Actae Apostolicae Sedis*] 6 (1914), 543.

In Zamora (Michoacán), the sacking of the bishop's palace
by Joaquín Amaro's troops was carved on the memory of its
inhabitants. But what the Catholics have not forgiven is the
spectacle of the old archbishop of Durango, who had taken
refuge there, sweeping the streets with the priests. On August
22, in Toluca, Brother Mariano González was shot, and the
churches of Carmen and La Merced were looted. In Puebla,
the cathedral chapter was destroyed and F. Escobedo was
appointed as administrator. The sites of the burned confes-
sionals were marked with Masonic emblems and the pulpit
was transformed into a platform open to all. Dances were held
in the chapel of the Jesuit college, the archepiscopal palace
was converted into barracks, and the religious were expelled.[23]

## THE CONSTITUTION OF 1917[24]

Carranza became the "first head of the constitutionalist army" until
new elections. To achieve an appearance of legality, a Constitutional
Congress was convened to issue a new national Constitution. The
Church's most radical opponents were called to this assembly. With
the new Constitution, they said, they were trying to respond to social
reforms demanded by the groups in favor of the Carranza revolution.

The debates began and the Constitution took shape in Querétaro.
In addition to having some valuable reforms in the social field, its
text it was influenced by the most radically anticlerical faction, which
eventually imposed its ideas into some articles. In fact, since it was
not a Congress with representatives from the entire nation but consisted solely of members of the Carranza party (with many anarcho-
syndicalist leaders), articles were added that tended to hinder, if not
in fact making impossible, the Church's action. What Bulnes came
to call the "most autocratic Constitution the world has ever known"[25]
was then approved.

Many articles could be discussed, but for our purposes there were
twelve in which the religious question was mentioned. The most
important discussed secular education (art. 3), the prohibition of
monastic vows (art. 5), the suppression of public worship (art. 24),
ecclesiastical property (art. 27), and the regulation of the clergy (art.
130), in which the juridical status of the Church was denied, requiring
the "registration of priests." Meyer summarizes thus:

[23] Meyer, La Cristiada, 2:78–79.
[24] See also Rius Facius, México Cristero, 1:113–16.
[25] Francisco Bulnes, Los grandes problemas de México (Editorial Nacional, 1952), 56.

In December 1916, the representatives of the Carranza faction, which had triumphed over the rival factions, met in Querétaro to revise the Constitution of 1857 and, after two months of tumultuous debates, finalized the text of the Constitution of 1917. From the religious point of view, this text further aggravated the legal situation of the Catholic Church. Article 130 denied any legal status and granted the federal government the power to "intervene by law in matters of worship and external discipline."

Monastic vows and religious orders were prohibited (Article 5). The Church had no right to own, acquire, or administer property, or to exercise any kind of dominion over property. All places of worship were the property of the state. It did not have the right to engage in charitable establishments or scientific research (Article 27). Ministers of religion should not criticize the fundamental laws of the country. They had no right to engage in politics, and no publication of a religious nature could comment on a "political fact" (Article 130), which immediately prohibited the entire Catholic press.

Article 130 established that the states of the federation were the only ones that could decide on the number of priests and the needs of each locality (this would be the starting point of the 1926 turmoil). Only a Mexican by birth could exercise religious ministry. It also outlawed political parties that had a religious affiliation. Article 3 provided for the secularization of primary, public, and private education.[26]

Let us analyze these points.[27]

With regard to *education*, secular education was made compulsory at all three levels, both for public and private schools, and was subject to official supervision. Thanks to the Regulation of Calles' future Secretary of Education, José Manuel Puig Casauranc, it was ruled that in school buildings there were to be "neither decorations, paintings, prints, sculptures, nor objects of religious intention or nature," "Ministers of any faith or member of a religious order of men or women" could not be their directors (see arts. 6 and 10). Later, starting in 1931, socialist education was compulsory.

With respect to *religious vows and orders*: no contract, pact or agreement establishing religious vows or monastic orders or orders of any other kind was allowed ("whatever the name or purpose for which they claim to be established"). Like the Lerdo Laws of 1873,

---

[26] Meyer, *La Cristiada*, 2:69–70.
[27] See Díaz Araujo, *La Epopeya Cristera*, 38–40.

simple secular confraternities were prohibited. Later, with the reform of Law 515 ( June 1926) of the Penal Code (art. 6) those who met in a religious community would be punished with two years in prison and the superiors of the orders with six years in prison, while women would suffer two-thirds of this penalty. And the penalty of arrest and fine remained for those who enticed someone to enter an order. In case of protest, the penalty was increased to six years of imprisonment (art. 8).

Regarding *worship*, the "crime of worship" was prohibited, and churches became state property. Religious beliefs could be practiced *in private* "as long as they did not constitute a crime," that is, spill out into the public domain. In addition, thanks to art. 19 of the penal reform established by Calles a few years later, churches that were not registered could be closed, with penalties of arrest and fines for offenders.

With respect to *property*, the Church was declared incapable of acquiring goods "through itself or through an intermediary"; all such goods passed to the State. In addition, public action was granted for their denunciation, with proof of "suspicion" being sufficient for their confiscation. On the other hand, by the reform of Calles (art. 21), those who concealed property could be punished with up to two years in prison.

*Marriage* was declared a mere "civil contract," and "the exclusive competence of public officials"; in addition, by Carranza's law, the legality of divorce was established.

Article 130 dealt with the *Regime of the Church*. It was decided not "to recognize any 'personality' on the part of the religious groups called Churches." Ministers of worship were considered persons "exercising a profession," requiring that they be "Mexicans by birth." Local legislatures would limit the number of priests in this matter, with the additional requirement that they be registered in each place of worship, without having the right to vote politically or to meet privately, or to criticize the laws or authorities or the government, like any other worker. For their part, lay Catholics could not make political comments in Catholic publications or form confessional political parties.

Moving a little ahead in order to see how the reform was enforced by the state legislatures, we see that already in October 1926, the State of Sonora established that only one priest was allowed for every ten thousand inhabitants, and in Tabasco, one for every thirty thousand inhabitants. (It was in Tabasco that Governor Garrido Canabal, in 1925, determined that "the priest should be from Tabasco, over forty years of age, with studies in the official school and *be married and of good morals*").[28]

A few paragraphs demonstrate the "spirit" of the famous Constitution of Querétaro. In one of the interventions, a certain convention member declared:

> Honorable congressmen: If ropes are lacking to hang tyrants, I will braid a friar's guts with my own hands. I began my debut speech on the rostrum of Mexico a few years ago in this way, and I have quoted this so that the assembly may appreciate my absolutely liberal reasoning.
>
> I will applaud from my seat anyone who besmirches the priests here... We all feel hatred against the clergy... Yes, on this point we are all in agreement, liberals, and radicals. Yes, all of us, if we could, we would eat the priests. Yes, honorable congressmen, I who am not a sectarian Jacobin, do not baptize my children, nor do I have any of the slavery of traditional Catholicism... I understand without strain that an ordinary deserving man, who is patriotic, brave, liberal, carefree, and only concerned with knowing how to fulfill his role as a revolutionary soldier in action, can come to the square of Querétaro and set fire in the public square to all the churches' confessionals, melt the bells, appropriate the schools of the clergy... and even hang some friars. All this seems to me perfectly reasonable among us, no one will condemn him in time of war, if he is an impartial and enlightened man... Finally, I declare myself in favor of the idea that to exercise the priesthood of any faith, it is necessary to be civilly married, if one is under fifty years of age, because I believe that the laws of nature are inviolable, and that the conservation of the species is a necessity...
>
> While Catholics believe that confession is a moral act, those of us who are not believers believe that it is an immoral

---

[28] "Tabasco, during the government of Carlos Greene, was the next state to take this step, decreeing, on December 15 of that year, that there could only be one priest for every thirty thousand inhabitants or fraction. However, as it seemed to the revolutionary clique that this law was too benign, Governor Tomás Garrido Canabal modified it on March 6, 1925, establishing that the necessary conditions to be able to exercise the priestly ministry there were: 1. Be Tabasco or Mexican by birth, with five years of residence in the State. 2. Be over forty years old. 3. Have completed primary and preparatory studies at the Official School. 4. Be of good record and morals. 5. Be married. 6. Not have been or not be subject to any [criminal legal] process" (Rius Facius, *México Cristero*, 1:301). The full law can be seen at Félix Navarrete and Eduardo Pallares, eds., *La persecución religiosa en México desde el punto de vista jurídico* (n.p., n.d.), 334-36.

act. But this immoral act cannot be prohibited by law, much less by the Constitution, because in this case we would have to prohibit a multitude of other immoral acts—for example, that onanism is forbidden [*laughter*], that it is as immoral as confession... [Priests] would not lack a "Daughter of Mary"—or someone else's daughter [*laughter*]... They would divorce, find another daughter of Mary more beautiful, and repeat the operation three, four, or five times... The only thing we would have achieved was to become suppliers of fresh meat for the priests [*applause and laughter*]... The truth is that none of us will need to find a wife for the priests [*applause*]...

I beg the prominent Catholics in this House to excuse me from heresies, which many will hear...without fear of excommunication, without fear of hell, without fear of eternal damnation [*applause and laughter*]... For me, all religious creeds have no meaning... I call [Christianity] a farce: I call it a pack of lies, of hoaxes [*laughter and applause*]... The Catholic religion brings us a dogma, which is that of the purity of Mary. I'm going to show you, gentlemen...[*whistles and laughter*]. If it is true, honorable congressmen, that the Virgin Mary is pure, then...[*laughs, whistles, and disorder; bell rung for order*]...

Honorable congressmen, we have already taken children away from clericalism, with the vote on Article 3. Now, why shouldn't we snatch the women away?... We cannot catalog how many prayers each individual needs... I am not trying to catalog the number of prayers..., but the number of friars that the people can bear... I will read you some important documents that, although they are not necessary for your vote in favor of the verdict, will show the situation beyond the Rio Bravo where our religious problem exists, and give in-depth knowledge of all the reasons and motives we Mexicans have had, not only to persecute, but even to exterminate that hydra called the priesthood...these vampires, which is the correct description that should be given to them... that black and fateful vestment that reveals nothing but the dirty and ominous spirit of those who wear it...with the sincere and firm purpose of not resting until we make the small number of vampires we have in Mexico disappear, and until we manage to exterminate them, because for me gentlemen, I confess, that would be the ideal... What great sense of justice the Mexican people have had when they have proceeded with such savagery, with so much cruelty,

sometimes with such incredible ferocity, to persecute what
we here call the clergy but who should be called a band of
thieves, outlaws, and swindlers![29]

It is worth remembering with Pereyra that these "reformers" were
submissively guided by skilled American mentors, such as the Protestant minister Samuel Guy Inman, the Freemason Robert A. Greenfield,
or the lecturer and journalist Lincoln Steffens. Among those who
benefited from this northern mentorship were Álvaro Obregón and
the future dictator Calles.

Obregón boasted of cursing the friars, while Deputy Monzón said
(to the constituents' laughter):

> Primary education, both in private schools and in offi-
> cial schools, *is rational*, because it combats error in all its
> strongholds, unlike secular education, which does not teach
> error, does not preach it, but, on the other hand, tolerates
> it with hypocritical resignation. Religious Ministers, espe-
> cially Catholic friars, do not have access to Sonoran primary
> schools, because we know that these gentlemen, when they
> intervene in the school, always find a way to instill their
> errors in the conscience of children, even when they teach
> shorthand, typing, music, or military tactics.... We know
> that the churches are veritable dens of corruption, because
> it is there that maidens' purity and also married women's
> honor are perverted. *Priests are the most irreconcilable enemies
> of civilization and libertarian revolutions.* I would like all the
> people of the Republic to be like my people.... Most of
> the inhabitants of that region aren't baptized. My children
> aren't either. They don't even have Christian names. Señor
> Bojórquez knows what my children's names are — they have
> numerical names...[30]

Once the Constitution was promulgated, some bishops were already
in exile because of the continuous harassment they suffered at the
hands of the Carranza supporters. This triggered a "Collective Pastoral Letter" in which it was noted that the Constitution of Querétaro
elevated religious persecution to legal status, sanctioning it definitively.

[29] Pereyra, *México falsificado*, 2:191–94, 206–8, 212–15, 217–19, 228. We have
limited ourselves to sentences based on Díaz Araujo's guidance, but the entire
speech that Pereyra includes is worth reading in its entirety.
[30] *Diario de los Debates del Congreso Constituyente*, 1:657; 2:1050. Quoted by
Meyer, *La Cristiada*, 2:82, emphasis ours. Let's look at the clarity of Calles'
thought: "secularism" was too soft. It was *a different worldview*, a different religion — in this case, rationalism.

"The Constitution," they said, "hurts the fundamental rights of the Catholic Church, of Mexican society, and of Christians, and proclaims principles contrary to the truths taught by Jesus Christ."[31] Therefore, Catholics, using the right that assists them, had to "work legally and *peacefully* to erase from the national laws everything that harms their conscience and their rights"[32] (note of the word "peacefully"). Even the aforementioned Benedict XV wrote a public letter to Mexican Catholics in which he urged them to resist peacefully, exhorting them to patience and to offer up sufferings unjustly endured.[33] We will return later to this pacific attitude of the Church.

The presidents who followed Carranza were Adolfo de la Huerta (1920) and Álvaro Obregón (1920–1924). Neither of them directly enforced compliance with the anticlerical requirements of the Constitution, yet anticlerical attacks were the order of the day. An example of this was the bomb that exploded in the archbishop's residence in Mexico City on February 16, 1921. The situation was increasingly complex and the impunity with which liberals acted against everything that was Catholic made the Obregón regime look like a government that supported underhanded persecution. However, it was still possible to survive, as Krauze states:

> With the Church, the tone of interactions was one of tense conciliation. Obregón congratulated the new Pope Pius XI in 1922 and privately insisted on the "complementarity" of the revolutionary and Catholic programs. But it wasn't the right time. In general, the Church was far from resigning itself to Articles 3 and 130 of the Constitution, and some bishops were fighting against the transfer of land or the unionization of lay employees. Obregón, despite his Jacobin displays in 1914 and 1915, did not entirely share the anticlerical ideology of Plutarco Elías Calles, his former Secretary of Interior.[34]

CALLES' ADMINISTRATION

On December 1, 1924, General Plutarco Elías Calles assumed the presidency of the Republic. During his period as governor of the state

---

[31] "Protest made by the undersigned Mexican prelates on the occasion of the Political Constitution of the United Mexican States, published in Querétaro on the fifth day of February, 1917" (Meyer, *La Cristiada*, 2:70).
[32] Cited by Fidel González Fernández, "Los 28 mártires mexicanos," *Ecclesia* 15 (2001): 32, emphasis ours.
[33] See Benedict XV, Epist. *Exploratum vobis*, 15-VI-1917, AAS 9 (1917), 376–77.
[34] Enrique Krauze, *Álvaro Obregón* (FCE, 1987), 95.

of Sonora (1915–1919), he had been known for his radical attitude in regard to the battle against the Church.[35]

His rise to power was like a bucket of cold water on the Catholic populace who had not yet recovered from a serious incident in their midst. At the start of 1925, supported by the government, a couple of priests tried to found a "National Church" (the attempt suited perfectly the government's desire to "de-fanaticize" Mexico). Under the guidance of a extraordinary person—the "pope" Joaquín Pérez, a Catholic priest affiliated with Freemasonry—this small group of clerics tried to become independent from Rome. For this, and with state support, the church of "La Soledad" in the Federal District of Mexico City was seized and the National Church began functioning there. The effort was a fiasco: there was minimal support from the faithful, who would not attend schismatic churches, and the madness of such an attempt in a country like Mexico, meant that soon they had to leave the church building because of rioting by the populace—which the government punished by confiscating the Corpus Christi parish church and donating the proceeds to them.

What did "Pope" Pérez want? He made it clear in his "exhortation" to Mexican priests entitled *To the Secular and Regular Clergy of the Roman Catholic Church*—a rehash of antique and modern heresies:

> Every good priest enlightened by the Holy Scriptures knows from the divine teachings of the Epistles of St. Paul that, in the first centuries of Christianity, national Churches were founded outside Jerusalem. Specifically based on this primitive practice and custom of the Church and making use of a legitimate right with the support of the Holy Scriptures, the Apostolic Mexican Catholic Church was founded.... Thus we established the Catholic Church of Mexico, inspired by a high patriotic ideal.[36]

It is worth noting that the schismatic fiasco was joined by only ten priests,[37] of which three were invalidly ordained and seven were later reconciled with the Catholic Church.

---

[35] "One of his most anticlerical measures, in fact unprecedented in the entire country, was to expel all Catholic priests from Sonora without exception." Enrique Krauze, *Plutarco E. Calles, Reformador desde el origen* (FCE, 1987), 32.

[36] Meyer, *La Cristiada*, 2:149–50.

[37] According to Meyer, Joaquín Pérez died in 1930 reconciled with the Catholic Church. However, *L'Osservatore Romano* places the date of his death in 1928, without saying a word about this supposed reconciliation (*L'Osservatore Romano*, 21-VII-1928, p. 2).

Around the same time, in March 1925, various Catholic movements of which we will speak later on formed the "National League for the Defense of Religious Liberty." This group had a markedly political nature and was "completely alien to the Catholic hierarchy both in its organization, its government and its actions."[38] The program of action of the "League" was reduced to a minimum of demands, such as freedom of education, and common law for citizens and the Church, and consequently called for the repeal of constitutional articles and the regulatory laws that violated them. It grew unexpectedly, perhaps due to the clever tactic of being parallel to the ecclesiastical hierarchy: in June 1925 it already had 36,395 members and a year later more than a million throughout the country.[39]

The "Calles administration" did not stand idly by when faced with this Catholic organization. Thus, on January 4, 1926, it issued a law implementing Article 130 of the National Constitution.[40] Ignoring the internal hierarchy of the Catholic Church, it set out to regulate the clergy's positions, functions, and assignments. The law also expanded the requirement for exercising priestly ministry, requiring "to be Mexican by birth and son of Mexican parents," so that hundreds of priests of foreign origin were excluded.

It also demanded the most difficult thing for the clergy: *the obligation to register with the government and obtain authorization from it to exercise their ministry*, in addition to other obligations. The problem was that, if these prescriptions were obeyed, the clergy must accept civil jurisdiction over ecclesiastical jurisdiction, forced to exercise

---

[38] "This does not mean that the League is in opposition to ecclesiastical authority, and that it wishes to act in complete independence from the council and the high direction of this same authority. But taking upon himself all the responsibility for his acts, he intends only to move with the freedom that rationally suits it." Quoted by Aurelio Acevedo, ed., *David VIII*, Estudios y Publicaciones Económicas y Sociales (México, 2000, first edition facsimile), 40. Acevedo's testimony is of great value: Aurelio Acevedo was born in 1900 in Potrero de Gallegos, Zacatecas. He belonged to the circle of Catholic workers of the ACJM (to be discussed below) and on August 23, 1926, he took up arms in defense of religious freedom, participating in several battles until he was named brigadier general in March 1929. He was distinguished not only by his courage but also for directing *David*, a monthly magazine that turns out to be an invaluable document for the knowledge of the Cristero point of view. Hundreds of firsthand accounts are collected there, as well as letters from the protagonists. This magazine appeared from August 1952 to December 1967; Acevedo died in January 1968.
[39] See Meyer, *La Cristiada*, 1:63.
[40] Failure to comply with the various regulatory laws of Article 130 issued thus far was especially penalized. The penalties and other articles can be seen in Navarrete and Pallares, *La persecución religiosa en México*, 135–43.

their ministry only where, when, and how the government wished and under its provisions.[41] In addition, in the case of compliance and given the enormous animosity being unleashed in the religious sphere, the priests who accepted or registered would remain in the eyes of the people simply as deserters and collaborators with the "regime." It was a question of making a pact with Caesar or not.

Three days after the law's publication, Calles had Congress grant him extraordinary powers to reform the Penal Code in view of compliance with this law. Thus, in the first days of 1926, a genuine campaign against the Church would begin.[42]

The "Calles Law," as it was known, consisted of thirty-three articles; here we shall quote the first twenty-three:

> *Article 1.* Punishes with a fine of five hundred pesos or fifteen days of imprisonment anyone who exercises the priestly ministry in Mexico, who is not Mexican, in addition to being expelled from the country.
>
> *Article 2.* For criminal purposes, a person is deemed to exercise a ministry of worship when he performs religious acts or ministers sacraments proper to the cult to which he belongs, or publicly pronounces doctrinal preaching, or in the same way performs religious proselytizing work.
>
> *Article 3.* The teaching in official and private schools shall be secular. An offender shall be fined five hundred pesos or arrested for up to fifteen days. In case of recidivism, the offender shall be punished with major arrest and a second-class fine, without prejudice to the authority ordering the closure of the educational establishment.
>
> *Article 4.* The same punishment as in the preceding article for religious bodies or ministers of worship who establish or direct primary schools.
>
> *Article 5.* Private primary schools may be established subject to official supervision. Penalty of five hundred pesos or fifteen days of arrest for offenders.
>
> *Article 6.* Religious vows and monastic orders are prohibited. Convents will be disbanded by the authorities, and those who meet again in community will be punished with one or

---

[41] Regarding this provision, it is worth bearing in mind that only one of the 3,600 priests in Mexico in 1926 registered with the government. He is Father Dimas Anguiano, from Alvarado, Veracruz, congratulated and received with great fanfare by Calles (see Meyer, *La Cristiada*, 2:286).

[42] See Meyer, *La Cristiada*, 2:262.

two years in prison and the superiors of the order with six years in prison. Women will suffer two-thirds of the penalty.

*Article 7*. Persons who induce a minor to enter a monastic order shall suffer the penalty of major arrest and a fine of the second class. If the person who hears such advice is of legal age, the penalty, for the person who induces someone, shall be minor arrest and a first-class fine.

*Article 8*. A penalty of six years' imprisonment and a second-class fine for a priest who, by word of mouth or in writing, incites disregard for political institutions or disobedience of the laws.

*Article 9*. If, as a result of such incitement, fewer than ten individuals intervene against the authority, either by using force or threat, each one shall suffer one year's imprisonment and a second-class fine. Priests who are held responsible for the attitude of the dissidents will be sentenced to six years in prison, plus aggravating circumstances from first to fourth class, according to the judge's opinion.

*Article 10*. Neither privately nor publicly may priests formulate any criticism of the laws, or of the Government, under penalty of one to five years' imprisonment.

*Article 11*. Nor may they gather for political purposes, since they shall be punished with minor arrest and a first-class fine.

*Article 12*. Studies made in establishments intended for the professional education of ministers of religion shall not be given validity. Offenders shall be dismissed, and the dispensation shall be null and void, and the professional title thus obtained shall be invalid.

*Article 13*. Religious periodicals, or those of religious tendencies by their program or title, may not comment on any political matter. The director of the publication shall suffer, in this case, the penalty of major arrest and a fine of the second class.

*Article 14*. In the absence of a director, the editor-in-chief, author, or whoever is within the reach of justice shall suffer the penalty. In the event of a repeat offense, the definitive suspension of the periodical publication will be ordered.

*Article 15*. No political group may bear a title that relates it to any religion.

*Article 16*. Meetings of a political nature may not be held in churches. In such cases, those in charge will suffer major arrest and a fine of second class and the Federal Executive may also order the temporary or permanent closure of the church.

*Article 17.* All religious acts of public worship must be celebrated only within the churches, which will always be under the supervision of the authorities. If they are done outside of them, the organizers or ministers celebrating them will be punished with major arrest and a fine of the second class.

*Article 18.* Outside the churches, priests and religious may not wear their characteristic garb either, under penalty of five hundred pesos or arrest for up to fifteen days. Repeating offense will merit a major arrest and a second-class fine.

*Article 19.* The person in charge of a church, within a period of one month from the entry into force of this law, or within the month following the day on which he has taken charge of a church intended for worship, shall give the notices referred to in the eleventh paragraph of Article 130 of the Constitution. Failure to give notice within the terms indicated shall incur a fine of five hundred pesos, or, failing that, imprisonment for not more than fifteen days. The minister of the Interior will also order the closure of the church until the constitutional requirements are met.

*Article 20.* Any member of the public may denounce the misdemeanors and crimes referred to in this law.

*Article 21.* The Church may not acquire, possess, or administer real estate, or capital imposed on it. Any member of the public may denounce the property found in such a case, and those who conceal it shall be punished with one to two years' imprisonment.

*Article 22.* The Federal Government shall determine which churches are to be used for worship, and bishop's residences, convents, rectories, seminaries, asylums, colleges, and any building intended for the administration, propaganda, or teaching of religious worship shall be expropriated by the Federation or the states in their jurisdictions.

*Article 23.* It is mainly the responsibility of the federal authorities to ensure compliance with this Law. Those of the states and municipalities are auxiliary to the former, and therefore equally responsible, when any of the precepts of this law are not complied with because of them.[43]

As is clear, it was almost a declaration of war.

---

[43] See Rius Facius, *México Cristero*, 2:8–11.

Although thus far only six states had tried to enforce the constitutional articles, they were prevented by popular revolts in defense of churches and their priests. Calles, determined to do anything, urged all the country's authorities both to apply the new regulatory law, as well as to regulate it locally in each state, mainly by limiting the number of priests.

In response to Archbishop José Mora y del Río's protest, Secretary of the Interior Adalberto Tejeda tried to accuse him of abetting crime and inciting armed struggle against the government. However, the accusation did not get far.

Once Article 130 of the Constitution was enforced, what remained was the struggle against the "retrograde" and "bourgeois." A month later (on February 22, 1926), Secretary of Public Education José Manuel Puig Casauranc took charge of this, enforcing Article 3, which referred to education. It stipulated not only the prohibiting the intervention of any minister of worship or member of any religious order, but also the existence of even the slightest religious symbol in the schools, this being sufficient cause for closure. For example, it rigidly declared in its implementation that "private primary schools shall not have a hall, or oratory, or chapel intended for the service of worship of any kind, and in the classrooms, in the corridors, in the hallways, in the workshops, in the gymnasiums, and in all the other dependencies of the campus, there shall be no decorations, paintings, prints, sculptures, or objects of a religious nature."[44] Not a single depiction of Michelangelo's *Pietà* could be kept under penalty of the institution being closed. After this legislation, a massive string of closures began without further ado, including the closure of Catholic schools and their subsequent conversion into barracks or public offices. Protests were of no use.

Immediately after, the expulsion of priests and religious of foreign origin was put into effect—though prior to April 1926, several hundred religious and priests had already been expelled from the country without a prior judicial order, as mandated by the Constitution. Although the Holy See protested, Mexico did not give in. Pius XI stated in the consistory of December 14, 1925, that "the condition of (Mexican) Catholics has been getting worse and worse and is all the more sad.... The hope of better times can only be

---

[44] Article 6 of the Regulations for the Operation and Inspection of Private Primary Schools in the State of Campeche.

placed in a special intervention of Divine Providence...as well as in a harmonious and disciplined work of Catholic Action promoted by the people themselves."[45] The Vicar of Christ was firmer when he declared on February 2, 1926, in his apostolic letter *Paterna Sane* (addressed to bishops), that the prescriptions imposed on Catholics by the "enemies of the Church" did not deserve to be called "laws," because they were not dictated according to right reason.[46] He also added that both bishops and Catholic associations should remain completely outside any political party, although he did not stop them from exercising the rights and duties common to all citizens. He ended by saying that "those who preside over the government of the Republic are waging *a war against the Catholic religion* that is becoming bitterer day after day."[47]

"What is to be done?" asked the Mexican Catholic world. Resignation or action?

Further, on April 21, 1926, the Mexican bishops published a pastoral letter that reminded Mexican Catholics of their political duties, telling them that they should "resolutely enter (into politics), since, as citizens, they should be concerned about their country's welfare, and as Catholic citizens, they have an obligation to work on legal grounds so that the Church's rights are respected and laws contrary to their freedom will be repealed."[48] The response was not be long in coming: boycotts, petitions, appeals for protection. Everything was tried, but—as we will soon see—all in vain.

※ ※ ※

The die was cast. Due to a succession of tragic decades, Mexico entered a war at once civil and religious, a war that could only end with the blood of its own people being spilled. In that people's veins flowed the religion of their ancestors; by attacking their beliefs, their very being was attacked. This was understood by those who refused to obey the laws and by those who offered their lives to stand against those laws—and often against the directives of those who should have defended them.

---

[45] Pius XI, *Consistorial Allocution*, 14-XII-1925, in AAS 17 (1925), 642, quoted by González Morfín, *La guerra cristera*, 103n383.
[46] See Pius XI, Epist. ap. *Paterna sane*, 2-11-1926, AAS 18 (1926), 175.
[47] Ibid., 176, emphasis ours.
[48] See *Pastoral colectiva del 21 de abril de 1926*, in Alberto M. Carreño, *El Arzobispo de México Excmo. D. Pascual Díaz y el conflicto religioso* (Victoria, 19432), 25-26.

*Arrest of Catholics who participated in the Guadalajara Tabernacle riot in 1926*

*Firefighters dispersing a demonstration in 1926*

*Cerro del Cubilete (dynamited);*
*miraculously, the head and heart of*
*the image of Christ remained intact*

*Joaquín Pérez, the Mexican "pope."*

*Cristo Rey of Mexico. Cerro del Cubilete*

# 2

# The Attitude of the
# Ecclesiastical Hierarchy

*There was no choice but the Lord's Prayer while throwing rocks.*
—Jeromito Gutiérrez, Cristero[1]

THE ANTECEDENTS OF THE CRISTERO WAR THAT we have summarized meant that the ecclesiastical hierarchy was almost forced to act. It wasn't the first time that the Church had endured similar persecution; it has happened from Diocletian's time to the present day. However, faced with increasingly widespread revolts and pressure from the people, the Mexican episcopate found it necessary to act. This led to the drafting, at the beginning and in the middle of 1926, of three collective letters that were to be read in all dioceses. These served as the "official" position of the Mexican bishops. In them, the impossibility of submitting to the government's regulations was declared; a new martyr's cry echoed the *non possumus* of the ancient Christians.

Below are the most essential statements from the first and third collective letters:

> The current conditions are already unsustainable and how correctly we believe that the time has come to say: *NON POSSUMUS!* WE CANNOT!...[2]

> If you persevere in your worthy and resolute resistance, friends and enemies will eventually understand that it is impossible to uproot the faith of your fathers without mortally wounding the soul of the Mexican people. But if, through shameful cowardice, you desert the ranks, or quit the fight, humanly speaking we are lost and Mexico will cease to be a Catholic people. You will have abdicated the noblest and most precious freedoms, and God forbid Jesus Christ's warning to his people be realized in us: "The kingdom of God will be taken away from you, and it will

---

[1] Meyer, *La Cristiada*, 3:5.
[2] *First Collective Letter of the Mexican Episcopate*, April 21, 1926, in Consuelo Reguer, *Dios y mi derecho* (JUS, 1997), 1:52.

be given to a people who will make it fruitful" (Matt. XXI, 43).... Imitate all true lovers of national freedoms, who in every period of history have known how to stand firm in the breach, until they win or die. Imitate the constancy of the first Christians...who died as good men, making their blood the seed of more and more converts.[3]

Clearly, it was initially the local hierarchy that—responding to the actual situation—framed it in terms of persecution. No call to arms, but simply a remembrance of the first martyrs. On the other hand, and at the same time, in Rome the official Vatican press, *L'Osservatore Romano*, declared Mexican people's state of emergency when faced with their government's arbitrariness when it said: "To the masses, who do not want to submit to tyranny, and who are no longer held back by the clergy's pacific exhortations, nothing remains but *armed rebellion*."[4] Barely ten days after this declaration, the same official press proclaimed more forcefully a statement in which the Secretariat of State officially transmitted papal guidelines to the nuncios, apostolic delegates, and the diplomatic corps. It affirmed that because Mexican Catholics were unable to "unite and organize themselves to attempt a defense by legal means...there remains for the masses, who are no longer contained by the clergy's pacific exhortations, only armed rebellion."[5]

Bear in mind, then, the bishops' call to martyrdom and *L'Osservatore Romano*'s call to armed rebellion.[6]

## THE BISHOPS' RESPONSE

Since the promulgation of the Constitution of Querétaro in 1917, the Mexican bishops had been protesting, along with peaceful resistance to abuses. The Constitution was rejected, but simultaneously any kind of violent protest was prohibited. Peaceful opposition was, as Meyer clarifies, the Mexican "official position":

> The 1917 legal code violates the most sacred rights of the Catholic Church, of Mexican society and the individual

---

[3] *Third Collective Letter of the Mexican Episcopate on the Occasion of the Current Religious Persecution*, September 12, 1926, in ibid., 234–36.
[4] *L'Osservatore Romano*, 2-VIII-1926; see Meyer, *La Cristiada*, 1:15, emphasis ours.
[5] *L'Osservatore Romano*, 11-VIII-1926; see Rius Facius, *México Cristero*, 2:127.
[6] It was, as *L'Osservatore Romano* said, a matter "of a persecuting government that wants the suppression of the Catholic Church in Mexico" (Rius Facius, *México Cristero*, 2:64).

rights of Christians; it proclaims principles contrary to the
truth taught by Jesus Christ, which constitutes the Church's
treasure and humanity's greatest patrimony; it also uproots
the few rights that the Constitution of 1857...recognized:
the Church as a society and Catholics as subjects. Not
intending to meddle in political matters, but to defend as
much as possible the religious freedom of the Christian people in view of the rude attack on religion, we limit ourselves
to protesting the attack vigorously and courteously.... 1) In
conformity with the doctrines of the Roman Pontiffs...and
moved also by patriotism, *we are very far from approving
armed rebellion against recognized authority*, without this non-
combative submission to the existing government implying
intellectual and voluntary approval of the anti-religious or
otherwise unjust laws emanating from it, and without it
being intended that Catholics, our faithful, be deprived of
the right that assists them as citizens, to work legally and
*peacefully* to erase from the national laws everything that
hurts their conscience and their rights.... Our only motive
is to fulfill the duty imposed on us by the defense of the
Church's rights and of religious freedom.[7]

A relative "Porfirian" peace could have followed for years if Calles
had not lit the wick that was smoking yet not aflame. By enforcing
the controversial articles of the Constitution that had lain dormant,
a natural reaction was ignited in the Christian populace.

Tempers were so heated that anything could mean a declaration
of war between the two sides. This was the case with respect to a
document that appeared in the newspaper *El Universal* in January 1926.
Making the most of the difficult situation that the Church was going
through, the journalist Ignacio Monroy requested an interview with
the Archbishop of Mexico, Mgr. Mora y del Río, whose statements
would later be branded as "seditious":

> The Church's teaching is invariable because it is divinely
> revealed truth. The protest that we Mexican prelates formu-
> lated against the Constitution of 1917 regarding the articles
> that oppose freedom and religious dogmas remains firm. It
> has not been modified, but strengthened, because it derives
> from the Church's doctrine. The information published
> by *El Universal*, dated January 27, with the meaning that a

---

[7] Memorandum of the Archbishop of Guadalajara, 31 pp., undated [1917] and
without place of publication, p. 9; quoted by Meyer, *La Cristiada*, 2:100–101,
emphasis ours.

campaign will be undertaken against unjust laws contrary to Natural Law, is perfectly true. The Episcopate, clergy, and Catholics *do not recognize and will fight* articles 3, 5, 27 and 130 of the current Constitution.[8]

Apparently, then, the conciliatory and peaceful idea of the Mexican episcopate was apparently coming to an end: "we will fight," declared the newspaper. This caused astonishment in the government. General Roberto Cruz, an eyewitness to Calles' reaction when he read the news, went so far as to say that the president exclaimed: "It is a challenge to the government and to the Revolution! I'm unwilling to tolerate it. Since the priests are in this plan, the law must be applied to them as it is."[9] It was useless for Mgr. Mora y del Río to later deny having used the verb "fight" printed by the journalist Monroy (something he maintained until moments before his death, when he said that "that false and premeditated news article…was the spark that produced the religious conflict").[10] Mexico and its bishops were thus divided between peace and the war incited by the government.

War and peace were being debated, and not metaphorically, but literally. The small state of Colima and its ecclesiastical hierarchy serve as an example. There, where in a few months there was a great counterrevolutionary center, the situation was far from peaceful: the legislature had limited the number of priests to twenty by forcing them to register with the authorities. The governor, Francisco Solórzano Béjar, a confirmed Freemason, had already become famous in 1925 for having meticulously regulated the ringing of church bells. Now he showed his zeal by going even further, attempting to apply the National Constitution to the letter. With a decree published on March 24, the bishop of the diocese was given a period of ten days to obey the provision on ecclesiastical demographics. Faced with this order, and after having obtained his priests' unanimous support, the prelate responded on April 19 with the following proclamation:

> Before God and all my beloved diocesan priests, I declare that I would rather be judged harshly by those who have provoked my attitude on this most delicate matter than to appear full of reproach and shame at the tribunal of the

---

[8] *El Universal*, February 4, 1926, emphasis ours.
[9] Meyer, *La Cristiada*, 2:242.
[10] *Excélsior*, April 23, 1928, p. 3. For Meyer, the "spark" was this act; but for Rius Facius (*México Cristero*, 1:244) the first symptom was the creation of the schismatic Church in 1925.

Divine Judge and deserve the condemnation of the Supreme
Hierarch of the Church... I repeat to you in the most formal
way my disagreement with the decree by which the civil
authority of the state of Colima is allowed to legislate about
the ecclesiastical administration of my diocese.... We are
branded as subversives, rebels, and systematic opponents of
the laws. We reject that accusation.... Knowing the Gospel, we have given to Caesar what is Caesar's.... Law and
humiliation do not mean the same thing. Bread is called
bread and wine is called wine, and we cannot confuse one
with the other. Catholics from Colima: for our deceived
brothers and sisters who have become unjustified enemies
of the Church, *we ask only for prayers*. Catholics, we reject
in advance the verdict of rebels. No, we are not rebels. As
God lives! We are simply oppressed Catholic priests who
do not want to be apostates, who reject the mockery and
criticism of Iscariots.[11]

Note well: "we ask only for prayers..."

## THE TWO POSITIONS: ARMS OR SUBMISSION

The stance was not uniform among the Mexican bishops. As early
as June 1926, the bishops were divided on the question of the "registration" of priests (the number and identification of priests as quasi-
state employees). The prelates were divided into three distinct groups:
those who spoke out in favor of active resistance (only political and
nonviolent), those who did so for passive resistance (even to martyrdom), and those who tried to persevere through juridical struggle.

As is clear, the bishops had not even contemplated armed resistance.
However, once it broke out, the majority left their faithful free to
defend their rights as they saw fit. A dozen would deny them that
right, and only three would encourage it.

In summary, the bishops fell into three major groups at the beginning of 1927:

1) Those who supported the LNDLR (National League for the
Defense of Religious Liberty) — the political arm of Mexican Cathol-
icism and therefore of armed struggle. This included Mgr. Leopoldo
Lara y Torres, bishop of Tacámbaro, Michoacán,[12] Mgr. José María

---

[11] Spectator [pseudonym of Fr. Enrique de Jesús Ochoa], *Los cristeros del volcán
de Colima* (JUS, 1961), 1:45–47, emphasis ours.
[12] Author of a beautiful work: Leopoldo Lara y Torres, *Documentos para la
Historia de la persecución religiosa en México* (JUS, 1954).

González y Valencia, bishop of Durango, and Mgr. José de Jesús Manríquez y Zárate, bishop of Huejutla (who was imprisoned for almost a year).[13] These three were prohibited from returning to Mexico after the "Settlements."[14]

2) The supporters of resistance and clandestine action, without going to war: Mgr. Francisco Orozco y Jiménez, bishop of Guadalajara (he did not agree with the armed actions of the Cristeros,[15] but he supported their activity, going into hiding before being exiled[16]), Mgr. Amador Velazco, bishop of Colima, Mgr. Emeterio Valverde y Téllez, Mgr. Gerardo Méndez del Río and Mgr. José Mora y del Río, Archbishop of Mexico. All were opposed to conciliation with the government.[17]

3) The supporters of the government: Mgr. Antonio Guízar y Valencia, bishop of Chihuahua, who formally forbade armed rebellion under threat of excommunication and would later greet President Portes Gil as a "new Constantine." Mgr. Ignacio Placencia, bishop of Zacatecas, who denied the right to self-defense also threatened the Cristeros with excommunication and disseminated the circular entitled "Red and Black" (the colors of the government) encouraging the faithful to denounce the Cristeros to the police; Mgr. Francisco Banegas y Galván, bishop of Querétaro, who sent his *compliments* to Portes Gil for having escaped a Cristero attack and expelled Canon Cañas from his diocese for making a case for the right to resist tyranny;

---

[13] See Andrés Barquín y Ruiz, *José de Jesús Manríquez y Zárate, gran defensor de la Iglesia* (Red-Mex, 1942).

[14] "Years after the end of the Cristero war, in 1943, two former leaders of the League declared in a newspaper: 'We deeply admire Monsignor Lara y Torres, a man of heroic memory, full of learning and burning with courage, who, when warning that unrestrained tempests would be awakened against the League, declared to us manfully: "I'll go down with you." In one of his virile pastorals, he proclaimed that "Force has a providential destiny to fulfill." José de Jesús Manríquez y Zárate, the *caudillo*, confronted Calles with those immortal words: "Mr. President lies." José María Mora y del Río, the Primate, the man with a sublime attitude before the Secretary of the Interior, in a tragic moment [said to him]: "*You* are not the Government." All were passionate about the freedom of the Church, because it is what God loves most on earth.... all were immersed in the bitter solitudes of Calvary'" (Sáenz, *La nave y las tempestades*, 347).

[15] The appellation by which those who had taken up arms or those who supported them were called, "*cristero*," seems to have arisen from their characteristic cry "Long live Christ the King!"(see Meyer, *La Cristiada*, 3:280–81).

[16] Rius Facius, *México Cristero*, 2:145.

[17] Mgr. Orozco y Jiménez and Mgr. Velazco, the only two bishops who went into exile on the battlefield with their faithful, administering the sacraments and fulfilling the mission of feeding the sheep *in situ*.

Mgr. Luis María Martínez, auxiliary bishop of Morelia, Michoacán, future archbishop of Mexico, a close friend of General Lázaro Cárdenas, the socialist President.[18]

Manifestly, of the thirty-eight prelates, at least three were truly committed to the armed uprising, although until the end of 1926 they preferred to pour cold water on the fratricidal clash.

Meanwhile, among the simple priests the question was also divided at the dawn of 1927[19]: one hundred would eventually declare themselves actively hostile to the Cristeros, forty would be favorable to them, five would take up arms, and sixty-five would be completely neutral. The rest (more than 3,500) left their rural parishes to take refuge in the cities.

## WEAPONS

Positions changed as the situation changed. As this was a matter of prudence rather than principle, not everything was black and white. This was the case with Bishop Manríquez y Zárate, an opponent of violence at first and later its defender. He went so far as to condemn violence on three occasions, as we read in his vehement pastoral letter of April 3, 1925:

> If the authorities appeal to violence, it will not be licit, neither for the faithful nor for the clergy, to appeal to brute force to repel aggression, rather they must observe the meek but dignified conduct of the martyrs of Christianity.... Consequently, we strictly prohibit riots and uprisings, and in general any manifestations of brute force against the constituted authorities.[20]

Two years later (on July 12, 1927, in his "Message to the Civilized World"), horrified by the viciousness that the government demonstrated against the people, he issued a call to arms:

> Our soldiers perish on the battlefields, riddled with the bullets of tyranny, because there is no one to reach out to

---

[18] Supporters of the "Settlements" were: Mgr. Leopoldo Ruiz y Flores, archbishop of Morelia, Michoacán, later primate of Mexico; Mgr. Pascual Díaz, bishop of Tabasco, later cardinal; Mgr. Rafael Guízar y Valencia, bishop of Veracruz; Mgr. Vera y Zuría, bishop of Puebla; Mgr. Fulcheri, bishop of Zamora; Mgr. Amador Villagómez, in charge of the see of Huajuapan. Mgr. José Othón Núñez, bishop of Oaxaca; Mgr. Jesús María Echevarría, bishop of Saltillo; Mgr. Nicolás Corona, bishop of Papantla, Mgr. Uranga, bishop of Cuernavaca.

[19] See Meyer, La Cristiada, 1:49.

[20] Originally in the Catholic weekly El Faro, no. 26, March 28, 1926, pp. 1 and 4, quoted by Meyer, La Cristiada, 2:256. See also Rius Facius, México Cristero, 1:273.

them, because there is no one to care for them, nor to support their heroic efforts by sending them food and war supplies to save the country. *We want arms and money* to overthrow the opprobrious tyranny that oppresses us and to found an honest government in Mexico.[21]

It must not have been easy for a bishop of the time to respond to Lenin's "What is to be done?" Rome, beyond its statement in the *L'Osservatore Romano*, faithful to Pius XI's conciliatory policy of the time,[22] was silent. Hence the heartbreaking utterance of Archbishop Manríquez: "If I only knew what the Vicar of Christ thinks!"[23]

As Meyer observes, the point of the Calles decree most disturbing to the bishops was Article 19, which obliged each priest to register with the authorities in order to exercise his ministry. The Episcopate could not decide. "*Rome did not know what to do* and was afraid above all to impose a solution on divided bishops."[24] Everything was uncertain and in the face of vital decisions — e.g., to support or not to support an economic boycott against the government — Pius XI's own Secretary of State, Cardinal Pietro Gasparri, responded evasively.[25]

However, there was some "moral" support from the hierarchy. In fact, Pius XI followed the painful events in Mexico very closely and on Holy Saturday of 1926 he addressed a letter to his Vicar asking the diocese of Rome to pray for the people and clergy of Mexico, where "the situation of the Catholics that we had already pointed out as not very consoling ... has deteriorated so much that it has become a real and proper persecution and a very great offense to the honor due to God and no less detrimental to the souls of that same people."[26]

On July 2, 1926, the same Cardinal Gasparri wrote a letter to all the nuncios in which he asked for prayer "for the cessation of persecution in Mexico and for the forgiveness for the guilty," adding that the government's imposition on priests of "conditions unacceptable to their conscience" would mean "they should avoid complying *at all costs*."[27] A commission of bishops, chosen from among the Mexican

---

[21] Meyer, *La Cristiada*, 1:19, emphasis ours.
[22] Pius XI was always careful not to speak about the lawfulness or illegality of the armed uprising (see Meyer, *La Cristiada*, 2:344).
[23] Ibid., 350.
[24] Ibid., 264, emphasis ours.
[25] See ibid., 265n101.
[26] Pius XI, *Chirographus ad Card. Pompili*, Holy Saturday 1926, in AAS 18 (1926), 181–82 (see González Morfin, *La guerra cristera*, 112).
[27] See Pietro Gasparri, *Litterae circulares de rei catholicae iniqua condicione in Mexico*, in AAS 18 (1929), 326–27.

prelates, went to Rome in mid-1926 to speak with His Holiness. On
October 18, 1926, Mgr. José María González y Valencia, Mgr. Emeterio
Valverde y Téllez and Mgr. Gerardo Méndez del Río, were received
by Pius XI. When asked about what the bishops' attitude should be
in the face of this painful situation that the Church in Mexico was
enduring, Pius XI replied: "Do not tell them anything. Let those who
are on the ground do what they deem appropriate." Mgr. Méndez del
Río asked him: "How should we be impartial?"—to which the pope
replied by banging his fist on his desk: "We cannot be impartial: we
must be on the side of justice."[28] This was an unambiguous answer.
That is, this silence was tacit support for what Catholics in Mexico
were doing: defending the Faith. The pope was with them.

There was no possibility of half-measures. The movement began
to accelerate, and Mexico could not wait for futile compromises.
In the middle of 1926 blood began to flow through the streets and
the bishops had to speak. Mgr. González y Valencia did precisely
that: from Rome, on February 11, 1927, he launched like a grenade
his famous "Pastoral Letter" to the Catholics of the Archdiocese of
Durango. "Be at peace in your conscience," he told them:

> We may now break the silence on a matter of which we feel
> obliged to speak. Since *in Our Archdiocese many Catholics
> have resorted to the use of arms, and ask for a word from their
> Prelate*, a word that We cannot deny, from the moment it
> is asked of us by Our own children. We believe it is Our
> pastoral duty to face the question squarely, and to assume
> with full awareness the responsibility before God and before
> history. We offer these words to you: We never provoked
> this armed movement. But *once peaceful means have been
> exhausted and this movement has arisen*, to Our Catholic
> children who take up arms for the defense of their social
> and religious rights, after having thought it over at length
> before God, and having consulted the wisest theologians
> of the City of Rome, We must say to them: *be at ease in
> your consciences and receive Our blessing.*[29]

Yet there were some who, contrary to this position, were inclined to
take a different path.

---

[28] Rius Facius, *México Cristero*, 2:133. A few days after this interview and thanks
to the summary of the situation in Mexico, the Pope published the encyclical
*Iniquis afflictisque*, 18-XI-1926, AAS 18 (1926), 465–77.
[29] José Maria González y Valencia, *Carta pastoral*, 11-II-1927, in Barquín y Ruiz,
*José María González y Valencia*, 43–44, emphasis ours.

PASSIVITY (OR DEFEAT)

As noted above, not all the bishops were of the same opinion. Mgr. José Juan de Jesús Herrera y Piña, Archbishop of Monterrey, in his pastoral instruction of March 10, 1926, stated, "once again, that it *will never be licit to resort to rebellion or violence* to recover the rights currently denied to Catholics. When evil cannot be prevented with the few legal means that remain, it is necessary to limit oneself to a *passive attitude*, without ever forgetting the respect due to the authorities, as God's representatives, because if they abuse power it is not our duty to call them to account"[30] (the majority of the bishops used more or less the same language). For his part, Bishop Francisco Banegas said something similar: "Once again, I earnestly recommend that Catholics refrain from any demonstration that could cause disorder. Prayer, suffering and penance will save us."[31]

Attitudes such as those of Bishop Herrera and similar statements could be cited extensively. Passivity, in this case, was taken for defeatism by the common people and defeatism meant the victory of the government. These were confusing times. Normal channels of command did not function in the Church and circumstances were pressing. This explains the attitude of "men of the Church," such as Father José Adolfo Arroyo (a priest from Valparaíso, Zacatecas), who, ignoring the calls by some pastors for peace, throughout the war remained at the side of his parishioners who had taken up arms. He said:

> The overwhelming majority of bishops and priests feared the enemy, soon sought compromise, and fell into criminal conformity. They plunged into accursed inertia, all of them waiting for pure miracles from heaven that would give freedom to the Church. They all agreed to give exhortations and recite a few prayers.... Hence, as at the time of Nero, they advised the people to passively offer their necks to the executioner.[32]

Still, unlike Father Arroyo, other priests went as far as to prohibit the use of arms, even after the unequal combat had begun. With bad theology and in some cases with much naïveté, more than one

---

[30] Meyer, *La Cristiada*, 1:98.
[31] *Pastoral Exhortation of Francisco Banegas, Bishop of Querétaro*, July 29, 1926, leaflet, in Meyer, *La Cristiada*, 1:98.
[32] *Algo sobre la persecución religiosa, defensa armada y arreglos* ( January 24, 1934), "Letter from P. A. Arroyo to his superiors," in Meyer, *La Cristiada*, 1:30.

tried to break the combatants' spirits. The people were astonished:

> We stumbled upon an issue *that we would never have even
> imagined: the same reverend fathers forbade us to fight for
> Christ*—for the religion that our parents instilled in us and
> then confirmed in us by baptism, confirmation, and first
> communion. And even more when we were mainly fight-
> ing to defend ourselves. "You must not resort to violence,"
> they told us. "A Christian must be humble and patient,
> allowing himself to be beaten. He must always turn the
> other cheek. Jesus was meek as a lamb, so he let himself be
> crucified.... In addition, since Moses, we have the Fifth
> Commandment, which forbids us to kill, to take the life
> of a neighbor. Even if it is our persecutor, this would be to
> do something that only belongs to the owner of life: God."
> And so on. Even the nine [priests] who fled through these
> mountains and ravines together with our families. The
> rebels wanted to ask them why, that although it was true
> that there was no other way but to turn the other cheek
> to Calles' soldiers, they were not going to turn themselves
> in so that they could be martyred once and for all. This
> was another mystery to us rebels.[33]

There were priests who ended up as martyrs due to this passivity—
which demonstrates that one does not need to be a good theologian
to give one's life for Christ.[34]

Thus, the vast majority of priests took a passive stance toward
the "uprising." Whatever their personal opinions were and without
judging their consciences, many of them left their parishes once the
"suspension of worship" was decreed and, breviary in hand, either
fled abroad or gathered in the big cities where persecution did not
necessarily lead to death. There were also among the lower clergy (it
must be said) exemplary priests who, even against the will of their
bishops, accompanied their sheep to their very death.[35]

---

[33] Meyer, *La Cristiada*, 1:34.
[34] "The martyred parish priest Mateo Correa preached against the Cristeros,
invoking the sanctity of patience and resignation, offering persecution as a punishment justly sent to make Mexico abandon its sins. And the other martyred
parish priest, Father Cristóbal Magallanes, said: 'The Church does not need
arms for its defense. God cares for her'" (ibid.).
[35] Such was, for example, the case of Father Isabel Salinas, parish priest of San
Miguel, who led a movement at the beginning of the Cristero war (Meyer, *La
Cristiada*, 1:142).

THE SUSPENSION OF WORSHIP: A COMPROMISING MOVE

The clashes and first hostilities took place on a small scale. It was only one event that, undoubtedly, motivated the widespread discontent of the Mexican Catholic populace: the suspension of worship. Indeed, in the face of the Calles regulatory law that came into force on July 31, 1926, the Mexican bishops, to avoid any occasion of conflict and to quench passionate spirits, decided, through the Mexican Episcopal Committee, to publish a collective letter on July 25, 1926. There it was announced that, although the churches would remain open, worship would be suspended from the moment the regulation came into force.[36] It was a temporary measure, it was declared, for the sake of being able to find the best way forward.

Did the Mexican episcopate act alone? It did not. At that stage everything was a matter for consultation, as appears from one of the telegrams sent to Pius XI:

> The majority of the Mexican Episcopate intends to suspend worship in the churches of the republic before the 31st of the current month (July), since they are unable to hold services in line with canon law, the new [civil] law coming into force on the 31st of this month. The Episcopate asks the Holy See for approval. The person in charge awaits your response.

The Apostolic Delegate in Mexico, Mgr. Jorge José Caruana, obtained the following response from His Holiness:

> "THE HOLY SEE CONDEMNS THE LAW AND AT THE SAME TIME EVERY ACT THAT MAY SIGNIFY OR BE INTERPRETED BY THE FAITHFUL AS ACCEPTANCE OR RECOGNITION OF THE SAME LAW. THE EPISCOPATE OF MEXICO MUST CONFORM TO THIS NORM IN ITS COURSE OF ACTION, SO THAT THERE IS A MAJORITY AND, IF POSSIBLE, UNANIMITY AND OFFER AN EXAMPLE OF CONCORD." (Signed: Card. Gasparri. July 22).[37]

This Delphic response gave rise to the policy of suspension of worship, via a collective letter from the bishops. We must quote its essential portions:

---

[36] Three months earlier and ahead of the rest of the dioceses in courage, Colima had already done so (see Rius Facius, *México Cristero*, 1:302 and 2:29–30).

[37] Historical Archive of the Archbishopric of Oaxaca, *Correspondencia del Obispo Pascual Diaz a Arzobispo J.O. Núñez y Zárate*, August 4, 1926, cited in Meyer, *El conflicto religioso en Oaxaca 1926–1929* (CIDE, 2005), 9; capitals in original.

His Holiness Pius XI, deeply moved by the religious persecution which has occurred for some time against the Mexican people, and which began even before the brutal measures were recently adopted, declared in his Apostolic Letter of February 2, 1926: "The decrees and laws published by a government hostile to the Church and applied against the Catholic people of Mexico are so unjust that we have no need to tell you, who have so long endured the yoke, that such decrees, far from being founded on reason, far from responding to the interest of the common good to which [the government] is bound, are in reality quite the opposite, and for this reason do not deserve the name of laws. With abundant justifications, our late predecessor, Benedict XV, approved of your attitude when, in all justice and holiness, you protested against these laws, and today we assume this approval on our own.

From 1917, the date of the protest to which His Holiness refers, until a few months ago, our attitude has been one of prudent silence since the anti-religion clauses were not then enforced to make the Church's life impossible. In reality, successive governments over the years have placed serious obstacles in the Church's path and subjected her to summary procedures, excessively severe and often in violation of the rights the Constitution grants us. However, they have not made the preaching of the Good News, the administration of the sacraments, or the exercise of public worship impossible.

Faced with this severe persecution, which we see clearly but which was in a certain way only temporary and intermittent, we have been able to adopt an attitude of expectation, to seek the best possible arrangements, to endure the humiliations with patience, as long as there was no violation of the rights that the Church, as such, has received from God, her founder.

The law promulgated on July 2 by the Chief Executive of the Federal Government violates these rights of the Church and, at the same time, man's natural right, the foundation and substance of civilization and religious freedom. This, in the opinion of eminent experts, constitutes a flagrant violation of Mexico's constitutional laws. In the face of such an outrage to the moral values we hold sacred, we can no longer remain passive. In such circumstances, our acceptance of it would be criminal. We cannot stand before the Divine Judgment with our only defense the lamentation of the prophet: "Woe is me, that I was silent!"

Who could deny that criminalizing those actions compelled by God Himself, actions favored by the laws of all civilized nations, actions that for centuries were the soul and life of the Mexican people, who could deny that making those acts crimes punishable by harsher penalties than those imposed for crimes against morality, life, property or the other rights of man, is a violation perpetrated by the Chief Executive against the inalienable rights that man has received from God and that these belong to man by nature, and that this law is a denial of those principles so dear and sacred to the Mexican people? Who could pretend that this decree is aimed at defending those rights? Who can deny that the sole purpose of this decree is to surround the Charter of Querétaro with a kind of sacred inviolability? That this charter can be reformed is foreseen by the charter itself, and there is not the slightest doubt that the Mexican people demand immediate reform for compelling reasons. Is it not clear that this decree, far from pursuing the common good, guaranteeing religious freedom, as the Constitution intends, has as its sole object the destruction of the Catholic religion in Mexico and can only drag the government into a useless conflict?

Therefore, following the example that the Holy Father gives us, before God, we protest against this decree. We protest before the heroes who have defended law and justice in the course of history. We protest before the civilized nations of the world. With God's help and your cooperation, we will work to achieve the reform of that decree and the Constitution's anti-religion articles, and we will not surrender until our efforts have been crowned with success.

In our recent pastoral letter, we demonstrated that this action is not a rebellion, because the Constitution itself provides for its own amendment and because our action is justified by the principles of justice and patriotism, superior to every law, and defends rights that law itself considers inalienable and sacred.

*Faced with the impossibility of exercising our sacred ministry subject to the requirements of this decree, and after having consulted our Holy Father, Pius XI, who has approved our attitude, we order that, as of July 31 of this year, and until further notice, all acts of public worship that require the intervention of a priest be suspended in all the churches of the Republic.*

We hasten to reassure you, beloved children: no interdict weighs on you: our sole purpose is to employ the only measure left to us to manifest our refusal to accept the Constitution's anti-religion clauses and the laws enacted to enforce them. The churches will remain open so that the faithful can continue to come to them to pray. The priests in charge of the churches will withdraw from them to escape the penalties of the presidential decree and because, in conscience, they cannot obey the order to go and obtain authorization from government agents to exercise their ministry.

We leave the churches entrusted to the faithful, not doubting that you will protect, with pious solicitude, the shrines inherited from your grandparents, or that, at the cost of great sacrifices, you built yourselves and consecrated to the worship of God.

The law now denies Catholic schools the right to teach religion as they should. We therefore declare to parents that it is an obligation of conscience to take the necessary measures to prevent their children from going to schools where their religion and morality are in danger of being undermined, where the books they use violate the constitutional clause which obliges the Government not to intervene in matters of religion. Let parents, in the family sanctuary, do all they can to fulfill the sacred duty of giving a [Christian] education to the children with which God has blessed them.

Our souls are filled with sadness and our hearts bleed at having been forced to take such austere measures. However, we have not hesitated to take full responsibility for our decision. We had no choice but to do so. Do not lose faith in us, just as we will never lose our faith in you, well-beloved children. As one people, let us place our faith in God. We recommend to you with hope and confidence Our Holy Mother the Virgin of Guadalupe. Days will come when the Divine Pilot seems to have fallen asleep. In need, He will not fail to console and comfort those who have put their faith in Him.

May our trust in God not lead us to inaction. Let us remember that Nineveh was saved from destruction by prayer and penance. Never cease to pray to Mary Immaculate and to her Divine Son. He will not be deaf to your persistence, to your penance, to your love. Think of the priests from whom all means of subsistence have been taken. Openly manifest the sorrow of your heart by refusing to take part in frivolous amusements. Strive to obtain, by all legal and peaceful means, the rejection of those laws that deny to you and your children the most precious of treasures: the freedom to adore God, your life of faith.

On August 1, the Vicar of Christ, our Holy Father Pius XI, will address the throne of God, and with him the Catholics of the whole world, in prayer for the Mexican Church. Let us join our voices to that of the Holy Father, to those of our brothers and sisters throughout the world, consecrating that day to prayer and penance.

In conclusion, let us find comfort in these words addressed by Jesus to His Apostles in foretelling His death and resurrection: "Let us go up to Jerusalem, where the prophecies must be fulfilled," and they will mock Him, and spit on Him, and on the third day He will rise again.

The life of the Church is the life of her Divine Founder. So, dear children, Mexico's church is today given over to its enemies, mocked, slapped, despised. It seems that it must die, but it will rise again with a new and vigorous life, with a splendor such as it never had among us. May this be our indestructible hope. And now, we end by giving you all our pastoral blessings, in the name of the Father, and of the Son, and of the Holy Spirit.

On the feast of the Apostle James, July 25, 1926. [Signed by eight archbishops and twenty-eight bishops] [38]

A total of thirty-six bishops signed the letter, attempting to give the reasons for their actions. The bishops have been accused — and continue to be — of provoking the armed uprising at the expense of Mexican religiosity. As we have seen, this hypothesis is unfounded when the statements and documents of the time are analyzed. It was exactly the opposite.

Furthermore, in August the Mexican president agreed to receive some prelates, who pointed out to him the lack of reason in adopting anti-religion measures for the application of the Constitution of Querétaro. Calles would not listen to reason. At the end of the interview, Bishop Pascual Díaz tried a proposal that seemed diplomatic: "It would suffice," he said, "to state that the registration of the priests is a purely administrative measure and that this does not mean that the government intends to get involved in matters of dogma and discipline" (he was asking simply for an act of good will, a declaration that the registration of priests was a mere administrative matter). Calles refused and ended the interview with these words: "You already know: *you have no other paths than laws or guns.*" [39]

---

[38] *El Universal*, July 25, 1926, emphasis ours.
[39] Acevedo, *David VII*, 239–40.

There was no turning back. The churches were closed and the people's pain at the suspension of worship was so great that the faithful could hardly bear it. "God was leaving the altars," they said. "He's not here" could be seen written on the abandoned tabernacles. These were terrible times for the vast majority of Mexicans.

> From the day the Episcopate announced its decision to sus-pend public worship, "people began to go [to church] in order to ease their consciences, despite it being time to begin working. Every day that passed, more and more people came to town, people came from all the surrounding ranches, and anxiety was perceived in all hearts, pallor was seen in all coun-tenances, sadness was seen in all eyes, and throats stopped speaking, and the question was nothing but "What is going on? And why are they closing the churches? What is happen-ing?" The only answer was: "Well, who knows? I don't know."
> In that parish there were three priests, but it wasn't enough to hear confessions for so many people; they didn't have time to rest or eat; they spent the days from very early until very late at night sitting in the confessionals, but it was not possible for them to confess that crowd. Days and hours elapsed and passed and vanished. And the people, downcast and thoughtful; they did not accept, did not understand: it did not fit within their judgement. They disapproved, they were not in conformity with that decree made known and executed so suddenly. It had struck like lightning in all hearts, in all minds...but there was no remedy, it was necessary to obey. Yet it was not only this: the arbitrary law dictated by Plutarco Elías Calles did not end there, in closing the churches—but God Himself had to leave them, although he had said: "Behold, I will be with you until the consummation of the ages." That promise had been broken, He had to go to the woods, He had to abandon his house, just as if on one day He threw out the money changers out of the Temple, telling them "My house is a house of prayer," and the next day He had to leave it and flee like a criminal because Calles had said so. The church was closed, the tabernacle was deserted, it was empty, God was no longer there. He had gone to be a guest of those who liked to give him lodging, fearing that the government would harm Him. The pealing of bells calling the sinner to go and pray was no longer heard. We had only one consolation left: that the door of the church was open and the faithful in the afternoon went to pray the Rosary and to weep for their sins. The people were in mourning, joy was gone, there was no longer any well-being or tranquility. Hearts were

oppressed and, to crown all, the government forbade meeting in the street as commonly happens when people stand with one another, because this [gathering] was a serious crime.

On that day there was to be a solemn Mass at 12 midnight, and in the end the nave of the church was wholly inadequate to accommodate the immense multitude of faithful. The visitors, kneeling from the door to the altar, followed one after another. Nobody wanted to see such a painful moment arrive, but God was allowing it. At 11:30 p.m., the bells, not with joyful pealing but with a gloomy accent, called for Mass. Nocturnal Adoration, the pious associations and the Catholic-social groups with their respective contingents and flags made an appearance as did all the faithful. At midnight the Most Holy Sacrament was exposed and then Holy Mass began. After the Gospel, our dear Father González occupied the sacred chair.... As soon as he appeared in the pulpit, the weeping of all the people gathered at the feet of Jesus in the Host began. Father's broken words, also full of pain, halted abruptly.... Holy Mass continued, in which there was general communion, and the Holy Sacrifice was finished, the blessing was given to us with His Divine Majesty....

Finally, Father, stripped of his vestments, knelt at the foot of the altar, with his eyes fixed on the image of the Lord of Mercy, then silently took leave of Him, and departed the dazed faithful: Christ and His minister were gone. On that day there was no more joy, no more tranquility. There was an abnormal feeling, all spirits were tense; there were exclamations of pain. "Good Lord! What is going to happen to us?" "Surely the end of the world," others said; and others said they did not know the meaning of this, it must be our sins. This all affirmed: that's what it is, and nothing else. They were everywhere in the streets like a swarm of bees when it senses rain coming. Indeed, it was quite astonishing to see this or that person who had kept away from the sacraments approach the confessor to receive forgiveness of their sins, and others who lived in cohabitation asking to be united in marriage as God commands; there were a number of baptisms. At last, the rosary was prayed with singular fervor, an eloquent sermon, then the Holy Sacrifice of the Mass, for it was midnight, nor was the church closed because of so many faithful who came to the sacraments.... No one slept that unforgettable night, discussing the future.... At the end of the Mass, the blessing with the Most Holy Sacrament was given as a farewell, leaving everything in darkness.

My God! How to describe that formidable time? My
nerves twitch and my hand trembles as I write what I saw,
what I heard. The children's own father had just vanished; we
were orphans.... The faithful departed the church in a sea
of tears, in the midst of darkness the people went out....[40]

The ecclesiastical hierarchy had preached peace, supported the
boycott, suspended public worship. However, everything was in vain
because the tensions did not ease, and the spontaneous uprisings
increased. It was a *fait accompli*:

At the end of September... Mgr. Orozco, alarmed by the
rumors of war, warned the Episcopal Committee that he
was absolutely opposed to any recourse to arms. And when
in November 1926 the League consulted the bishops about
the licit nature of armed resistance, its decision had already
been made: in the face of the spontaneous, isolated, impul-
sive uprisings that were taking place in the countryside, and
in view of the boycott's failure, he proposed to manage the
rebels in order to unify them and make their fight effective.... The League placed the Episcopate before a *fait
accompli*, which it could not change or condemn in any way.[41]

It was not a struggle of the poor against the rich, nor of the bourgeois
against proletarians. The motive, as shown by countless testimonies,
was primarily religious, rather than political. For example:

On July 31, 1926, some men acted to remove the Blessed Sacrament from their churches, from the altars, from the homes
of the Catholics, but other men tried to get Him to come
back again. Those men did not see that the government had
many soldiers, a lot of weapons, a lot of money for making
war on them. They did not see that. What they did was to
defend their God, their Religion, their Mother who is the
Holy Church. That is what they saw. Those men did not
care about leaving their homes, their parents, their children,
their wives and their property. They went to the battlefields
to seek God our Lord. The streams, the mountains, the hills,
are witnesses that those men spoke to God Our Lord with
cries of "LONG LIVE CHRIST THE KING! LONG LIVE THE
BLESSED VIRGIN OF GUADALUPE! LONG LIVE MEXICO!"

---

[40] Cecilio Valtierra, *Memorias de mi actuación en el movimiento cristero en Jalpa
de Cánovas*," Guanajuato, in *David*, 312 and 317, and Josefina Arellano, *Narración
histórica de la revolución cristera en el pueblo de San Julián* (Universidad de Guadalajara, 2002), 14, 15 and 16, quoted by Meyer, *La Cristiada*, 1:95–97.
[41] Meyer, *La Cristiada*, 1:72–73, emphasis ours.

> The same places are witnesses that those men soaked the
> ground with their blood and, not content with that, gave
> their very lives so that God Our Lord would return again.
> And seeing that those men were truly seeking Him, God
> our Lord deigned to return once again to His temples, to
> His altars, to the homes of Catholics — as we are witnessing
> now — and He charged the young people of today never to
> forget the example left us by our forefathers, if ever in the
> future it becomes necessary again [to imitate it].[42]

A few months after worship was suspended, the armed movement
began to spread naturally, and the uprisings happened without structure and planning. Any statement from the Mexican episcopate could
do great good or irreparable damage at that point. The silence was
deafening. In response to this, the Directing Committee of the National
League for the Defense of Religious Liberty, heeding the expressed
desires of the Cristero leaders, who had slowly coalesced, resolved to
take the lead in the crusade to give it some unity. Before doing this,
however, they wanted to consult the episcopate on the legality of the
right to armed rebellion by Mexican Catholics. For this they wrote
to the secretary of the Episcopal Committee, Mgr. Pascual Díaz y
Barreto. Accepting the request, the League Committee convened a
joint assembly on November 26, 1926.[43] What the "League" asked
of the Episcopate was summed up in the very words of the petition:

> Never in the history of our country has the collective con-
> science been formed in the direction of armed resistance.
> This movement cannot and must not be ignored by the
> episcopate, because whether we like it or not, the battle flag
> raised is that of religious freedom and the cry of "Long live
> Christ the King" is unavoidable. The movement cannot be

---

[42] *Letter from Francisco Campos, Santiago Bayacora, Durango* (cited by Meyer, ibid., 93, emphasis ours).

[43] It is worth remembering who attended on behalf of the Church's officials: Mgr. Leopoldo Ruiz y Flores, archbishop of Morelia and vice president of the Episcopal Committee. On this occasion he held the presidency due to illness of the archbishop of Mexico; the Archbishop of Oaxaca, Mgr. José Othón Núñez y Zárate; the bishop of Aguascalientes, Mgr. Ignacio Valdespino y Díaz; from Saltillo, Mgr. Jesús María Echevarrieta y Aguirre; from San Luis Potosí, Mgr. Miguel María de la Mora; from Tulancingo, Mgr. Vicente Castellanos y Núñez; from Chiapas, Mgr. Gerardo Anaya y Diez de Bonilla; from Chihuahua, Mgr. Antonio Guízar y Valencia; from Tacámbaro, Mgr. Leopoldo Lara y Torres; the mayor of Papantla, Mgr. Nicolás Corona; Mgr. Pascual Díaz y Barreto, bishop of Tabasco and secretary of the Episcopal Committee, and Mgr. Luis María Altamirano y Bulnes, then-bishop of Huajuapan de León.

condemned because it is the gravest case of legitimate defense
of the most cherished rights and interests. If the movement
were to be resisted, the only thing achieved would be to
corrupt it and a feeling of dislike would be created against the
Episcopate and all action of defense, even peaceful defense,
would be weakened.[44]

After deliberation on the issue, the Committee resolved:

Attentive to these considerations, we reverently request of
the Episcopate: 1) A negative action, consisting in not condemning the movement. 2) A positive action, consisting of:
a) Sustaining unity of action, by means of agreement on one
plan and one leader, b) Forming the collective conscience,
by the means within the reach of the Episcopate, in the
idea that this is a laudable, meritorious action of legitimate
armed defense, c) Canonically enabling military vicars.... d)
Encouraging and sponsoring a collection vigorously developed with wealthy Catholics, so that they may provide funds
that will be designated for the fight, and that, even just once,
they may understand their obligation to contribute.[45]

Four days later, Mgr. Díaz y Barreto, through Juan Lainé, delivered
the response to the memorandum of the 26th of the same month.
The short interval meant that only Rafael Ceniceros y Villarreal, Luis
G. Bustos, Miguel Palomar y Vizcarra, and Juan Lainé attended the
meeting, accompanied by the ecclesiastical advisors of the League,
Reverend Fathers Alfredo Méndez Medina, S.J., and Rafael Martínez
del Campo, S.J. There they limited themselves to not condemning
the movement, and as we will see, granting the people freedom of
conscience and thus recognizing the counterrevolution's lawfulness.

✳ ✳ ✳

Two worldviews, two religions, were about to face off. Something
unprecedented was about to happen in Latin America: a religious
war between countrymen. In the words of St. Augustine, echoed by
Dickens, they were "two cities" that, from their opposing principles,
could not yield in their positions.

The second part of our work lays out the Mexican populace's
actions when faced with the suppression of their religious rights, and
the evolution of the conflict.

---

[44] Rius Facius, *México Cristero*, 2:130.
[45] Ibid.

*Anacleto González Flores and a group of lay Catholics*

*Part of the Mexican episcopate at the time of the Cristiada*

*Mgr. Francisco Orozco y Jiménez*

# PART II

# The Perspective
## OF A
# Counterrevolutionary
# People

# 3

# Non-Ecclesiastical Catholic Groups

*The government cannot win a war of this kind except by fighting its own people.*

— Porfirio Díaz

THE HISTORY OF THE CRISTEROS CANNOT BE understood, in our opinion, without taking into account the crucial role of the lay Catholic movements, often "independent" of the ecclesiastical hierarchy. What follows is a brief review of what were the foundations of the future Cristero uprising during the painful three years during which Mexico endured religious persecution.[1]

## FR. BERGÖEND AND THE FOUNDING OF THE NATIONAL CATHOLIC PARTY[2]

The Church in Mexico, beginning in the mid-nineteenth century and more precisely as a result of the Constitution of 1857, began to view with some suspicion the positivist education initiative in the country and its effects in the social sphere. For its part, Rome was engaged in intense magisterial labor, publishing various social encyclicals. Among these stood out the famous *Rerum Novarum* of Pope Leo XIII on political and economic changes in society. Following the dissemination of these encyclicals, four Catholic congresses were held in Mexico (Puebla and Morelia, 1903; Guadalajara, 1906; and Oaxaca, 1909). These resulted in several practical accomplishments and did not fail to exercise a certain influence on society (e.g., reduction of working hours, wage increases). The work of laity took on a new momentum and not everything was the work of "the priests."

Yet it was not until the arrival of the French priest, Father Bernardo Bergöend, a Jesuit, that the future of the militant laity began

---

[1] The most well-documented book on this subject is, without a doubt, Rius Facius's already-mentioned *La juventud católica*. It is included in the first volume of his *México cristero* to which we have referred.

[2] See Rius Facius, *México Cristero*, 1:18–27.

to take shape. With his excellent academic training and great political intuition, he saw the need for better organization of lay endeavors. In 1907, knowing that the people must also be won for Christ the King, he organized the first spiritual exercises for workers in Guadalajara. He also quickly contacted the Guadalupan Workers' two prominent members: Miguel Palomar y Vizcarra and Luis B. de la Mora. The idea was to have a Catholic political society ready when the "Porfiriato," already decadent, would fall like a ripe fruit.

Thus, inspired by the principles of the French Catholic party "Popular Liberal Action" (*Action libérale populaire*), Bergöend drafted the groundwork of the party that would be called the Political-Social Union of Mexican Catholics. Among other things, it declared itself against the "more or less Jacobin groups that, for the sake of obeying a maxim coming from foreign Masonic centers, are preparing in the imminent future to renew enforcement of the Reform's laws." The idea was to make Catholics aware of the imperative to throw themselves "without fear into the political battlefield."[3] It was a complete apostolic program.

The Jesuit proposed the creation of two different bodies — one definitely political, independent of the ecclesiastical hierarchy in its direction and action, and the other specifically for Catholic social action, dependent on episcopal authority (bear in mind this political independence).[4]

Meanwhile, as the fall of Don Porfirio Díaz was imminent, in order to save what could be saved, the old general created a party that officially called itself Catholic but, in reality, depended directly on him. It was an old political trick. Once his intentions were discovered and without wasting time, the Archbishop of Mexico, Mgr. Mora y del Río, deemed the time had come for a true Catholic party. Hence, in August 1909 he told Gabriel Fernández Somellera, founder of the National Catholic Circle, that they should implement a plan for the foundation of their own lay party. This was accomplished on the night of May 3, 1911, when the National Catholic Party was founded, based on the principles and advice of Father Bergöend.

---

[3] Rius Facius, *México Cristero*, 1:21.

[4] Mgr. Orozco y Jiménez, who can be labeled anything but pusillanimous, went so far as to declare the independence of Catholic movements by saying that "if Catholics want to give the groups that they form the status of *official* or unofficial *representatives* of the Catholic Church in Mexico, perhaps we prelates would find it necessary to publicly deny them such a status" (Andrés Barquín y Ruiz, *Relaciones y copias de documento en el archivo del autor*, quoted by Rius Facius, *México Cristero*, 1:156–57, emphasis ours).

Before Díaz's fall, the Catholic Party made its debut within the framework of the 1911 elections where, contending for power with the Maderistas and the Constitutionalists, it won several votes despite its inexperience.

## THE FIRST YOUTH SOCIETIES AND
## THE LEAGUE OF CATHOLIC STUDENTS

Under the influence of the Catholic Party, the opportunity for young people to form a student organization with the same objectives arose. For this, the young Luis B. Beltrán and Jorge Prieto, members of a philosophical circle called *Jaime Balmes*, explained their plans to a Fr. Vicente M. Zaragoza. He encouraged them to present the project to the party's president, the aforementioned Fernández Somellera. He received with open arms the idea of starting the Catholic Student Club. Soon after it took the name of the Catholic Student Party and, finally, the League of Catholic Students.

Under the wing of the Party, the students Beltrán, Cordero Sevilla and Arévalo were in charge of drafting the program and the statutes, documents that would be, in the future, the basis of the Catholic Association of Mexican Youth (ACJM, its Spanish acronym). With social objectives, and with the motto "God, Fatherland and Freedom," the group not only sought to "unify Catholic students throughout the Republic," but also to educate workers through conferences "to instruct them about their rights and duties."[5]

After some difficulties, the League of Catholic Students began to publish a weekly entitled *La Libertad*, with markedly political content and supporting the Catholic Party's nominees. Thanks to the connections of a renowned Jesuit, Father Carlos Heredia, the students were able to form a connection with the Association of Catholic Ladies who provided them with the means to have their own building. As a result, the Student Committee of Mexican Catholic Women, made up of young women, was also founded, as well as the Center of Mexican Catholic Students. It was blessed by Mgr. Mora y del Río on February 2, 1913. Ten years after its foundation, the Catholic leader René Capistrán Garza recalled:

> When the Center was inaugurated, the founders' plan did not have the broad horizons that later it acquired, thanks to the heat of action and struggle, and more contact with

---

[5] *Archive of the Central Committee of the ACJM*, cited by Rius Facius, *México Cristero*, 1:32.

reality. The object was to organize the Catholic students to provide them with elements of culture. This caused frequent and extremely interesting descents from the realm of ideas to that of blows; on many occasions it became indispensable to demand a measure of respect.[6]

## THE CATHOLIC ASSOCIATION OF MEXICAN YOUTH (ACJM)

After the elections and the long years of the "Porfiriato," Francisco Madero rose to power. The country finally had an "elected" president, but peace didn't last long: rebellions led by Generals Bernardo Reyes and Félix Díaz, in addition to General Huerta's betrayal, Madero's military right-hand man, ended not only the government of the "anti-reelectionist" Madero, but also his life after he was arrested and executed in a mock escape. U. S. Ambassador Henry Lane Wilson was behind the plot.

After Madero's assassination, Huerta took the reins and governed for a little more than a year (February 1913 to July 1914). However, he was not trusted by Woodrow Wilson to continue with the Monroe Doctrine and "good neighbor" policy.[7] This is why he supported the governor of Coahuila, Venustiano Carranza, at the end of May 1914. He seized absolute power.

In this context, the largest and most influential Catholic group in Mexico was born: the ACJM, whose purpose was to unite the different Catholic organizations, especially youth organizations. To this end, and based on the "Catholic Association of French Youth" (known in Mexico from the influence of Father Bergöend), a solid and consistent group was founded at young Manuel de la Peza's request (a member of the Catholic Student Center) and with the help of Father Bergöend. Its purpose was to "cooperate in the restoration of the Christian order, through serious religious, social and civic formation."[8]

It is worth considering the enormous independence the ACJM had from the hierarchy. This was reflected in its bylaws, drafted by the French priest:

---

[6] René Capistrán Garza, "Speech delivered on April 13, 1922," in *Juventud Católica* no. 5, first period, cited by Rius Facius, *México Cristero*, 1:39.

[7] Woodrow Wilson's government set four clear objectives: 1) to remove the Mexican government's nominations, 2) to put an end to the Tehuantepec National Railway, a real obstacle to controlling the rates for passage through the Panama Canal, 3) to end the influence of the clergy, and 4) to end the landowners who represented the class most attached to the country. See also Rius Facius, *México Cristero*, 1:60–61.

[8] Bernardo Bergöend, S. J., "Discurso sobre la historia de la ACJM," *Juventud Católica* no. 5, first period, quoted in Rius Facius, *México Cristero*, 1:46.

The ACJM, like the Conferences of St. Vincent de Paul, is clearly a lay association, because:

A. In fact:

a) It has not been founded by the Ecclesiastical Authority and continues to be composed of lay elements (General Statutes, Arts. 2, 5 and others).

b) It governs itself (Art. 3), although from its beginnings it has always had very close connections with Ecclesiastical Authority, so much so that it is a necessary condition for a Local Group to belong. For this reason it has an Ecclesiastical Assistant appointed and approved by the diocesan Prelate (Arts. 6 and 20).

B) By law, it meets each and every condition that Canon Law supposes in an Association for it to be lay and not ecclesiastical.[9]

Clearly comprised of laity, it was sustained by piety, study, and action. With respect to the latter, it had to be "purely Mexican," committing itself to the reconstruction of social institutions and "energetically resisting both revolutionary individualism...and collectivism." All this and without neglecting the electoral sphere, since "its members as citizens will always keep in mind that it is an essential duty for them to defend political and religious freedom, even in the electoral sphere."[10]

On August 12, 1913, and united with the previously founded National League of Catholic Students, the two consolidated with the Marian Congregations and the Center of Catholic Students (without losing their internal hierarchies), to join forces in a single association: the ACJM. Finally, Catholic youth were combined with the consecration of Mexico to the Sacred Heart of Jesus, on January 11, 1914, which declared, moreover, that Christ was King of the Mexican nation.

The confused situation that the country endured due to Obregón and Carranza supporters, added to the religious persecution it suffered, made the development of the ACJM temporarily impossible (from 1914–1917). However, far from remaining in vague apathy, not only did its members continue to work, they even showed their support for the rights of the Church.[11]

---

[9] *General Statutes of the Asociación Católica de la Juventud Mexicana*, first edition (Sacred Heart Press, Mexico, 1913), cited by Rius Facius, *México Cristero*, 1:49.
[10] Rius Facius, 1:50.
[11] As evidenced by the protest that members of the Catholic Student Center made in February 1915 against the arrest of some priests, which earned them

In the first four months of 1917, the study circles of the ACJM regularly continued. They elected in January René Capistrán Garza as president of the Board of Directors and Julio Jiménez Rueda as vice president and had the great joy, in August of that year, of bringing the Association to Guadalajara, the heart of Jalisco. This was where, after its proclamation in 1917 and despite the protest of the bishops, one of the first public demonstrations against the government took place, prompted by the arrest of some priests. This, plus the closure of several churches, caused the new group to publicly demonstrate against "the attempted search of the churches" and "the imprisonment of our priests." Afterwards, on June 24, some twenty-six demonstrators were arrested, nineteen of whom were "acejotaemeros" (as ACJM members were called).[12] The group had undergone its baptism of fire.

Little by little, various Catholic centers throughout the country were affiliated with the new group. Among the places where new groups opened were Morelia, Colima, Sonora, Querétaro, Celaya, Acámbaro, and Michoacán. Given the association's scope and the great need to be prepared for the growing religious persecution, that they decided to initiate the first General Committee. It was placed under the presidency of René Capistrán Garza, a young man barely twenty years old, known for his feeling and eloquence.

Government pressure on the states had led to the implementation of the anti-religion decrees of the Constitution of Querétaro. In mid-1918, in Jalisco, for example, the famous 1913 decree was promulgated. Among other things, it regulated the number of priests and prevented the administration of the sacraments without prior authorization from the State. Catholic protests were swift in coming, especially when the Archbishop of Guadalajara, Mgr. Orozco y Jiménez, was arrested for his public opposition to the anti-religion policy, which had led to the closure of all churches in retaliation. His arrest provided the ACJM with one more reason to form a defense.[13] On July 22, thousands of people gathered in Guadalajara to demonstrate their discontent with the exasperating laws. General Diéguez attempted to address the crowd:

---

arrest and, if there had been no foreign representatives, possibly execution (see Rius Facius, 1:100–101).

[12] See Rius Facius, 1:118.

[13] On July 17, 1918, in Guadalajara, a "protest" was drafted in the form of 10,000 leaflets, denouncing the persecution against Mgr. Orozco y Jiménez, as well as the arrest of several members of the ACJM, which led to new persecutions (see Rius Facius, 1:142–43).

> "You have been gathered here by deception..."
> "No! No!"—the people roared—
> But "your priests deceive you..."
> "No! No! No!" replied the crowd.
> "Well, gentlemen, you have only two paths: either to
> abide by Decree 1913 issued by Congress...or abandon the
> state as pariahs..."—after which a loud laugh resounded as
> Diéguez turned his back on the crowd.[14]

Repression was not long in coming, so the ACJM responded with
a call for a huge boycott, which had immense popular support. The
General Committee of the ACJM, in a manifesto published on August
18, concluded by ridiculing Mexican democracy:

> They have attempted to make exclusionary laws against Cath-
> olic priests. Exclusionary laws against Catholicism already
> have a name in history: they are called laws of persecution.
> And these laws of persecution have been put into our Magna
> Carta—that is, they wanted to establish religious persecution
> in Mexico in a permanent way as an institution of the State!
> And this is the procedure of a *democratic* government, of a
> public power that emanates from the people, and is instituted
> for the benefit of the people (Art. 39), who are almost entirely
> Catholic? In a democratic republic, citizens should be treated
> equally—we are either all sons or all stepchildren.... Good
> for the heroic Catholic people of Guadalajara! Long live
> Jesus Christ, Immortal King of all nations![15]

So great was the effect caused by the protests that the Jalisco Chamber of Deputies was forced to repeal the decree at the beginning of
1919. It was a resounding victory for the Catholics of Jalisco. A few
days later Mgr. Orozco y Jiménez and Mgr. Leopoldo Ruiz y Flores
were able to return from exile, thanks to the efforts of Mgr. John J.
Burke, a priest from the United States,[16] despite Carranza, who was
against softening the persecution.

---

[14] Rius Facius, 1:145–46.

[15] *Archive of the Central Committee of the ACJM*, cited by Rius Facius, 1:146–47.

[16] "John J. Burke, priest and secretary general of the NCWC (National Catholic
Welfare Conference), was the priest who most closely followed religious hostilities
in Mexico, from 1916 until the time of his death in 1936. He advised four U.S.
presidents on the subject, deployed humanitarian aid on behalf of all refugees,
negotiated with the Vatican and, finally, used all his influence to get Calles to
mitigate the persecution. The arrangements of 1929 owed a great deal to his
involvement. A good biography on him has yet to be written." Luis A. García
Dávalos, review of Jean Meyer's *La Cruzada por México. Los católicos de Estados*

## THE CIVIC LEAGUE FOR RELIGIOUS DEFENSE

Almost as a necessity and given the simmering religious persecution, the ACJM's inspiration, Father Bergöend, formulated another measure: a League that, without the characteristics of a political party, "would take charge of defending the universally recognized rights of the Church and freedom of education, denied in Article 3 of the Constitution."[17] It would thus be a body defending religious freedom, understood as the Church's right to practice religion publicly without interference from the State.[18]

Some years earlier, the French priest had told Palomar y Vizcarra his intentions to found a "League" that, remaining outside any political party,[19] would give its moral support, and its vote to the candidates who could guarantee the essential freedoms and the Church's rights. This League was not ready. Five more years passed before the plan was executed.

## ACEJOTAEMEROS IN THE NATIONAL REPUBLICAN PARTY

Álvaro Obregón's rise to power in 1920, after the coup d'etat and assassination of President Venustiano Carranza, were among the many events that continued to mobilize the Catholic laity politically. Some adherents of ACJM took an active part in the organization of the National Republican Party, whose main objective was, if it came to power, changing the Constitution of 1917.

In Morelia, in May 1921, there was a brawl between socialist and Catholic students as a result of a demonstration by the former. After an attack on one of the churches, a large protest happened on May 12, which provoked violent police intervention by order of the police chief, Vicente Coyt:

---

*Unidos y la cuestión religiosa en México* (Tusquets/Océano, 2008), in *Estudios de Historia Moderna y Contemporánea de México* 26 (2008): 283–84.

[17] Rius Facius, 1:155.

[18] It is worth clarifying that what was meant by "religious freedom" at that time was simply this: the freedom of the Church to manifest herself publicly and to exercise her ministry independently of the claws of the state.

[19] "The League recognizes its dependence on the Episcopate in the sense that, in moral and religious matters, it follows the orientation and suggestions of the Bishops. But in practical actions it considers itself independent: organization and government. Theoretically this seems clear to both the League and the Episcopate." Andrea Mutolo, *Gli "arreglos" tra l'episcopato e il governo nel conflitto religioso del Messico (21 giugno 1929). Come risultano dagli archivi messicani*, Pontificia Università Gregoriana, 2003, p. 32.

"This demonstration is hereby dissolved, or we will dissolve it with bullets!"

Rómulo González Reyes answered: "No! This demonstration is not dissolved because the voice of the people is the voice of God. Go ahead, men. Go ahead... Go ahead... Go ahead...!"

Coyt, his two assistants and a few other officers stationed themselves behind the pilasters of the aqueduct that crosses the road. From there, Vicente Coyt fired his gun at Rómulo who fell mortally wounded. This shot was a signal to attack. Several policemen hidden in the aqueduct canal appeared and from there riddled the unarmed citizens with bullets.

Above the confusion, rifle and pistol fire, there were shouts: "Long live the Virgin of Guadalupe!"

Julián brandished a pistol, exposed the smallest possible area of himself as a target, and began firing while shouting at the same time "Long live Christ the King!" Next to him, a man — a water carrier — fell with his heart pierced, further on, a lady climbed a bench and shouted "Long live Christ the King! Long live the brave men!" She fell as if struck by a bullet in the chest.[20]

The first *acejotaemeros* to offer their lives were nine in all; two government soldiers fell as well. The war began and the ACJM was ready: "Faithful to its principles... to repel by force, when necessary, the attacks by which decadent Jacobinism and advancing communism seek to claim their victims."[21]

The protests of the ACJM grew as the anti-religion offensive increased and began to toughen its strategy. There was — among so many not included here — an episode that further roused spirits for the conflict. Near Guanajuato is Cerro del Cubilete, the geographical center of Mexico: a mountain which rises to an altitude of 800 meters. There was a plan to build a large monument dedicated to Christ the King there. The foundation stone was laid on January 11, 1923. It was not done in a public space (at that time, it was private property) so that it would not violate any existing law. Mgr. Ernesto Filippi, apostolic nuncio in Mexico, was received with great joy by the populace of Guanajuato and on the morning of January 11 the faithful began the ascent up the mountain. The ceremony took place calmly but the outburst of faith there caused the government to

---

[20] Rius Facius, *México Cristero*, 1:175.
[21] Rius Facius, 1:178.

impose a peremptory deadline of three days for the apostolic nuncio to leave the country, citing a "violation of Article 33 of the National Constitution" ("foreigners may not, in any way, interfere in the political affairs of the country"). René Capistrán Garza, president of the ACJM, commented on the events:

> I have just learned, without any surprise, that the Government has given His Excellency Filippi three days to leave the country. I said "without any surprise" because I have always feared acts like this on the part of a government which I cannot but judge to be utterly oppressive. The great and most Christian act carried out in the Cerro del Cubilete, a true and genuinely popular act, is the best demonstration of the immense store of energies that still exists in Mexico, and reveals that ours is a truly Catholic country. That action has been the full, admirable and beautiful use of a sacred right. It has been the correct use of true freedom, which has been so much proclaimed and so much mocked. Yet precisely because it is the use of a right, it is repressed, because it is the exercise of true freedom, it is punished. Is there anything strange about this? Revolutionary history has been and will be a history of oppression. To think otherwise or to expect the opposite is either naive or stupid. This, it seems to me, is the pure and simple truth without ambiguity or euphemisms.[22]

Catholic organizations increasingly began to have much more public participation and did so in proportion to the government's provocations. This happened in several states, such as Durango, when the legislature in May 1923 limited the number of priests. When Obregón was asked to intercede, he brazenly replied that "to reduce the number of these [Catholic priests] is to alleviate the burden on the people and is, at the same time, to create a more comfortable situation for the ministers of worship themselves, since, by diminishing their number, they will be better able to live."[23] The matter escalated and during a demonstration in front of Durango's Government Palace ten people lost their lives defending freedom of worship. For the ACJM, it was one more battle. Similar incidents around the same period happened in San Luis Potosí, Guadalajara, and Zacatecas. This was the seedbed of the *Cristiada*.

---

[22] Alfonso Taracena, *La verdadera revolución mexicana* (Jus, 1962), cited by Rius Facius, 1:210–11.
[23] Rius Facius, 1:230.

## THE FOUNDING OF THE "LEAGUE": A GROUP INDEPENDENT OF THE EPISCOPATE[24]

As mentioned above, it had not been time for founding the Civic League for Religious Defense. Now, circumstances led the leaders of the ACJM to implement the plan, and once again, it was in reaction to the government's oppression.

The rise of Calles to the presidency in 1924 and the schismatic attempt on the part of "Pope" Pérez that we have already discussed, led the ACJM to call for a boycott against the newspaper *El Globo*, the only one that had not repudiated the fact of the taking of the Soledad church. Moreover, due to fears that something similar would happen at the Basilica Shrine of Our Lady of Guadalupe in Mexico City, some members of various groups from the ACJM took turns protecting it from a possible assault. Hours passed slowly until one Sunday morning, a convoy with men harboring evil intentions sent by the government arrived. The young defenders and several pilgrims prepared to defend the basilica of Guadalupe from "the alleged assailants." One of the defenders, Andrés Barquín y Ruiz, said that they "limited themselves to contemplating us and, turning around, withdrew."[25]

All this made Miguel Palomar y Vizcarra think that it was the first step of a well thought-out plan against Catholicism in Mexico. The time had come to implement Father Bergöend's earlier project to found a national association to defend religious freedom. So, he began to discuss this with René Capistrán Garza and Luis G. Bustos. On March 9, several representative members of the different existing Catholic societies met at the premises of the Order of the Knights of Columbus to consider whether the project was appropriate or not, and ended up approving it unanimously. In reply to the question asked by Ramón Ruiz y Rueda, a participant, about "whether all the means used by the League should be exclusively legal," Capistrán Garza stressed that, as the manifesto said, "the means will be constitutional and those demanded by the common good."[26] These final words were not entirely pleasing ("demanded by the common good" implied the right to a violent response). The declaration was signed on March 14, 1925,

---

[24] "The League acknowledges its dependence on the Episcopate in the sense that, in moral and religious matters, it follows the guidance and suggestions of the bishops. However, in practical matters, it considers itself independent in terms of organization and governance. Theoretically, this seems clear to both the League and the Episcopate." Mutolo, *Gli "arreglos" tra l'episcopato e il governo*, 32.
[25] Text in Rius Facius, *México Cristero*, 1:251.
[26] Rius Facius, 1:254.

hence constituting the National League for the Defense of Religious Liberty. To make it known, it was agreed that all national Catholic groups would send a flyer to their local associations accompanied by the program of "the League," as it was known from then on.

The communiqué to the Catholic people made clear that the new entity was not a confederation of associations, but a distinct organization with specific purposes, although it was encouraged, sustained, and spread by other associations. By virtue of this, the ACJM, adding its efforts to that of the other existing institutions, proposed to cooperate intensely in the success of this enterprise. As González Morfín correctly noted,

> since its foundation, the League assumed responsibility for its actions, disassociating itself from the hierarchy. This does not mean that it is in opposition to ecclesiastical authority, and that it intends to act with complete independence from the council and the senior management of this same author- ity; but that it "takes upon itself all the responsibility for its actions, and aims only to move with the freedom that reasonably suits it," stated its statutes.[27]

Capistrán Garza was in charge of publishing the League's pro- gram in the metropolitan newspapers *Excélsior* and *El Universal*. On March 20, the program appeared and, on Sunday, March 22, the press published the following statements by the Secretary of the Interior, Gilberto Valenzuela:

> The work that the Catholics who are part of the League propose to carry out is, judging by the tenor of the manifesto they launched, illegal and seditious.... (Since) the group that intends to be formed is not a religious group, as its purpose is not to write propaganda to obtain a greater number of followers of a certain religious sect, but it is a political group, since, what it intends to do is of a political nature, such as reforming the Constitution, defending the civic rights of citizens, etc. (therefore I will) make a careful study of the manifesto of the Catholics that intend to form the league, to see if it is appropriate to report the aforementioned manifesto to the competent authorities, since it contains subversive paragraphs and because the group has been constituted in a form prohibited by article 130 of the Constitution, or to issue the appropriate resolution on the matter.[28]

---

[27] Acevedo, *David VIII*, 140, emphasis ours.
[28] Rius Facius, *México Cristero*, 1:255.

The die was cast, and Valenzuela knew where the Catholics were headed. Faced with such a statement, Capistrán Garza, honorary president of the ACJM, denied that it was a "political party," since its function was not electoral, but a

> defensive organization for the rights of Catholics. It is evident that, even if it is not a political party, the League will be forced to act in the political field… (because) the religious question in Mexico is a political question, much to the chagrin of Catholics… The fact that we Catholics finally decided to defend ourselves should not surprise anyone. It had to happen one day. It seems to me that we have given truly remarkable evidence of extravagant patience.[29]

Something to keep in mind, again, is that the "League" was founded without the express approval of the ecclesiastical hierarchy, to avoid repeating the events of 1919 when Mgr. Orozco y Jiménez had opposed such an enterprise. The League was born, then, as an association completely separate from the bishops.[30]

The group was established under the presidency of Rafael Ceniceros y Villarreal, one of its first promoters. René Capistrán Garza and Luis G. Bustos were elected as co-directors. Independent of the ACJM, it was almost like its subsidiary (the first directors were, without doubt, members of the Association) and in a few weeks it had the support of several related societies throughout the country already operating in support of religious freedom.[31]

## THE "PEOPLE'S UNION" OF ANACLETO GONZÁLEZ FLORES

In Jalisco, the "People's Union" had already existed for several years, led by the lawyer Anacleto González Flores and independent of the bishops as far as its governance was concerned. Enthusiastic about the undertakings of the German Catholics who, with their peaceful resistance against Otto von Bismarck's harsh campaign, had managed to prevail in the country's affairs, he believed that in Mexico, otherwise

---

[29] Rius Facius, 1:256, emphasis ours.
[30] Even in Morelia, there was a possibility that the foundation would be condemned by its archbishop and, apparently, at the behest of Monsignor Luis María Martínez, creator of the "Asociación del Espíritu Santo" (Association of the Holy Spirit). See Rius Facius, 1:256–57.
[31] In Guadalajara, the great *acejotaemero* and future martyr Anacleto González Flores, president of the association "People's Union," joined instantly, although the People's Union retained almost absolute autonomy and its own name (see Rius Facius, 1:259).

so different from Germany, the same results could be obtained. Hence, inspired by Ludwig Windthorst, the great adversary of the Reich Chancellor, he established an organization which he called the "People's Union."

There was room for all Catholics. Each one had a place, according to his abilities, so that the group's actions would become unstoppable. The plan was to fight on three fronts or "crusades": spreading good newspapers (along with the declaration of war on ungodly newspapers), which implied that bad newspapers shouldn't be accepted or tolerated at home. Second, that of the catechism, to ensure that all parents take their children to church to receive religious instruction. And third, the book crusade, which meant clearing homes of bad books and ensuring that in every home there was at least one serious book for religious formation.

González Flores wanted the People's Union to reach everywhere: the press, the workshop, the factory, the home, the school — every place there were individuals and groups. This organization grew significantly, spreading even to neighboring states. With a weekly publication, *Gladium* (which by the end of 1925 had a circulation of 100,000 copies), he explained his purpose was to make all the nation's Catholics form a bloc of disciplined forces, conscious of their individual and social responsibility, and in a position to mobilize quickly and constantly, either to resist the harsh Reform or to set in motion the reconquest of the freedoms taken from Catholics.

With simple equipment and without bureaucratic offices, the People's Union had more than 100,000 members, distributed throughout all social spheres, both urban and rural. No one was to remain inactive.

> To be a member of the People's Union at the most basic level required only a very simple act of the will. No age, no condition, no determined quota, no compulsory attendance at specific events. You became a member of the People's Union when you least expected. But as soon as someone became part of the organization, a continuous and effective link was established between him and the hierarchy of leaders. The demand on its members was minimal, and according to the thinking of the director [Anacleto González Flores], it could be reduced to this: that someone be willing to listen to us.... On an urban block, a man would appear as a salesman of a tiny newspaper and a visitor to homes. That man spoke periodically with another person from his parish. Was there anything in this that exceeded the

normal relations in a neighborhood? Yet that was enough for the individual sensitive to this minimal influence, and by spending a penny a week, the price of the newspaper, to change indifference into cooperation. "It's enough," said the founder, "for each Catholic to look for his neighborhood's head and ask to register so that in the future he can be aware of everything that is being done for God's cause and cease being a Catholic paralytic and become a standard-bearer of life's fundamental freedoms." An elementary hierarchy, as solid as it was simple, linked the newest member with the Head of the five-member Directory who ruled the Union. Block, zone, parish: the person in charge of each of these areas had close contact with his subordinates and with his immediate superior. There were no ceremonies, solemnity, and protocol. There were almost no books and nor were any orders issued. The paperwork was replaced by the effectiveness of personal relationships.[32]

When the "League" appeared on the scene, González Flores, far from feeling jealous, enabled both organizations to work together for the same purposes. For a time, the People's Union remained within the orbit of the League but maintained its autonomy. However, over time and thanks to the national reach of the "leagues," it was necessary to unify them completely, the People's Union eventually becoming an auxiliary and confederate society of the League.

The League viewed Augustin de Iturbide, Lucas Alamán, Miguel Miramón, and Tomás Mejía as exemplary heroes, and likewise repudiated the adversaries that its mentor Anacleto González Flores would point out as the "three heads of a single enemy": the liberals, Freemasons, and Protestants. He had been born to defend the rights of God and in a peaceful way, but there came a time when he could not continue in this manner. As González Flores himself declared, they were forced into war:

> You will have noticed that our position as militant Catholics has led us, almost without realizing it, to the inevitable crisis that will necessarily make each of us reflect on the impact that our present resolution may have for our lives. The League has embarked on the revolutionary adventure with a determination that may be, more than anything, a heartfelt intuition. Hopefully, the intuition is accurate. For

---

[32] Demetrio Loza (pseudonym of Antonio Gómez Robledo), *El Maestro* (Xalisco, 1937), cited by Rius Facius, 1:266.

my part, I can say that I have decided on my personal position, which can be none other than what my post seems to
demand: I will stand with the League and place everything
I am and all that I have on the line. But I feel obliged to
declare my message for posterity before you: The People's
Union was never an organization whose proper aim was to
initiate a civil war. Mixed up as you are going to be, I know
too well, in the whirlwind of a struggle by resorting to force,
you run the risk of forgetting the doctrine: the sword blade
is not the best support for institutions like ours. Beyond
triumph or beyond defeat in the future, we must continue
to maintain that Mexico's problem is a problem of culture,
of apostolate, of civilization. Today, however, everything
pushes us to the mountain. Let's go forward. The People's
Union is too important to lose it all in a venture in which
we will be left alone. May God make this collective sacrifice
bear fruit.[33]

A Mexican ballad remembered it this way:

> Gentlemen, listen carefully
> To what I am going to sing to you:
> They rose up in arms,
> Those of the People's Union.[34]

### THE WOMEN'S BRIGADES OF SAINT JOAN OF ARC

Not everything was a male affair, as there were groups especially
dedicated to action made up only of women. Although discussed
more later, we mention here the famous Women's Brigades of Saint
Joan of Arc. This society was founded in Jalisco and whose initial
purpose was the moral defense of female trade-workers, office workers, and seamstresses, recruiting its affiliates from the middle class
and the common people. Directed and founded by the lawyer Luis
Flores González and María Goyaz (alias "Celia Gómez"), it eventually
had more than 25,000 members and became part of the "League."[35]
Completely secret, a rigorous oath "on one's knees and before the
crucifix" to defend the Fatherland and the Church was required in
order to enter it. Its members were young, mostly single, between
15 and 25 years old.

---

[33] Heriberto Navarrete, *Por Dios y por la Patria. Memorias de mi participación en la Defensa de la Libertad de Conciencia y Culto, durante la Persecución Religiosa en México de 1926 a 1929* (Tradición, 1980), 121–22.

[34] Navarrete, 117–19.

[35] See Meyer, *La Cristiada*, 3:122.

Within the war zones, the "BB" (as they were known) would have a very prominent logistical function: "These true heroines who came and went, by train or on the back of a mule, [hid] ammunition under their clothes, in vests that were made with gathered fabric so that a multitude of folds were formed where the cartridges were kept, from 500 to 700 per person."[36] Father Ochoa, who under the pseudonym "Spectator" wrote about the Cristeros' exploits in Colima, described the character of these young women as follows:

> With self-denial, joy and holy commitment, without measuring fatigue or danger, they took on their shoulders the task of providing the Army of the Crusaders of Christ with everything that was necessary: arms, equipment, clothing, medicines.... They were discovered more than once, were tortured, without the pain of torment ever making them disclose anything.... And the one who writes this gives formal testimony that this whole army of women was always, without exception, truly without any exception, equal to Christian duty regarding purity of life. Never a vulgarity, much less any moral stain that would have been so easily explained in the circumstances in which they worked, mixing with the Callista soldiers to buy war supplies. Always dignified, honest, pure, joyful, and heroic.[37]

Still, their work was not always peaceful during the war and there was more than one who took up arms in defense of their faith, as Meyer points out.[38]

## THE SECRET ORGANIZATION "U"

Although all Catholic organizations maintained a certain "clandestinity," there was one that especially characterized this: the "U" (Union of Mexican Catholics).

Founded by Father Luis María Martínez, who eventually became Primate of Mexico, and by Adalberto Abascal, a Catholic leader, this organization became a major force in the Mexican religious conflict.

Salvador Abascal wrote that the organization "was born in Morelia, more precisely it was planned in Santa María de los Altos, a small town

---

[36] Alfredo Sáenz, *La ascensión y la marcha* (Gladius, 1999), 259.
[37] Spectator, *Los cristeros del volcán de Colima*, 1:335–36.
[38] "They took their war mission very seriously, not hesitating to resort to violence, kidnapping, execution, to obtain ransoms, protect combatants and punish spies. Using every means, they organized dances in the villages to gain the trust of the officers, dispel their suspicions and obtain information." Meyer, *La Cristiada*, 3:132.

in the hills of Morelia in 1918," whence his father spread it throughout
the country from 1920 to 1925. The "U," as it was called, "managed
to control under the table, secretly and decisively, all Catholic organizations, both civic and religious, from the Knights of Columbus...
to the Catholic Ladies."[39]

It is interesting to see how the teenager Salvador Abascal found
out about the existence of it, through his father's adventures.[40] The
way it was managed was like a "white Freemasonry": with initiation
rites and rigorous secrecy for its members, its goal was the defense of
religion and the fatherland. Jesús Degollado Guízar, general in chief
of the Liberation Army after General Enrique Gorostieta Velarde's
death, recalled that while living in Atotonilco El Alto, Jalisco, one
day in early 1920, he received a message from the parish priest, Don
Macario Velázquez, in which he asked him to come by that night
because he had an urgent matter to deal with. He recalled:

> As I promised, at eight o'clock I was present at the rec-
> tory.... He invited me in. Guided by him, we arrived at a
> room where forty people were gathered.... Among them
> were the priest Don Vicente Camacho, Anacleto González
> Flores, Miguel Gómez Loza.... After greeting us, the priest,
> addressing me, said: "We have seen with our own eyes that
> you are an honest man and a true Christian. We have received
> reports about you from different places, and the informa-
> tion we have received is in accordance with your way of
> life.... This group will be honored if you agree to belong
> to it. Do you give your word of honor not to tell anyone
> what you are told?
> "Yes," I answered. The priest continued:

---

[39] Salvador Abascal, *Mis recuerdos. Sinarquismo y Colonia María Auxiliadora*
(Tradición, 1980), 142.

[40] "When I was on my tour in 1935–1936 as a member of the secret organization
of the Legions [promoting it] in each diocesan see, I visited the bishop of the
town to place myself at his service. So I arrived with the bishop of Saltillo, and
he asked me if I was the son of Adalberto Abascal, then he told me about the
U to which I had belonged and about my father and there I learned what he did
when on vacation we accompanied him to the ranches, my brothers and I and
we saw how he met for hours with the gentlemen of the ranch. We didn't know
that he was founding an organization. When I told my father, he was upset with
the bishop because he said that they had committed to secrecy. That secrecy
was about the government, not about the Church. The founder was Luis María
Martínez, he conceived the idea, my father helped him to finish planning it and
he made it. The idea was the union of all Mexican Catholics to save Mexico.
They both said, 'They beat us because we are divided.'" Fernando M. González,
*Matar y morir por Cristo rey. Aspectos de la cristiada* (UNAM, 2001), 32.

"There is an organization established throughout the Republic called the Union of Mexican Catholics, better known among us as the "U." This group is fully organized in the states of Jalisco and Michoacán, in others it is now being organized. The purpose of the "U" is to seek by all lawful and possible means the restoration of the reign of Christ in our country. To achieve this object, one must commit oneself to obey one's superiors in everything that is licit and honest, and to give one's life, if necessary, in defense of the rights of God and the Church. We, the group, invite you to calmly consider and respond as you see fit."

"Father," I answered, "no one who loves Christ as I love him can refuse his assistance in securing, with his effort and with his life, Christ's full reign in our country.... I gladly and freely accept membership in this honorable group..."

The priest... invited me to go to the makeshift altar that was in the room, and before an image of Christ crucified and the book of the Gospels, I took an oath to obey my superiors.... Then they gave me the signs and passwords with which I could identify myself with all the group's members throughout the Republic.[41]

According to Fernando González, this testimony of an initiation into the "U," prior to the Cristiada, is the only one that has been discovered so far, given the ironclad oath that existed between them. Perhaps it was because of this secrecy that the ecclesiastical hierarchy tolerated it until 1929, after which Pius XI ordered its immediate dissolution, with the resulting possibility of breaking the oath.

The "U" was an organization in which, at least since 1923, according to González,[42] had in mind the possibility of armed struggle against tyranny and even tyrannicide, based on the texts of theologians St. Thomas Aquinas and Francisco Suárez.

The conflict became, in fact, more and more aggressive, and everything suggested that a new stage was beginning for the Mexican laity.

## HERIBERTO NAVARRETE AND THE INDEPENDENCE OF ANACLETO GONZÁLEZ FLORES

Being deeply involved in a lay movement in counterrevolutionary Mexico had very unusual features. Among innumerable cases that could be recounted, the case of Major Heriberto Navarrete is of

---

[41] Jesús Degollado Guízar, *Memorias de Jesús Degollado Guízar. Último general en jefe del ejército cristero* (JUS, 1957), 11–12.

[42] See González, *Matar y morir por Cristo rey*, 35.

particular interest because of his later career, which will be discussed later. Born at the beginning of the twentieth century in the state of Jalisco and educated as a Catholic from his childhood in Guadalajara, Navarrete became a militant in the ACJM when he was still a teenager. There he had the opportunity to meet someone who would become his intellectual and moral mentor, the aforementioned Anacleto González Flores.

The ACJM's mode of operation did not differ, initially, from any serious parish group: as we said, piety, study, and action were the pillars of the formation of an "acejotaemero." These pillars did not prevent healthy fun, serenading at night, or the endless popular ranchero music sessions. In the atmosphere of the Association, however, difficult times were coming, and it was necessary to prepare.

One afternoon Navarrete, still a young man, met the "Maestro" González Flores: his language and his enthusiasm captivated him. Both Heriberto and other young people were called to live in a different, more heroic, and more virile way:

> Let us go back to the subterfuges of the cowardly little man within each of us: there are ways and means of loving God. Are you perhaps one of those who believe that this infinite ambition is fulfilled by those ordinary practices of the cardboard Christian who attends Mass on Sundays and already feels entitled to heaven because he sometimes listens to a sermon? No. That's not being a Christian. That is the way of paganism. It is an easygoing desertion of the Christian life, passing by the tabernacle while wearing a carnival mask, smiling at the world and vice, while in the vague gloom of a church corner, hastily, in a few minutes painfully stolen from the week, he makes the sign of the cross on his painted comic face. The conscientious man cannot deceive himself so miserably. [43]

The Catholic leader's words inflamed the hearts of his listeners. Navarrete was one of those captivated by it. Later he would recount how the lay movements were so independent of the ecclesiastical hierarchy that even González Flores himself denied some requests from certain priests. For example, the *Gladium* newspaper published a weekly "blacklist" of recognized Masonic merchants so that the Catholic people could "boycott" their wares, avoiding purchases from them. Everything worked perfectly, especially in Jalisco. One

---

[43] Navarrete, *Por Dios y por la Patria*, 23.

morning in the Archbishop's palace, the following dialogue took place between Anacleto González Flores and a certain priest named Castro.

*Fr. Castro*: Maestro, I have been looking for you.

*Anacleto:* At your service, Father.

*Fr. Castro*: My issue is very simple. In your newspaper, Alfonso Emparán appears on the blacklist of Freemasons. I promised him that you will remove him from it because Alfonso Emparán is not a Freemason.

*Anacleto:* In the Secretariat of the People's Union, reliable data were found, Father. Alfonso Emparán is a Freemason. We know very well the serious responsibility we would face if we carelessly published his name in the absence of evidence.

*Fr. Castro*: Well, you are committing an injustice. Because if at one time he belonged to Freemasonry, today he does not.

*Anacleto.* I am ready to withdraw his name and place a free advertisement on it, if he makes a public retraction to our satisfaction.

*Fr. Castro*: I don't think it's necessary. Alfonso Emparán went to confession with me.

*Anacleto:* Forgive my frankness, Father — to try to fool us, Alfonso Emparan, like any Mason, is not only capable of confessing, but also of receiving minor orders.

Respectful, yes, but not submissive. Emparán continued to appear on blacklists.[44]

❋ ❋ ❋

Lay groups were forced to mobilize, and they did so with the same principles as the hierarchy but outside the sphere of their control. The shepherds were overwhelmed, and the sheep were achieving an increasing influence, as we will see.

---

[44] Navarrete, 108–9.

*Peaceful resistance: the boycott*

*Women of night-time Eucharistic adoration, arrested*

*The defense of the churches*

*Cristero women*

# 4

# A People's Uprising

*Without their permission or their command, we launched this blessed struggle for our freedom, and without their permission and without their command we will continue until we win or die.*[1]

I
T IS NOW TIME TO ANALYZE THE PUBLIC CHARAC-
ter of the Cristero War. Keep in mind, however, that when we
refer to "popular,"[2] we do so not in a Marxist sense—that is,
presuming a binary dialectic of poor against rich—but in the broadest
sense of the term: of the people, that is, the Mexican population.

Given the various meanings of the term, we offer some parenthetical
remarks. The word "people" has magnetism, an irreplaceable force for
the development of politics, whether in traditional or current terms.
Since modern politics tends to replace tradition with the force of will,
it is the people, directly or through their representatives, who are the
most clearly legitimized to erect new political systems. It is also true that
conventionally it was always accepted that the "people" in the political
sense is "an association based on the consent of the law and on the community of interests," in the words of Cicero. This implies their being
holders not only of civil obligations and rights, but also of political ones.

Applied to nation-states in modern times, the concept of "people"
also is a key point of reference for constitutional law, in view of the
growing demographic, social and cultural heterogeneity. Hence, eliminating castes or social classes is considered a prerequisite for framing
its definition. For many, this constitutes a shift in the thought of
traditional *bourgeois* constitutional law, for which the idea of "people"
was the set of inhabitants who held political rights that enabled them
to form a government.

Likewise, and in this same way, the distinction between the people
and the masses cannot be ignored either, since the latter is made up

---

[1] Letter from Aurelio Acevedo, in Meyer, *La Cristiada*, 1:35.
[2] Taking up the question of whether or not one can speak of a "popular uprising,"
Meyer replies: "Can one speak of 'popular' to designate the Cristeros? Undoubtedly, since it was an exceptional movement due to its intensity, its geographical
extension, and the number of combatants it mobilized. Without a doubt, since it
encompassed all rural groups and crossed all structures." Meyer, *La Cristiada*, 3:43.

of individuals who do not assume any responsibility voluntarily in the development of social life, but limit themselves to consuming what is presented to them in a predetermined way. Perhaps for this reason, for centuries, the masses were considered an enemy of democracy since it supports every tyrant who can dazzle it. Modern authors prefer to replace the expression "masses" with "mob," without essentially changing its characteristics. The people have will and action, while the "multitudes/masses" would be only a "plane of singularities" that is not homogeneous but something to which the people tend.

For our purposes, demographically and ethnically, Mexico has been characterized since its inception as the *mestizo* country par excellence.[3] The literature is abundant on this subject and, more recently, even the results of the Human Genome project support this hypothesis. Some have argued in recent studies that 85 percent of the Mexican population is mestizo, with two major components: Caucasian and Amerindian, while "in almost all cases (the Mexican) has an indigenous origin."[4] From this to identifying mestizo with indigenous there is a gap measurable in millimeters... Other studies go so far as to say that racial mixing reaches 93 percent.

Even the modern Mexican Constitution takes the situation into account in its first articles. It seems to ignore or implicitly assumes the social fact par excellence, racial mixing, thus concluding that there is a kind of historical debt to indigenous races, which borders on the absurd. I limit myself to quoting a few paragraphs and then offer a clarification that is no less relevant because it is obvious.

> *Article 1.* Any discrimination motivated by religion... or any other that violates human dignity and seeks to deny or annul the rights and freedoms of the people is prohibited.

> *Article 2.* The Nation has a multicultural composition originally based on its indigenous peoples, who are those descended from populations that inhabited the current territory of the country at the beginning of colonization and who maintain their own social, economic, cultural and political institutions, or part of them...

> The right of indigenous peoples to self-determination will be exercised in a constitutional framework of autonomy that

---

[3] *Mestizo*, derived from the Spanish word meaning "mixed," is a term primarily used in Latin America to describe individuals of mixed European and Indigenous American ancestry. It often refers to people with Spanish and Amerindian heritage.
[4] Juan Arturo López Ramos, *Oaxaca: cuna y destino de la Civilización Americana* (Fundación Cultural Fernández Pichardo, 2010), 25.

ensures national unity...deciding on their internal forms
of coexistence and social, economic, political and cultural
organization.[5]

Oriented by an indigenism of questionable outlook, it is nevertheless useful for framing certain aspects of the Cristero movement, since
its popular character was actually synonymous with mestizo, if not
indigenous (although enculturated by centuries of evangelization and
mainly Spanish admixture), depending on the region, as noted above.[6]

Taking into account these propositions of the most modern social
constitutionalism, the aggression by the government in religious matters (the Constitutions of 1857 and 1917 already recognized the right
to religious freedom), the persecutions of the faithful and priests, the
confiscation of Catholic property, the indiscriminate massacres of the
faithful, not only in villages and towns, the persistent and suffocating
discrimination and so on, formed a typical picture of the violation of
modern human rights, and were a preview of what would be tried
in Europe fifteen years later. These are the worst conflicts — in this
case, mestizos armed by state force against mestizos and indigenous
people, translating into social ruptures that are difficult to address,
as our explosive political history has demonstrated.

However, we must include the following reflection that we believe
is important and that we hesitantly propose: the Cristero counterrevolution developed the most and with enormous success in the area
called Los Altos de Jalisco, east of Guadalajara and in the state of
Jalisco. A field study has enabled us to observe that most of the "alteña"
population — that is, people from Los Altos de Jalisco — is of European
heritage in a very high percentage (the visitor seems, at first glance, to
be more in Spain than in Mexico because of the type of people: the
people are blonde and tall, compared to the average Mexican who is
rather dark of complexion and *chaparritos*, that is, short in stature).
According to what we have been told, there were two waves of Spanish

---

[5] Political Constitution of the United Mexican States.
[6] The weak argument that the Constitution refers to peoples that are preserved
as the Spaniards found them would be of no use; except in the south of the
country, not even a century ago, and even less now, were there pure indigenous
populations in significant numbers. It should be borne in mind that the 1930
census shows that 16% of the Mexican population spoke indigenous languages,
a percentage that varied between 2% or 3% and 30% depending on the state
(now it is around 6%). Unless one wants to discriminate between mestizos (85%
to 93% of the population) and indigenous people, in favor of the latter — which
would be unconstitutional as well as ridiculous.

immigrants. The first occurred between the 16th and 17th centuries and the second between the 18th and 19th, mainly from Navarre and Galicia, the latter settling where no one wanted to be. In fact, Los Altos has an endless number of small towns whose lands had been left uninhabited not only by the first waves of colonization, but also by the indigenous people themselves who preferred to take advantage of the land's natural fertility rather than work in semi-arid regions such as this (in fact, it is a good livestock grazing area and not very arable). These small towns boasted not only an enormous number of combatants but also martyrs at the time of the uprising. But let us leave aside this digression, which falls outside the scope of our analysis.

Let us conclude by emphasizing that the government's aggression, as is clear on the factual level, was driven by religious hatred towards a humble, mestizo, Christian people. It is true, it cannot be denied, that the leadership of the counterrevolutionary fight by the Cristeros was in the hands of a few more or less educated people, as happens in all wars, but it was the common people who fought the most. It was a war "against the people," hence the people rose up. Not only did it rise up, but it also acted civically, that is, as an organized population, as evidenced by the political, economic, and educational development of the municipalities under Cristero rule, exercising rights that only the modern Mexican Constitution recognizes (art. 2). It is not unreasonable, then, to affirm that in certain respects the modern ideological Constitution ends up recognizing rights denied by a government characterized by the worst absolutism, that of Plutarco Elías Calles.

Let us take it a step further. At the beginning of 1926, when the "Calles Law" was to be enforced, several factors converged: the atmosphere was heated and, faced with government pressure and the consequent disorientation of the bishops, the situation for the Mexican laity became extremely tense. Opinions were more or less the same and — especially in the central part of the country — it was said that patience was running out. Jean Meyer recalls that after Holy Week that year, when the movement began to accelerate, the vast majority of the faithful began to do long public penances to ask for mercy for sins, both their own and those of others (the government). However, such exercises were ignored by the government. The Almighty's aid was besought because the new laws "could not be tolerated"; they were nothing more than "a betrayal by the government" towards which there was enormous hatred, "more than of Satan himself."[7]

---

[7] See Meyer, *La Cristiada*, 1:102.

Catholic lay leaders found it increasingly difficult to contain the common people. Among them was the famous lawyer Anacleto González Flores—later martyred—who had not consented to the armed uprising of even a single man from the People's Union group that he led. Only at the end of December 1926 did he accept the recourse to force decided by "The League" and read to the convention of the People's Union. The text read: "The LNDLR orders its delegations to...*immediately organize an armed movement to overthrow the government of the Republic* and secure by force the people's liberties."[8] The situation was escalating and questions of fact preceded those of law.

## THE BOYCOTT AND PETITIONS

To achieve the repeal of the regulations, the Mexican laity proposed through the "League," the application of an economic boycott. On July 7, 1926, they declared to the bishops:

> As of July 31, this year and while the decree is in force... from June 14.... The inhabitants of the Mexican nation who love freedom will carry out a widespread action of defense and blockade throughout the country, which will consist of the paralysis of social and economic life by the following means: refraining from giving advertisements and buying those newspapers that oppose this action or do not give it assistance. Silence will be understood as a lack of support. With regard to the newspapers of Mexico City, there will be no action except by express determination of the League. Refraining from making purchases that are not essential for daily subsistence.... The greatest possible limits on the use of vehicles.... Do not attend amusements, neither public nor private. Limit the consumption of electrical energy. Total and definitive refusal to attend secular schools.[9]

For his part, the Archbishop of Mexico, Mgr. Mora y del Río, supported peaceful measures in order to exert pressure on the government's intransigence. When asked for necessary support, he replied that after having "carefully examined your project, it seemed to us worthy of all praise, both for the purpose it puts forward, and by the orderly and peaceful manner in which it will be carried out."[10] As is obvious, this measure, simply recognized and vigorously adhered to a popular sentiment that came "from below," that is, not from the ecclesiastical hierarchy.

---

[8] Meyer, 1:120.
[9] Meyer, 2:288.
[10] Rius Facius, *México Cristero*, 2:12–13.

This decision was a success in several states and was applied by the majority of the people. It is impossible here to explain each of its effects, but it could be said that, for some, the consequences became great anxiety: the American emissaries informed their government that business had fallen by 75 percent from August to December 1926 because of the combined effects of the fall in cotton, silver, and lead and the boycott. A "general economic depression" was predicted. Cinemas, affected by the crisis, asked for complete tax exemption, a 30 percent drop in the price of films and the salary of employees, suffering a 75 percent decrease in tickets. As Rius Facius rightly points out,

> in a few days fifteen cinemas and three theatres were closed, which was equivalent to a very high percentage in relation to the theatres that then existed in the capital. Trade was also seriously affected, mainly those businesses dedicated to the sale of luxury goods. From the Bank of Mexico, recently made by Calles into a state bank, seven million pesos were withdrawn, an enormous amount for its reserves.[11]

Among all the cities, Guadalajara most strictly observed the measure: girls gathered at the entrance of the stores, forming strike pickets. The city became one of pedestrians; people dressed in mourning and the streets were paralyzed, economically and socially. As for education, eight hundred primary school teachers resigned to avoid serving the government, and twenty-two thousand children (out of twenty-five thousand of school age) stopped going to school.[12] In the villages, keeping in mind the sizes, the spectacle was similar: in Pénjamo, electricity was stopped to switch back to candles, to the extent that the power plant was forced to stop. The slaughterhouse was limited to slaughtering two cows every three days (for the sick) instead of twelve cows a day, as before. No merchandise entered the space of the city, and the municipal government, deprived of its fiscal resources, was in enormous trouble, such that both the chief of police and the mayor had to resign; they were replaced by a shoemaker and a tailor at the town's expense.

The economic boycott wasn't the only strategy. The League, for its part, and as a last resort before taking up arms, went so far as to call for legal reform by collecting more than two million signatures (in a country that did not have fifteen million inhabitants). The petition sent to Congress was immediately filed without further action.

---

[11] Rius Facius, 2:26.
[12] The People's Union, the Catholic movement inspired by the ideas of Anacleto González Flores, was in charge of housing and feeding the teachers who stuck to the boycott.

## THE PEOPLE AND GUNS

After the boycott was completely ignored by the government, the Mexican people began staging spontaneous disturbances: civil war was already looming in mid-1926, as we have seen. The people were exasperated, and for them "it was clear: patience, penance, and prayers over the course of five months had been of no use, because Calles' heart was hardened,"[13] they said.

> As the only recourse we had left to defend our rights was that of arms, secret meetings were being held, and when the number of those committed reached three hundred, the date of the uprising was set for January 6 (1927).[14]

There was "no other recourse." Even the government itself proposed the use of arms in contempt of the Mexican people (we have already cited Calles' provocation when he said "either the laws or arms"). Evidence of this provocation to violence were three "public controversies" that were documented and that took place in a theater in Mexico City called *Iris* on August 2, 1926. A government official spoke in defense of "legality" and a delegate of the ACJM refuted it in the best style of a medieval *disputatio*. In these public debates, the young René Capistrán Garza, a popular Catholic leader, demonstrated his brilliance:

> In reply, Luis N. Morones blustered that Catholics, if they were not satisfied with this state of affairs, should take up arms to defend their rights. He didn't have to wait long for the answer. Luis Mier y Terán, in the midst of a great uproar, challenged the Minister of Industry and his henchmen with these words: "Morones invites us Catholics to take up arms. I answer that we have not done it because we do not feel defeated in the dispute of reason, which is why he challenges us to dispute by force."[15]

The call to arms was sounded and the laity, not out of pacifist principles but for reasons of prudence and moral principles, did not want to use them except as a last resort. But it all seemed in vain. Everything had been tried. Faced with a situation of fait accompli, even some bishops began to change their position:

> On March 27, 1927, Mgr. Mora y del Río wrote to Mgr. Valverde y Téllez in Rome: "Mestre and Obregón have wanted to have some conferences...but since they have all been on

---

[13] Meyer, *La Cristiada*, 1:125.
[14] Testimony of Rosendo Flores (Tapalpa), registered by P. N. Valdés (Meyer, 1:93), emphasis ours.
[15] Rius Facius, *México Cristero*, 2:48.

the basis of being bound by the so-called laws...nothing
has been achieved.... *There is, therefore, no other recourse
than armed defense*," and Mgr. Díaz declared on April 5 to
the American press: "I do not believe that there is any possibility of an agreement between the Calles regime and the
Church...because when one thinks rationally, nothing can
be settled with an irresponsible tyranny... *The Church is not
leading any armed rebellion*. It is, for example, a ridiculous lie
to say that the Archbishop of Guadalajara, Mgr. Orozco y
Jiménez, is directing the revolt in Jalisco. Instead, *it is solid
Catholic doctrine to resist any unjust tyranny*, just as this is an
imperative duty of every citizen. Once and for all I must say
that the Calles government does not represent the people of
Mexico. That is why thousands of citizens are up in arms in
determined rebellion against it, while millions more of the
country's population contemplate the movement with silent
sympathy, under the ruthless tyranny that has at its disposal
every means of oppression... What is now called the Mexican
Constitution...is nothing more than the unbridled expression
of a savage political theory imposed by an egotistical oligarchy
to give the veneer of constitutional legality to its evil actions."[16]

With less learning but with great common sense, the Cristero Ezequiel Mendoza said the following, showing the general popular feeling:

I think it is better to die fighting for Christ the King, the
Virgin of Guadalupe, and for all one's family, and not take a
single step against the one true God, even if the devil gets
angry. The war is certainly just, and in a just war it is right to
kill God's enemies, because *if we do not kill them, they will kill
us*, and we would also be guilty if we could avoid evils and
not do so; since the person who helps someone kill a cow is
as guilty as the one who kills it.[17]

The Cristero "corridos," the accounts sung by the common people,
described it this way:

Calles is the reason
That we rise up in arms.
Only God knows where
So many poor souls will go.[18]

---

[16] Archives of the Compañía de Jesús, provincia de México (Puente Grande y
San Ángel), cited by Meyer, *La Cristiada*, 2:308–9, emphasis ours.
[17] Interview between Meyer and Ezequiel Mendoza Meyer, *La Cristiada*, 3:288,
emphasis ours.
[18] "Santiago Bayacora's Ballad" by Francisco Campos, cited in Meyer, *La Cristiada*, 3:292.

Thus, the Mexican people were driven by circumstances to defend churches, families, and beliefs. This, we repeat again, was not guided by an ecclesiastical hierarchy, but often in spite of it. In order to understand the decisions that led many Cristeros to take up arms and almost anticipating the objections that might be raised, in a truly precious work done on the basis of personal interviews, Jean Meyer[19] summarized the reason for the uprising in the form of a florilegium. Asked in a thorough interview "what had been the reason for joining the revolt," those who participated in the Cristero movement answered without hesitation:

"To defend the Cause."

"For the love of the cause of religion."

"To defend the Church."

"For Christian rights."

"For religion, the faith."

"For the rights of Christ and of his Holy Church."

"For religious freedom."

"By the faith of Christ."

"For the freedom of Christ the King."

"For the cause of God and my fatherland."

"For freedom of belief."

"For the rights of the Church and the Fatherland."

"For God, the Fatherland and freedom, my life and my religion."

"Since President Calles denied us all the freedoms of religion by peaceful means... I thought that only by means of arms would we defeat them!"

"Because, in disagreement with Calles' persecutory laws, I regretted not having religious freedom."

"So that the persecuted priests would return."

"Because God touched my Christian heart and drew me to it."

---

[19] See Meyer, 3:292-93. "This war was their war without them having wanted it, without them having run to meet it, from the moment they made their decision. 'I have a commitment with the Virgin,' Quintanar told his wife. Castañón did not want to deny that he is a Christian. Epitacio Hernández's mother sent, after the latter's death, her twelve-year-old son. The father who had lost two sons awaited the death of the third.... If the victory of Christ the King, and his advent, refer to the hazy promise of a new secular world, it highlights particularly the idea of a contract between the Mexican people and God who has twice distinguished it, who has twice made Mexico his Kingdom, sending it the Virgin of Guadalupe and proclaiming in it the Kingship of His Son." Meyer, 3:243-44.

"Because of not finding another solution to the religious conflict provoked by Calles."

"Out of conviction."

"For love."

"Out of duty."

"From a pure heart."

"Because I felt a real obligation."

"To cooperate in the Church's liberation, the Holy Religion to which I belonged and to which I belong, thanks be to God."

"By inspiration of God."

"Because they forbade worship and there was no Mass."

"Because Calles attacked the clergy."

"Because of my faith."

"Because as a Catholic it was my duty."

The Catholicism that ran through Mexico's blood responded from within.[20] It was, in Meyer's words, "a self-defense reaction, only natural."[21] The Cristero Joaquín de Silva y Carrasco affirmed his motives to a priest who tried to dissuade him from embracing the cause:

---

[20] Francisco Campos, a Cristero from Durango, stated his reasons: "On July 31, 1926, some men took God our Lord from His churches, from His altars, from the homes of the Catholics, but other men brought Him back again. Those men didn't consider that the government had many soldiers, a lot of weapons, a lot of money to make war on them. They did not consider that. What they considered was defending their God, their Religion, their Mother the Holy Church. That's what they considered. Those men didn't mind leaving their homes, their parents, their children, their wives and what they had. They went to the battlefields to seek God our Lord. The streams, the mountains, the ridges, the hills, are witnesses that those men spoke to God Our Lord with the holy motto of long live Christ the King, long live the Blessed Virgin of Guadalupe, long live Mexico. The same places bear witness to those men watering the ground with their blood and, not content with that, they gave their very lives so that God Our Lord would return again. And God our Lord seeing that those men were really looking for Him, deigned to come again to their churches, to their altars, to the homes of the Catholics, as we are seeing now, and charge the young people of today that if in the future they come to offer themselves again that they not forget the example that our ancestors left us." Meyer, *La Cristiada*, 1:93.

[21] "If armed resistance could express its purposes, its ideology, it would be in religious terms, and this was not surprising since it is the rebellion of a persecuted people, who have exhausted legal means, who have a vision of the world, a religious ethos. Those who too often pretend to have empty brains and who are likened by their silence to idiocy knew how to distinguish between Caesar and God." Meyer, 1:388. Hence certain authors' opinons are strange, then, or at least partial, who insist on seeing a mere economic motive at the root of the

He told the priest of his desire to confess. When he finished doing so, he revealed that an hour later he would leave for Michoacán, to take up in arms in the Church's defense. The priest, surprised, tried to dissuade him by making him see that he was leaving his mother and sisters.

"Ah, father!" replied Joaquín. *They are the ones who have encouraged me the most in my mission!* No, no. If we young Catholics aren't going to fight for Christ the King, the wicked will soon have finished off Catholicism in Mexico...They have already taken away our churches...They have already forced our bishops to suspend worship...our schools are closed... our hospitals became secular...the priests are killed after being tortured...and under the leadership of a Jewish rabbi, Martin Zielam, numerous bands of Russian émigrés are arriving to replace our peasants fleeing persecution to the United States... no: enough is enough! *We don't want to be Catholics in name alone*...I'm going to the army of Christ the King![22]

Among the many letters available we have chosen one in which a Cristero tells his wife the reasons why she should embrace the "cause." It is a good example:

*My dear wife,*

The pencil is unsteady in my hand, I don't know whether to write to you or not: I say this because if I write to you, perhaps it will increase your pain. If I do not write to you, you will form the idea that I do not love you, that I do not remember you or those children, my life's treasure, for whom I have shed so many tears.

I'm going to tell you: Will you have the courage to listen to me? On April 27, 1927, I left, as I told you in a letter I wrote to you in Mexico from Tepalcatepec, and I believe you have received it. I left San Isidro for Coalcomán to see Don Guadalupe Lucatero, with the aim of settling the matter of the cattle that you knew about. On my arrival at that place, I found that Señor Lucatero had

---

uprising: see Andrés Fábregas Puig, *La formación histórica de una región: Los Altos de Jalisco* (Ciesas, 1986), 195; Ramón Jrade, "Inquiries into the Cristero insurrection against the Mexican Revolution," *Latin American Research Review* 20 (1984): 53–69; idem, "La organización de la Iglesia a nivel local y el desafío de los levantamientos cristeros al poder del Estado revolucionario," *Estudios del Hombre* 1 (1994): 65–80. See also the work of Eduardo Camacho Mercado, *Reforma eclesial y catolicismo social en Totatiche y el Cañón de Bolaños (1876–1926)* (CIESAS, 2012), 17–19.
[22] Rius Facius, *México Cristero*, 2:96, emphasis ours.

taken up arms, and a multitude, not to say all, seconded him, including the gentleman you know. I arrived and saw that rejoicing, that the people *en masse* acclaimed Christ who, exposed in the Monstrance, perhaps saw with a pleasant smile the enthusiasm of children desirous of their God, whom men without conscience wanted to expel from churches, homes, etc.

Seeing that uproar and feeling enthusiastic were one and the same. The blood was boiling in my veins, and, do you want me to tell you? Aren't you angry? There were a few moments when I forgot about my wife and my children and was filled with feverish enthusiasm. I too went out and shouted with all the strength of my lungs: "LONG LIVE CHRIST THE KING!" From that moment on I became Christ's soldier, and you will see your husband not paying his servants, not trading livestock, not doing business, but you will see me with a gun in my hand defending the faith of my wife, my children and myself. Isn't this proof of the love I have for you?... Here I am doing a Christian duty and burdened with a cross so heavy that I can hardly bear it. So many things! Hunger, cold, persecution, and slander, but what hurts me the most and makes me suffer is the memory of you... I know that you suffer greatly, my dear, you are not accustomed to any misfortune in life, an only child and always treated with the greatest care!

And now I will be the cause of your sufferings. But what can I say, if I know that you are also a Christian and will support my work in a different way! I with a rifle and you with resignation. I, burning in the sun and hungry, and you in your prayers, we are united in the same crucible working for the same ideal and our eyes fixed on the same point... God... Imagine that there are times when we have battles that last ceaselessly twenty-four hours and that left and right our brave soldiers fall lifeless. Many have died in my arms and when they die, do you know what their last word is: "LONG LIVE CHRIST THE KING!" And immediately they go to receive their palm in Glory... I hope to see you here on earth, but if I die, have the courage of Mrs. Gutierrez — Sra. Carmen Alfaro Madrigal, widow of Navarro Origel. Do not cry for me. On the contrary, offer to God the sacrifice of my life, and say long live God! For if you lose me on earth, you will have me more attentively watching over you in Heaven. From that mansion of peace, I will pray for you and for all those who do you good… Here they talk about Settlements. Hopefully, hopefully, this will be as we have demanded. We will not give up for a moment: to win or die, so we have proposed, sworn with an oath, and if it's not as we have intended, may God take my life instead.

I embrace you from these desolate regions, and although I am not personally with you, I am present with thoughts and ideals. I have not abandoned you, I am with you, though a superior and irresistible force compels me to leave. There is something greater than wife, children, and belongings, and it is Christ for whom I fight, for whom I suffer, for whom we must leave the dearest things of this world. He touched my heart once, then again, and so I ran like Saul and said, "Lord, what do you want from me?" "Come," he told me, "defend me because my enemies are harassing me." Without waiting any longer and without any hesitation, I left everything I had: interests, businesses, and what was greatest and dearest: my wife and my children. It is very sweet to suffer for CHRIST the KING.

In our sufferings we have much to console us. We know that they call us: bandits, robbers, in short, a heap of slander. But what does it matter? Christ was also slandered, and did he not say: "Blessed are those who are persecuted for righteousness's sake?"… Do not grieve for me but be content with your husband. Don't worry about the future. God will be with you. Do you think he will leave the family of the one who left everything for Him? Impossible. I have already made my pact with God: almost daily, if not every day, I receive Him in my heart, and everything boils down to talking to you… For my children, help them see that if I left them, it was for God's sake, then they won't think they were abandoned for another reason. Always talk to them about God…

Farewell, my dear companion, the only refuge of my sorrows and joys. I embrace you and my dear children, and you know that if we do not see each other on earth, I will live for you in heaven.

Your husband, José María Fernandez
God and my right.

LONG LIVE CHRIST THE KING!
LONG LIVE OUR LADY OF GUADALUPE!
LONG LIVE THE POPE![23]

---

[23] Joaquín Blanco Gil, *El clamor de la sangre* (Rex-Mex, 1947), 175–76. José María Fernández died in combat on May 9, 1929.

It is interesting how, in most cases, the uprising in rural areas was purely lay and very spontaneous, as it was in these areas where the Church's pastoral care had been quite limited for decades:

> After 1860, the Mexican Church returned to the people, who had suffered sixty years of revolutions and wars, and to the countryside, which had been generally neglected. It is curious that the countryside, which in the twentieth century was the bastion of Christianity, had not always been so. Before 1860, the clergy was practically urban, and the peasants fashioned a Catholicism often without priests; they did not attend Mass, for lack of a priest. This was because religious orders had declined. After Independence there were no longer any Franciscan missions, the regular clergy left, and the only convents that remained were urban.[24]

Paradoxically, it was from the rural districts "neglected" by the Church since 1880 that that those bearing arms would come. The simple and uneducated people were the main supporters of the insurrection, as General Gorostieta himself would testify: "With this kind of men do you think we can lose? No, this cause is holy and with those defenders it is impossible for it to be lost!" After having received twenty cents in San Julián from the hands of a beggar, he said to his assistant, very touched: "If [the cause] is lost, it will be because we can't defend it. But no, it cannot be lost."[25]

So popular was the uprising that the fighters themselves were surprised at the support they received from the laity they met:

> Not a single penny has been spent on food, because the *rancherías* (simple houses in the countryside) support the Catholic combatants. This effective supply was patiently ensured by thousands... of men or women who carried food, in their baskets, each one to a few Cristeros. They transmitted messages learned by heart, served as couriers, delivered letters written on silk paper and concealed as well as possible. Many were discovered and shot.[26]

Even the Federal Army complained about how difficult it was to win in a war that, in addition to being without quarter, had the support of the masses: "All the federal generals agree in denouncing the support of civilians for the Cristero movement as one of the rebels'

---

[24] Meyer, *La Cristiada*, 2:45.
[25] Meyer, 1:203.
[26] Meyer, 3:113–14.

main forces because the people who say they are peaceful were the
ones who sustained the movement, from every town."[27]

## MUNICIPALITIES, SCHOOLS, AND PARALLEL GOVERNMENT

It would have been impossible to maintain a struggle for three long
years without some organization. The Mexican laity was organized
as a state within a state. In fact, in the towns that had been taken by
the Cristeros, parallel authorities were quickly installed to govern in
an exceptional way. The municipal authorities were established in the
towns held by the Cristeros. They were in charge of the civil registry,
collecting taxes, postal service, education, and the administration of
vacant property or property confiscated from enemies, as well as the
battle against gambling, prostitution, cohabitation, adultery, public
amusements, and the sale of alcohol, the latter two items for political
and military reasons.

They collected ordinary city taxes, state, and federal taxes, as well
as the profits from the administration of confiscated property. Fifty
percent of the funds went to the army, twenty-five percent to regional
defense and the other twenty-five percent to the municipality. The
latter ensured the operation of the schools, which, in some cases, was
limited to two teachers and a blackboard under the trees. Parents who
did not send their children to class were sent a first warning, after which
they were punished. From 1928 on inspectors visited open schools
and established new ones. For example, at the end of 1927 there were
nineteen schools in the municipality of Valparaíso alone, attended
by six hundred children of both sexes. Two years later these figures
had doubled. In June 1929, the town of Huejuquilla had thirty-six
schools scattered among the most remote ranches: Tenzompa, Llanos,
Soledad, Puesta de Lagos, Paisanos, San Nicolás, Sauces, Rancho
de Abajo, Adobes, Tecolotes, Salitres, Mesa de Piedra, Muralla, etc.

## WOMEN AND CHILDREN

More is being written every day about women in the time of the
Cristiada.[28] Apparently, without their participation, things would
have gone very differently. Organized mainly within the scope of the
"Women's Brigades" under the name of "Saint Joan of Arc," they played
a fundamental role, reaching more than twenty-five thousand associates

---

[27] Meyer, 3:109.
[28] See the book by Soledad Reynoso de Alba, *La actuación de la mujer en la Cristiada* (APC, 2005).

committed to the Cristero cause.[29] On this topic, Meyer wondered:

> How many wives of generals and politicians fought for three years, like so many Penelopes, to undo at night what was done during the day? How many, like General Amaro's wife,[30] attended clandestine worship, worked against the government, and took care of the Cristero orphans? This was even more the case among the common people. They were the ones who forced men to shoulder their responsibilities, shaming them, and Anacleto González Flores praised them as the main force of the People's Union. This newly awakened feminism even led the Women's Brigades of St. Joan of Arc to want to manage the war, placing each regimental commander under the "protection" and patronage of a colonel. Gorostieta restrained this ardor, limiting it to the essential activities of quartermaster, finance, care, propaganda, and provisioning. Yet there were some women's groups that prepared explosives, taught men the art of sabotage, and even engaged in direct action.[31]

The Women's Brigades worked secretly, offering support on diverse fronts, and even risking their lives. Its statutes read:

> This is an exclusively female, civic, free, autonomous, and rightly secret Mexican society, that is, its members swear to keep every secret necessary to safeguard the life of the Institution, that of its members and the broad development of its purpose and its object.... Its object is to provide for the crusaders.... The means by which it will achieve its objective will be the following six points: organization, war, finance, research, communications, charity.... War: manufacture, acquisition, and transportation of war supplies to the battlefields.... Finance.... Espionage, both in one's own spheres and in those of the adversary, so as to discover in time our disloyal members and traitors, as well as the movements, plans, and conditions of the enemy. Communications: it will be in charge of conducting all kinds of letters. Beneficence: health branch and beneficence proper (lodging and provisions for the crusaders and their families)....
>
> Secrecy is complete, reasonable, legitimate, and temporary. The organization is secret from all those who are strangers to it. The oath shall be twofold: that which shall be imposed

---

[29]  See Meyer, *La Cristiada*, 3:25.
[30]  Secretary of War under Plutarco Elías Calles.
[31]  Meyer, *La Cristiada*, 3:25–26.

on any person before she is invited, and that which shall be
taken by each and every one of the members upon entering (the second after acceptance).... The second oath shall
be taken on one's knees before the crucifix: "Before God,
Father, Son, Holy Spirit, before the Most Blessed Virgin
of Guadalupe and before my fatherland's face, I., N., swear
that even if I am martyred or killed, even if I am flattered or
promised all the kingdoms of the world, I will keep absolute
secrecy about its existence and activities as long as necessary,
about the names of people, addresses, signs, that refer to its
members. With God's Grace, I will die rather than become
an informer. Members shall endeavor to ignore one another
ENTIRELY.[32]

This was a risky task for these women, yet without them it would
have been almost impossible to carry out a large part of the war. Combatants were "pushed into action by their wives, mothers, sisters"; the
women were absolutely necessary to the soldiers because they acted
as spies, suppliers, organizers, and propagandists. It was the women,
in fact, who were the first to declare war, and the worst enemies of
the federals, who, when they could, paid them back with interest.
The women were frequently the most determined to stand guard in
the churches and in sacred places. They were the ones who provided
logistical support, mainly transporting messages, ammunition and arms
that they smuggled under their long skirts. In fact, for the transport
of the *"parque"* (ammunition) a kind of internal vest was devised
that went over the body and that allowed several kilograms of cargo
to be carried without being discovered. This would be attested to
in 1928 by the enemies of the Cristeros when they discovered them:

> Thick fabric, a kind of bodice for the bust and a wide sash
> for the hips formed by bandoliers also made of fabric strips
> added to each other, which once full of "parque" (ammuni-
> tion) are sewn to prevent the cartridges from being dropped,
> and the ladies put them under their dresses, 800 cartridges.[33]

Still, the women were not limited only to logistics: in some cases,
they even participated in violent activities, not hesitating to resort to
kidnapping to obtain ransoms, protect combatants, and punish spies.
They deployed various means. For example, they organized village
dances to gain the confidence of the officers, dispel their suspicions,

---

[32] Extracted from Meyer, 3:125-26; the capitals are in the original text.
[33] Meyer, 3:115.

and obtain reports.[34] It is even said of the mother of Father Reyes Vega that she had no qualms about stabbing to death a schismatic priest, Father Felipe Perez, who was a government spy.[35]

As an example of female courage, here is the text describing the attempted occupation of the Guadalupe shrine on August 3, 1926:

> Inside the shrine, the rosary had ended. Outside, a group of children ran through the garden in front of the Shrine of Guadalupe and asked all passers-by to shout: *Long live Christ the King!* As a car passed, the children intercepted it and asked the driver and its occupant to give the usual shout, which they refused, continuing on their way amid the children's shouting. They threw a stone at the vehicle. The general in civilian clothes who was in the car ordered his driver to stop, got out and fired his pistol without further provocation. To this unexpected attack, some men who were nearby responded in the same way, which forced the officer to flee to the Military Hospital, located a short distance away. From there he asked for federal troops from the Operations Headquarters and, half an hour later, twenty-five soldiers under the command of an officer appeared in front of the church, where a large number of people had already gathered. Twenty soldiers were spread out in the garden and five made the attempt to enter the church. *From the crowd outside, a girl from the village approached the officer and plunged a dagger into his back.* His soldiers, faced with such an act of audacity, remained hesitant, seeing the brave woman pick up the sword and pistol of her victim. These she handed over to the men who were watching the scene behind the church gate, saying to them: *"Take this so that you may defend yourselves."* [36]

The Mexican women of that time were fierce.

Let us describe here what happened that night during the defense of the Guadalupe shrine. The text is long, but it is worth seeing the participation of the common faithful in the Cristero uprising. Heriberto Navarrete provides an account:

> July 31, 1926 arrived, which was the date indicated by presidential decree for the law against religion to come into force. It was also the date that the Episcopate set to suspend worship in all churches.

---

[34] Meyer, 3:132.
[35] See Meyer, 3:133.
[36] Rius Facius, *México Cristero*, 2:71–72.

Emotion was at its highest: the priests left the churches, which were automatically left in the care of the faithful, on the night of the 31st.... Heightened public imagination created an endless number of speculations. What if troops are going to seize the churches to loot and demolish them? What if they are going to burn all the images and altars?

August 4, 1926. In the morning, I went to the Maestro's house. He looked at me with wide eyes. He was anxious to know what happened last night. I gave him a detailed account.

About fifteen "acejotaemeros" boys left the Shrine of Guadalupe at about 8:30 p.m., after having prayed the Rosary. The church was full.... A band of boys from the village, with flags, branches, sticks and pieces of old banners, walked the streets around the garden, in a continual demonstration of protest and reparation. The cries of "Long live Christ the King," "Long live the Virgin of Guadalupe," "Death to the persecutors of the Church," were heard continuously. For three days now, this kind of activity has continued outside the church. During the three nights that have passed since the closing, the Shrine's nave has always been full of faithful who devoutly remain in prayer, asking the Lord to have mercy on His people.

In these circumstances, we were standing and chatting on the garden sidewalk, in front of the main door of the church, when suddenly we noticed that the mob stopped a car and, surrounding it, tried to force a man who was in civilian clothes to take off his hat (for he was in front of the church) and shout "Long live Christ the King." The stranger replied with a loud curse and ordered the driver to drive the car through the crowd. His driver did so, tossing several boys here and there, and risking a serious collision. The group's irritation surged and stones pelted the car, which came to a halt. A man emerged, wielding a revolver, and fired shots in several directions. The answer was immediate: at the church's entrance, revolver shots were heard and the car had to flee at high speed.... But the group of those who "stood guard" in the tower had already started pealing the bells, an agreed signal for the inhabitants of the neighborhood to go to the Sanctuary at times when the government attempted an attack. So, small groups of neighbors began to arrive from all directions, armed with pistols, the occasional carbine, knives, machetes and even axes and railroad picks. Everyone asked about the assailants. The excited crowd was churning and the bells continued to ring out.

Moments later, decisively making its way through the crowd, a truck from the Military Operations Headquarters advanced until it stood in front of the main door of the church. Then another and another truck, from which platoons of regular troops dismounted, with rifles cocked and in an attitude of defense and attack. They formed a line along the street bordering the Sanctuary, advancing little by little trying to clear out the garden. Thus far, the crowd had only attacked them with words, calling them "servants of Satan," supporters of Calles the devil, etc. The soldiers, with marked patience, continued their task, but suddenly an altercation arose, in the middle of the garden, between an officer and a young worker. There were two loud shouts, and the worker fired his pistol at the soldier.

This was the signal that began the fight. The soldiers began to fire their weapons, first into the air. Inside the entrance and on the Shrine roof there were many armed Catholics. Furious shooting began. Here and there wounded soldiers fell. Some peaceful residents were hunted by the enraged soldiers, and five dead and many wounded were left lying after the first volleys in the streets adjacent to the church. Ambulance sirens began to sound. The streets were deserted and only rows of soldiers could be seen, pressed to the walls or crawling through the flowerbeds, maneuvering to take positions. The shooting continued to intensify by the minute.[37]

Tempers were heated, then, and neither the young people nor the children, as is clear, were left out. The youngest acted as messengers, flag-bearers, and even brave combatants when the occasion called for it.

There were ten-year-old boys whom the superiors refused to enlist and whom they got rid of by setting conditions they thought were impossible... and one day the child would appear with the horse or rifle seized. It was usually an orphan or a child who wanted to avenge his brother, or even a son sent by his mother, who had already lost all the men in her family.[38]

Another proof that women's participation was not always peaceful is this beautiful dialogue that happened during the defense of the churches:

---

[37] Navarrete, *Por Dios y por la Patria*, 101–3.
[38] Meyer, *La Cristiada*, 3:27, emphasis ours. One of the exemplary lives spent in service to the Cristeros, from earliest childhood, is that of St. José Sánchez del Río, horribly martyred on February 10, 1928 at just fourteen years old.

The fight in the Shrine of Guadalupe in Guadalajara would be repeated in many churches in the city and with worse consequences for the Government in other localities if the military authority had not tempered its eagerness to outrage the people.

In the Chapel of Jesus, the parish church of one of the most populous neighborhoods of Guadalajara, rigorous shifts of volunteers were established to prevent the official inventories that were to be made by the Government for enforcing Article 130. On one of the first days of August, I had the opportunity to overhear, in the Shrine's garden, a conversation between two women from the village:

"How are you doing, little Pastorcita? How have you been doing around here with those barbarians?"

"Let's just say it's fine, Nicolasita. We won't let them anywhere near the Sanctuary. This government is already doing a lot. It makes you want to be a macho man and stand up to them, man to man. And over there in the chapel, how have they managed?"

"The Chapel of Jesus does not give up, Pastorcita. This morning, by God's grace, we killed one wretched man. He was one of the police leaders. He thought he was going to have fun with us."

"How did that happen, Nicolasita?"

"Well, it was nothing. We were leaving to pray our Mass that one of the *jota eme*[39] reads to us every day, and passing by the Inspector laughed at us and said: "Pray, you chattering old hens, all you ever do is gossip." And to make long story short, in a split second, we surrounded him and, with the help of some boys who jumped on him and took his pistol, we threw him face up in the middle of the street. Oh, Pastorcita! You should have seen how angry he became. But we didn't even let him move. Then we told him to shout 'Long live Christ the King!' and he didn't do anything, just his hellish mouth spouting gross profanities. He asked for it, Pastorcita, nothing would have happened to him, but he asked for it. Then we began to beat him and some heard him using blasphemies, and we asked him if he wanted a priest, because he was going to die soon. We grabbed an exceptionally large stone and let it fall on his head. By that time, when the poor guy was about to die, the firemen arrived, and we all went into the entrance of the Sanctuary, and the boys in the market all threw stones at them and hit their shiny helmets. They were spraying water everywhere and the poor dead man was drenched, he

---

[39] That is, "JM," a reference to the ACJM.

was bathed there in the middle of the street, with his head crushed. It was a good thing that the firefighters just poured water so it was only a bath."[40]

## A GRASSROOTS MOVEMENT DESPITE OPPOSITION FROM SOME BISHOPS

As we have seen, the uprisings were not so much prompted by the pastors, but on the contrary, as Melchior Cano, the theologian of Charles V in Trent, said: "when the shepherds sleep, the dogs must bark." In support of this view, we quote here some examples showing that the uprisings were a "question of fact," accepted *a posteriori* by the ecclesiastical hierarchy.

At the beginning of the war and when everything began, the bishops' position was extremely stark about the possibility of an armed revolt. However, circumstances forced prudence to take a different view. This was the case, as already mentioned, with Bishop González y Valencia, who, submitting to the facts, declared: "We feel obliged to speak. Since in our Archdiocese many Catholics have had recourse to arms and ask for a word from their Prelate.... We offer these words to them...: be at ease in your consciences and receive Our blessing."[41]

In fact, in most cases armed conflict began independently of the hierarchy. The Episcopate wasn't sure what to do or say and initially limited itself to saying only that it "did not show solidarity," as we read in the declaration of the Episcopal Committee at the end of 1926:

> There are cases in which Catholic theologians authorize, not rebellion, but armed defense against the unjust aggression by a tyrannical power, after peaceful means have been exhausted without result. The Episcopate has not released any document declaring that there is such a case in Mexico.... If any Catholic, lay or ecclesiastical, following the doctrine cited, believes that the case has arisen regarding the lawfulness of this defense, *the Episcopate does not agree with this practical resolution.*[42]

Faced with the uprisings, the Church was in a bind, as little by little, and forced by the situation, it had to declare the lawfulness or unlawfulness of what was happening. In fact, on November 26,

---

[40] Navarrete, *Por Dios y por la Patria*, 101–2.
[41] José María González y Valencia, *Carta pastoral*, 11-II-1927, in Barquín y Ruiz, *José María González y Valencia*, 43.
[42] Barquín y Ruiz, 46–47, emphasis ours.

1926, as we mentioned above, the League had made a request to the Episcopal Committee by means of a "memorandum" where, essentially, it requested that the grassroots action not be condemned.

The response was not long in coming from the hierarchy: on November 30 of that same year, according to Rius Facius, the delegates Mgrs. Ruiz y Flores and Díaz y Barreto stated:

> That the study of the declaration had been made by the illustrious prelates who attended the aforesaid meeting of the Committee; that it had been brought to the attention of the Honorable José Mora y del Río, Archbishop of Mexico, and that the various points indicated in the memorandum had been approved unanimously, regarding the part that, according to the same document, concerns the episcopate, with these two modifications: The Committee could not grant the consent of military vicars in the terms expressed in paragraph (c) of point 2, because it lacks the faculties to do so, but the necessary authorizations or permits could be granted to each priest who intends to exercise his ministry among those who rise up in arms. They should report to the secretary of the Committee, since the most illustrious prelates agreed to give the corresponding licenses with regard to their respective dioceses. The Committee considers it quite difficult, almost impossible, and particularly dangerous to take action with regard to the rich Catholics, as requested in point (d). *With this declaration, the Church recognized the lawfulness of the Cristero rebellion.*[43]

Other prelates were obliged to speak in Rome as well. Mgr. Pascual Díaz did so in *L'Osservatore Romano* of March 1, 1927, occupying a large part of the front page. He held office as bishop of Tabasco (in exile) and secretary of the Episcopal Committee, and explained that both the clergy and laity had resorted to all the legal and peaceful means in their hands without achieving a change in the laws that made the exercise of the sacred ministry impossible. Only after having exhausted all these means did *"the people themselves resort to armed resistance. Have they done right or wrong? It has been our duty,"* the bishop points out, *"to report, as we have reported, that when all peaceful means have been tried, the people are justified in resorting to arms, not to carry out a revolution, but to defend their own rights against revolutionary usurpers."*[44] Immediately afterwards the bishop

---

[43]  Rius Facius, *México Cristero*, 2:131.
[44]  *L'Osservatore Romano*, 1-III-1927, p. 1, italics in the original.

explained the attitude of the clergy regarding the concrete problem: "The clergy have enunciated this doctrine. However — and let this be very clear — they have not wanted to go so far as to declare that the situation that exists in Mexico is such that it justifies its application."[45]

The Church spoke, but again in Sibylline terms.

In response, General José Álvarez, Chief of State of President Calles accused the clergy of fomenting the rebellion by simply referring to this statement:

> *Regarding armed movements*, other prelates were obliged to speak also in Rome, although ... *the episcopate is unrelated to them*, we have already declared, and it is no mystery to anyone who knows the Church's teaching and the unanimous authority of the great Doctors, that there are circumstances in the life of peoples in which it is licit for citizens to defend by arms the legitimate rights which they have vainly sought to safeguard by peaceful means.[46]

On the part of the hierarchy, answers and speeches, analogies and parables were published, but not all of them were like that. Some brave prelates, as already mentioned, accompanied the Cristeros to the field, sharing their fortunes for years, but without bearing arms. This was the extraordinary situation of the archbishop of Guadalajara, Francisco Orozco y Jiménez, who was in hiding for more than three years while exercising his ministry clandestinely, and supporting peaceful resistance, at least in the beginning. He went as far as to write to the pope the following:

> Of the directives that I left for the social groups of the Diocese, the main one was that they not get involved in any armed conflict, even when fairly demanding their rights. The People's Union, which was attached to the National League for the Defense of Religious Liberty, received orders from the General Directorate [of the league] and independently from me, as I have said, *in spite of my directions* (which it thought perhaps it was not contravening by acting on a higher order). It entered fully into the effort of January 1927 and still remains in armed conflict. I present this to explain what my feeling was on the matter.[47]

---

[45] Ibid.

[46] Acevedo, *David VIII*, 79–80, emphasis ours.

[47] "Carta del arzobispo Francisco Orozco y Jiménez al Papa Pío XI," March 14, 1928, in *Archivo Cristero de la Compañía de Jesús en el ITESO* (Universidad Jesuita de Guadalajara), diocesan archive, italics in the original.

Other bishops, not as daring as Orozco y Jiménez in their pastoral support during the conflict, likewise opposed the popular revolt. This was the case with the bishop of Chihuahua, Antonio Guízar y Valencia, who managed to prevent the uprising in his diocese's territory, and the bishops of Querétaro and Zamora, Francisco Banegas and Manuel Fulcheri, who attempted to do so but were partly disobeyed. The fact is that the clergy were for the most part "passively against the Cristeros," as Meyer wrote:

> *This was the attitude of the vast majority of priests,* whatever their personal opinion, given the simple fact that they abandoned their parishes, fleeing abroad and to the big cities, where persecution never went so far as death and was generally limited to mere humiliations. Thousands of priests spent three years in an uncomfortable situation at times, more often comfortable, housed in the homes of well-to-do Catholics, even in the homes of persecutors, celebrating [Mass] in private. Between 1926 and 1929, the majority of the clergy was gathered in the Federal District and in some large cities, while the countryside remained literally abandoned.... In the large towns where they still remained, the combatants said, "the priests did not want to get involved in anything, they didn't even show their faces."[48]

The majority of the clergy at most dared to ask the laity to "pray." The situation got out of hand, for the matter escaped the bishops and passed into the hands of lay Catholics, who, placing themselves solely on the terrain of faith, became much more intransigent than the heads of the episcopate. An uneasy agitation erupted from all sides, and public anxiety increased. For all these reasons, when we describe the Cristero uprising as one "independent of the hierarchy," we do not mean that it went directly *against* it, but rather took place without its express consent. The statement does not seem as harsh as it might seem: the people had ceased to obey the "official" position that oscillated between the ups and downs of diplomacy, and this allowed them to act independently, as circumstances warranted.

---

[48] Meyer, *La Cristiada*, 1:37–38, emphasis ours. Mutolo thought the same: "The government's version of the *Cristero* war claims that the clergy incites the humble and ignorant people to rebel against the legitimate government through deception. The truth is that the clergy, in general, oppose violence. Unfortunately, the people have no other choice. The clash has long been sought by the government." Mutolo, *Gli "arreglos" tra l'episcopato e il governo*, 45.

In Michoacán, a very isolated state, except in the precincts of Jalisco and Guanajuato, the guerrillas continued operations around Hidalgo City and La Piedad. On the coast it began in Santiago Tangamandapio, Chavinda, Jacona, and Cotija. In Cotija, the unrest had been extreme in August: men armed with machetes, and women with ground chili peppers to throw in the soldiers' eyes, guarded the crowded churches day and night. Very peacefully, the peasants then went to ask Bishop Fulcheri for permission to take up arms. The prudent bishop sent them to his theological advisor, Fr. José Planearte, who told them that the boycott was enough and that there was no need to think about war. But when General Tranquilino Mendoza shot Pepe Sánchez because no one wanted to be part of the committee in charge of guarding the church, *they ceased obeying him.*[49]

※ ※ ※

Therefore, we are faced with an initiative of the people: a people who were forced to act in the face of an invasion by the state and inaction on the part of the Church's hierarchy. Those were not easy times, granted, and perhaps that is why the bishops and Pius XI himself had to tread carefully when speaking. Be that as it may, and as Meyer rightly says, "the Church's personnel never directed or inspired the Cristiada," that is, it wasn't the hierarchy but Catholic faithful who conducted it. They did not inspire or direct it — after all, "when the [Church] concluded the peace with the government, they did not consult the combatants."[50] The world had underestimated the attitude of the Christian people who, from the summer of 1926, began to take on a primary role, while "behind the scenes, the government and the bishops never stopped negotiating."[51] It was not a matter of defending "stones" — the stones of the church buildings — but of defending the Catholic religion that had become embodied in a nation.[52]

---

[49] Meyer, *La Cristiada*, 1:140, emphasis ours.
[50] Meyer, 1:385. Here, we read that the Cristeros said — exaggeratedly, in our opinion — that "the people of the Church will never be the Church."
[51] Meyer, *La Cristiada*, 2:285.
[52] "The determining element was the attachment to the church and the will to defend it, to protect it as a deeply embodied religion. The church was more than just a building of stones, and popular sensibilities had been affected in their very life, as the profane and the sacred are inextricably blended. As soon as the government comes out of its books, its parliament, its laws, to attack the life of the faith, its intervention appeared as a sacrilege and provoked a real rebellion that prepared the subsequent uprisings." Meyer, *La Cristiada*, 1:101.

*Blessed Miguel Gómez Loza*

*Caves where the Cristeros took refuge*

*Cristero soldiers*

*Cristero soldiers*

*Fr. José Reyes Vega, newly ordained a priest*

*Fr. Vega as Cristero general*

# 5
# The Morals of a People at Arms

*It was anticipated that, after the religious war, a large number of Cristeros would become bandits. This did not happen.*[1]

A FTER EXPLAINING THE UPRISINGS' POPULIST character, it is worthwhile to state briefly what kind of men and women fought to the cry of "Long live Christ the King!" Although the morality of the soldier and his supporters has been seen throughout the current pages, we want to emphasize once again their Christian character, a character that is not accidental in a case like this. In other words, the counter-revolution would not have been possible without the Catholic spirit that animated it.

By this we do not mean that the cause they were pursuing made thousands of men and women into "saints," no. There were archetypal examples for virtue and also the opposite, since they were still children of Adam. However, overwhelmingly their behavior was exemplary — even to their enemies.[2]

## THE STUBBORNNESS OF THE COMBATANT

Those who had left home, father, mother, farm, and even their own family to pursue a cause that seemed humanly lost knew they were facing a challenge not only posed by the government but also their own passions, their own interests. This was also clear to the Cristero chiefs who from the start tried to point out the difference between their troops and the federal troops, that is, of the national government. Among the Cristero ranks at that time, the slightest

---

[1] Words of the U.S. military attaché after the "Settlements" between the government and the Church; see Meyer, *La Cristiada*, 1:329.

[2] Because of the importance of the role of the Catholic priest in Mexico, the bad example of certain priests who rose up in arms are often cited for these cases, among whom there was everything from martyrs to not very exemplary clerics. At one end we find Father Aristeo Pedroza, alias *"el puro,"* and, at the other, General José Reyes Vega, nicknamed the "Pancho Villa in a cassock" (both were generals). The latter was a man with more vocation for military sacrifice than for the altar; he was too passionate with women and found continence difficult. But the bad examples were few. For the most part, the Catholic priesthood had plenty of examples of heroism, even to the point of martyrdom.

theft was not allowed, and no women were admitted into the ranks. There were those who prevented their soldiers from having any other companion than their lawful wife: "Don't let them stain my troops, I don't want people like that," said the Cristero chief Valentín Ávila Ramirez[3] when female "escorts" were offered for the troops. "The spirit of the liberation movement is entirely moral," said the Cristero Aurelio Acevedo, "which essentially distinguishes it from previous movements.... We do not tolerate scandals involving women. Whoever is not properly married either marries according to the law, or separates with guarantees, or is sent to prison."[4]

The women were the first to have no intention of offering their charms in times of war. It was not that fun or love were forbidden, but that the juxtaposition of drink, gambling, and women could be distracting and even dangerous in times of war and mourning. Hence, almost naturally, festivities were prohibited: it was said that "where there is music, there is wine, and the enemy can surprise us while we're drunk."[5] It is worth bearing in mind that this mentality was not puritanism but a political, structural decision. For example, once the parish priest of the town of Huejuquilla tried to set forth rules on modesty: women's skirts and sleeves should be longer, their hair should be shorter, and they should wear no "flesh-colored" stockings. Faced with this, the Cristero general Aurelio Acevedo grew angry and told him that his people were not "pious" and did not bother with such things. The combatants were already doing enough.

What were the reasons for the fight? The general himself said:

> Our movement is the defense of the rights of our Holy Mother Roman Catholic Apostolic Church and of ours as Catholics and citizens of this nation. Our leader is Christ the King, and that is why it is a movement of order in which are found those who never took part in previous revolutions.... The soldiers from previous wars in our ranks are to forget personal grudges and hatreds, like every soldier of Christ.[6]

The morality of the Cristeros was one thing and the aims of the struggle were another. Those who entered its ranks needed to know what to expect: sacrifice, obedience, and courage.

Serving as Catholic troops meant renouncing pillage and immoral

---

[3] Meyer, *La Cristiada*, 3:226–27.
[4] Quoted in Meyer, 3:143.
[5] Interview Meyer-Acevedo, in Meyer, *La Cristiada*, 3:144.
[6] Meyer, 3:144.

living, so there were several for whom the armed militia was the bridge to the unarmed Truth. Those who refused to change either deserted or underwent punishment. Such was the case of Nemesio López, a Cristero fond of money who had stolen a certain sum. After being reprimanded, his weapons were taken and he was discharged in December 1926, a few months after the war had begun. Another Cristero, J. Rosario Guillén, a leader serving near Cocula and who refused to mend his ways, was shot by General Gutiérrez. Cases like these are few. Here are examples:

> General Esteban Caro, head of the western sector of the Southern Division and the East of Nayarit, famous for his superhuman courage, began to slide into banditry in 1928, and when the Atenguillo people went to accuse him of rape before General Degollado, the latter decided to intervene. A circular was sent to all leaders stipulating the death penalty for this crime. Caro returned to his old ways in Soyatlán. Degollado, disregarding the danger, went alone to speak to this man whom he had never seen, and sternly reprimanded him in front of his troops. He then ordered Esteban Caro's bodyguard to arrest him and was obeyed. Caro repented and asked permission to return to service as a simple soldier, on the condition that a chaplain accompany them. Degollado returned him to command and sent him to Fr. Lorenzo Plascencia, who was able to testify to the reality of the soldier's conversion. He died in 1929, in a machete charge. One of his officers, Jesús Zepeda, "el Zarco," believed that the time had come to return to the old practices of his commander, and was tried for insubordination and banditry in April 1929 . . . .
>
> *Robbery, revenge, and rape* were punished very severely, usually with the death penalty. Manuel Frías, who was horrified by the shedding of blood, had thieves shot, and *rape was never forgiven* . . . .
>
> The fight against alcohol was a military necessity. This is demonstrated by the story of Fr. Ramón Pérez, chaplain of the Southern Division, who, when confronted with Cristero officers who were jubilantly celebrating the victory in an inn in Cuautla, went in and began to break the bottles and the guitar, to the drinkers' intense anger. However they respected him as a friend, as a father, and after the first moment of rebellion they acquiesced, which is praiseworthy, because with weapons in hand, power, and all, it's not so easy to submit.[7]

---

[7] Meyer, 3:227–28; emphasis ours.

For all this, the Cristero generals made known to their troops a series of rules they must live by:

1) First and foremost, they must observe strict morality among their soldiers.

2) They will be inexorable with the enemies, confiscating all the goods that belong to them, which they will distribute equally and with their own hands among their soldiers.

3) When finding wares on the roads...they will demand the proof of purchase...They will issue a receipt in duplicate... reporting to headquarters...

4) When they find cars or trucks, they will search them thoroughly...

5) When confiscating goods, if liquor of any kind is found among them, it shall be thrown away immediately.

6) When taking merchandise from any establishment, they will ask the owner to deliver it, noting its value in duplicate...

7) For no reason will they allow their soldiers to take anything on their own.[8]

The existing order was such that it almost made them incorruptible, so that already at the end of the war Calles himself said to Portes Gil: "We will not win against the Cristeros, so look for a way to enter into Settlements with the priests and put an end to this war that annihilates us."[9]

## THE CRISTERO OATH

Yet it was not enough to count on the natural goodness of man, not even that of a Christian. Clear and precise rules needed to be imposed. This happened as soon as General Gorostieta took command of the Liberation Army, as the Cristeros called themselves. He had an oath drafted that every combatant had to take:

---

[8] Huejuquilla el Alto, January 3, 1929, A. Acevedo, cited in Meyer, 3:228–29.
[9] Meyer, 3:229. To all this we should add *the Cristero did not desert:* "Underpaid, poorly fed, recruited against his will for a struggle that was not his own, the Federal soldier, who certainly did not fear death, was a potential deserter. Desertion, frequent in peacetime, became massive in wartime, even more so since the brutality with which General Amaro tried to discipline, modernize, and motivate his army was terrible. According to an American report, the desertion rate was as follows: in 1926, 9,421 deserters; in 1927, unknown; in 1928, 28,000 deserters; in 1929, 21,214 deserters.... This is why General Amaro could not put more than 70,000 men in line, although he spent his time recruiting: 20,000 deserters a year, out of 70,000 soldiers!" Meyer, *La Cristiada*, 1:152–53.

> Any individual who wishes to have the honor of becoming
> a soldier of Christ must swear to the following obligations:
> a) He is obliged to serve at least six months, without leaving
> service, under penalty of being considered a deserter before
> the enemy, b) He is obliged to blindly obey his superiors...,
> c) He is obliged not to get drunk while he is a soldier of
> Christ, d) He is obliged to endure, without any pecuniary
> reward, all the privations that a campaign entails, and for
> no reason may he complain about the poor quality or small
> quantity of food, that the fatigue is too much or the work
> is too heavy, e) He is obliged not to complain about the
> dispositions or orders of his superiors, nor to say anything
> that could damaging performance and spirits and that might
> demoralize his companions, f) All those who are not willing
> to take the oath...will be discharged, and arms and horses
> collected from them.[10]

The war was on completely unequal terms, so the "moral factor" was the mainstay that counterbalanced the enemy's arsenal in a war of David against Goliath, as the Cristero chief Aurelio Acevedo liked to recall. It is impressive to turn the pages of history and confirm the strength that reigned in those men:

> The Cristeros began without arms and without money. They
> took weapons from soldiers, but they always lacked money,
> and this constitutes a great difference with revolutionaries
> like Villa or even Zapata, who at one time or another in
> their ventures received large sums and large quantities of
> ammunition.... The Cristeros never counted on anything
> but themselves, without support either in the nation or
> outside it: "All the arms and ammunition with which we
> fought the government, we took from the government itself,"
> said Federico Vázquez, "and as proof, the horses that we gave
> to the government when we surrendered were all from the
> same government." And as Acevedo said: "Who will be able
> to deny that I began on the 26th with twenty men and three
> weapons and my chief with five armed men? And who will
> deny that on the 29th we both had more than 2,500 perfectly
> armed? Why were we, so few, poorly armed, without military
> discipline, to fight with those, so prepared for war, with so
> many supplies to fight the poor ranchers — why the miracle?
> The little ones conquered the big ones like David."[11]

---

[10] Meyer, *La Cristiada*, 3:232.
[11] Meyer, 3:213–14.

Their moral vigor made them fight with everything they had to hand. Such was their courage and even recklessness that anything might serve the purpose:

> In these battles, stones played an important role: they were rolled over the enemy who climbed up slopes. When the cavalry spurred their horses, each time they were repulsed not only with bullets, but also with stones. And the government soldiers shouted: "Cristeros dying of hunger, you fight with Our Fathers and Hail Marys," and the Cristeros answered with: "Yes, here goes a Hail Mary," and a rock rolled downhill. Another told them: "Here goes an Our Father," and another "Here goes a bull, fight it." The rain of stones was so heavy, and the rocks were so great, that they could not escape.[12]

## DEALING WITH THE ENEMY

In wars where martial law prevailed, execution by firing squad was a reality. However, the Cristero army was not a normal army: the way in which it recruited its troops, the religious motivation, and the lack of military experience made the executions cause a certain horror at the beginning of the war. On the other hand, the systematic shootings practiced by the federal troops were the order of the day for enemies.

Did the Cristeros execute people? Without a doubt, but on a vastly smaller scale than their opponents. The first public execution took place on March 15, 1927, after the victory in San Julián against the troops of General Espiridión Rodríguez. Victoriano Ramírez, alias "El Catorce,"[13] had twenty-eight soldiers executed (with a dagger, to save bullets). The carnage caused such a scandal among the Cristeros that witnesses still spoke of it forty years later: it seems that an old woman told El Catorce, "Good Heavens! Even those with the Union are killing people!" Somewhat fiercely, he replied: "What did you think, that it was a pilgrimage? I could not find a way to defeat my enemies without killing them. Show me how, then." It is interesting to note that, after this, El Catorce avoided shooting common soldiers; they were released once their weapons were taken.[14]

---

[12] Meyer, 3:247.
[13] An almost mythical character about whom much has been written and recognized for the accuracy and bravery he showed in combat. It is said that in one battle, he killed fourteen federal soldiers alone, hence the nickname (*catorce* is fourteen in Spanish).
[14] See Meyer, *La Cristiada*, 3:261.

The general rule was to avoid the useless spilling of fraternal blood. In the Catholic sphere, those who applied the maximum penalty for enemies were career military leaders, as was the case of General Gorostieta; the only criticism among his soldiers was the ease with which he ordered executions. General Degollado Guízar, head of the Southern Division, and later supreme commander of the National Guard, always opposed this practice and in March 1929, during the march on Cocula, he harshly reprimanded the officer who executed some federal prisoners without having been ordered to do so:

> "The individuals I shot," replied the officer, "prevented me from marching at every moment, seeking to escape, and I thought it would be better to shoot them. After all, what do you want them for? If you or I fall into their hands, they will not only shoot us but even torture us."
>
> "All right, but we are not murderers, and if you repeat this, I assure you that you will suffer the same fate," replied Degollado.[15]

In practice, military and political necessity led the Cristeros to shoot most of the federal and agrarian leaders who fell into their hands, as well as individuals who had been especially pointed out for their ferocity or for crimes and sacrileges. This punishment was often preceded by a summary trial. In the event of a death sentence, they sought to impart the sacraments, if the convict asked for them, as ordered by the general of Colima, Dionisio Ochoa:

> Never shoot [via firing squad] an enemy, no matter how evil and wicked, without first giving him at least the time necessary to repent and prepare for death. When possible, make it easier for him, if he wishes, to receive the Holy Sacraments.[16]

Regarding treatment of the enemy, we mention a fact that seems to have been taken from medieval knights, showing the nobility of the Cristeros:

> In mid-March 1929, General Degollado Guízar gathered the main commanders of his forces operating in southern Jalisco to take the important town of Cocula, Jal. It was noon on March 18 when the column, made up of seventeen hundred men, made its entrance into the town under a rain of flowers and confetti that the people threw with their hands onto the liberators. The joyful ringing of the bells and the cheers to

---

15 Meyer, 3:261.
16 Spectator, *Los cristeros del volcán de Colima*, 1:154.

Christ the King and Holy Mary of Guadalupe thundered
in the area....

When he was about to take a brief rest at midnight, before
embarking on hard journey next day, General Degollado
received notice that a Callista column of fifteen hundred
men was approaching the town. It was necessary to draw up,
in haste, a new battle plan. It consisted of leaving the town
at six in the morning and provoking the enemy's attack on
the plain, since it would be difficult for the enemy to enter
a town where the Cristeros were established.

And so they did. When the rear guard of the Cristero
troops left Cocula, they were attacked on the plain by the federals, but all the movements of the counterattack were already
foreseen and, in a few minutes, faced with the serious risk of
being annihilated, the Callistas fled in disorder towards the
town.... The next day, Lieutenant Débora of the federal army
unconditionally surrendered his troops. General Degollado,
who could honor manliness, after disarming the vanquished,
released them and, in a gesture of chivalrous recognition of
courage, allowed the lieutenant to keep his own arms.[17]

## CULTURE AND WORSHIP IN TIMES OF WAR

Although the Cristeros were mostly humble people, they did not
lack culture — not, of course, a "bookish" culture, but that which
comes from one's ancestors and the worship of God. Meyer himself,
a European and to top it all a Frenchman, was impressed in his youth
by these almost medieval characters. Catholic and Western culture
had penetrated deeply into the country that emerged from Spain. He
gave an account of the legacy received over the years:

> If writing is often clumsy and awkward, elocution is remark-
> ably loose, yet it cannot be said that the mostly illiterate
> masses are in "the darkness of ignorance." *The unlettered
> leader who has a secretary demonstrates a remarkable culture
> in which the oldest references abound, coming from the Middle
> Ages and the Renaissance.* The conversations recorded on tape
> also show that "the stupidity of the countryside" is more a
> lie than a reality, and that these people know how to express
> themselves remarkably well about everything that matters to
> them.... A table of biblical, historical, and geographical refer-
> ences wouldn't be surprising, and it would not be sketchy, but
> would demonstrate the firmly rooted existence of a *popular*

---

[17] Rius Facius, *México Cristero*, 2:452–53.

*culture based on the Bible, the Christian oral tradition, books of chivalry and court poetry.* Clovis, Geneviève of Brabant, and Joan of Arc were familiar characters, as were Charlemagne and the Twelve Peers of France, or Bertoldo, Bertoldino, and Cacasenno. The reading aloud by someone who knew how (regarding the Bible, it is read standing, out of respect for the Holy Scriptures) or the theatrical performance, constitute the vehicles of this knowledge. As late as 1970, in Chalma, in the atrium of the church, one could see and hear a company from Tenango del Valle represent *Charlemagne and the Twelve Peers of France.* It had accompanied Ezequiel Mendoza's childhood, and in it he saw a prefiguration of the Cristiada.[18]

The religion of the Cristeros was the traditional Catholic religion, "strongly rooted in the Hispanic Middle Ages."[19] The culture of the warrior and the Christian worldview were difficult to separate; as the Argentine Carlos Disandro says, the divine "cult" or worship was its center.[20] So deeply rooted was the Catholic *cultus* and such was the love for the Church that although the churches remained closed, the Cristero heart remained open to the mysteries for which, in some cases, even "dry Masses"[21] or "white Masses" were celebrated, so as not to lose the memory of the sacred rites.

However, strength and nobility in wartime intensified when the sacred mysteries could actually be celebrated, thanks to the courage of many priests who, without bearing arms, had taken seriously the duty of being good shepherds.[22] When a chaplain could be had among the ranks, Holy Mass was normal, giving meaning to resistance:

> Daily Mass, Mass of thanksgiving the day after a victory...,
> Mass for the repose of the soul of the deceased, solemn
> Mass for troops attended by the entire populace and in
> which the soldiers paid homage to the Blessed Sacrament,
> extraordinary solemnities of Holy Week experienced with

---

[18] Meyer, *La Cristiada*, 3:272–73, emphasis ours.
[19] Meyer, 3:307.
[20] Carlos Disandro, *Las fuentes de la cultura* (La hostería volante, 1965), 17.
[21] See Meyer, *La Cristiada*, 3:277. This name is sometimes given to the representation of the Mass when its texts are recited by a layman so as not to lose the memory of what the Sacrifice was. It should be borne in mind that the Cristeros did not know how long the churches would remain closed and, therefore, how long they would be without the sacraments administered by the Church. Something similar is happening today in communist China.
[22] The whole book was beautifully written by Father Enrique de Jesús Ochoa, although — as noted above — under the pseudonym of "Spectator," being the chaplain of the counterrevolutionary army of Colima.

a new fervor in their shared experience of the Passion, great Eucharistic and Christological feasts, the greatest of which was that of Christ the King. In the Cristero camps, when possible, the Blessed Sacrament was exposed, and the soldiers, in groups of fifteen or twenty, held perpetual adoration...The priests who remained with the Cristeros spent their time confessing, baptizing, marrying, organizing spiritual exercises, and doing missions.[23]

As for prayer outside of liturgical worship, the recitation of the Holy Rosary was also a habitual and daily practice. Many of the combatants, at the end of the prayer, specially invoked Our Lady of Guadalupe, and recited the following prayer that Anacleto González Flores had drafted in his own handwriting, as recounted by Father Ochoa:

> Among the acts of piety that were strongly recommended to all groups of soldiers was the collective prayer of the Holy Rosary. And the one who writes this is a witness to the piety and fervor with which this took place everyday in the evening, even in the most unfavorable and distressing circumstances.... At the end of the recitation of the Rosary, the following act of contrition was recited daily, which is a poem, a monument of greatness, faith and sublime love for Jesus Christ and the Church. It is believed that it came from the heart and pen of Maestro Anacleto González Flores. Here it is, verbatim and complete:
>
> "Merciful Jesus, my sins are more than the drops of your precious Blood that you shed for me. I am not worthy to belong to the Army that defends the rights of Your Church and fights for You. I wish I had never sinned, so that my life would be a pleasing offering in your divine eyes. Wash me from my iniquities and cleanse me from my sins. For your holy Cross, for your death, for my most holy mother of Guadalupe, forgive me. I have not known how to do penance for my sins, so I want to receive death as a merited punishment for them. I do not want to fight, nor live, nor die, but only for Your Holy Church and for You. My Mother of Guadalupe, accompany this poor sinner in his agony. Grant that my last cry on earth and my first song in heaven may be: *Long live Christ the King!*"[24]

Prayer during the war became a necessity for the combatants. They took advantage of the opportunity, in some places, to expose

---

[23] Meyer, *La Cristiada*, 3:278.
[24] Spectator, *Los cristeros del volcán de Colima*, 1:154–55.

the Blessed Sacrament for adoration. Once again, we quote Father Ochoa, a privileged spectator of the uprisings in Colima:

> On the eve of the first Friday of October (1927), General Dionisio Eduardo Ochoa arrived at Cedillo, accompanied by his escort and with Father Chaplain, his brother [it was Ochoa himself]. All the Cristeros who worked in that place had met beforehand. A makeshift chapel was set up, and the next day, Jesus in the Blessed Sacrament, after Holy Mass, remained in the small tabernacle to receive the adoration of his soldiers.... On their knees, in groups of fifteen or twenty, the crusaders took turns to make reparation and praise the Divine King. He did not remain alone for a moment, neither day nor night, and at all hours and at all times, until dawn on Friday, and the religious songs of those fervent worshippers did not cease to resound on the mountain. On that Mass of the First Friday, all the Cristeros present received Holy Communion, which filled them with the sweetest strength.[25]

### THE CONVERSION OF ENEMIES (AND OF ONESELF)

It is impossible to relate the enormous number of accounts about the life of the Faith in this war. We want, however, to mention only one case, because it is paradigmatic.

Mother María Concepción Acevedo ("Mother Conchita," as she was affectionately called)[26] was abbess of the Capuchin nuns in the city of Tlalpan. In 1927, victims of a cowardly betrayal, they were exclaustrated under orders and, like the Carmelites of Compiègne during the French Revolution, began to move from house to house with the intention of continuing to live religious life. Ending up in Puebla, they tried to live as cloistered nuns, though dressed in lay clothes. Here Father Miguel Agustín Pro, S.J., visited them in September of that year. He came with a specific intention: to propose to the superior that they offer themselves as propitiatory victims for the conversion of Plutarco Elías Calles.

"Offering oneself" implied that, if God accepted such a request, whoever offered himself would have to suffer much in this life in exchange for the president's conversion. Aware of their spiritual responsibility, both Father Pro and Mother Conchita made a solemn vow on September 23, 1927, that sealed the love they had for souls and for the Mexican people. Two months later the Jesuit priest achieved martyrdom, while the nun

---

[25] Spectator, 1:340–41.
[26] See Rius Facius, *México Cristero*, 2:398–400.

spent more than twelve years detained in the Islas Marías federal prison, having been accused of conspiring against the government.

That is just one example of the interior life of those who fought not with arms, but with prayer and sacrifice.

General Gorostieta himself, who for years had been considered an agnostic (baselessly, as it turns out), was described in this way, in a battle on June 2, 1929, in El Valle, about 18 miles from Atotonilco:

> The Cristeros had breakfast. Some went to a small shop across from the hacienda, others up to the roof: from there you can see the plain.... Surprisingly, the first soldiers of the 42nd Cavalry Regiment appeared there.... General Gorostieta got up quickly, gauged the danger threatening them, and ordered: "We have to get out of here in any way. Mount your horses, all of you, and let's get out before they surround us."
>
> But the horses, at the sound of the gunshots, bucked, and only General Gorostieta managed to mount his. He grasped the crucifix on his chest in his hands for a moment, looked at it and rushed towards the exit. A volley of gunfire caught him outside, and his horse fell. He returned to the house.
>
> "These filthy men killed my horse and took my files," he said indignantly.
>
> One of his men asked him: "What do we do, general?"
>
> "Fight bravely and die like men."
>
> The Cristeros boldly resisted their enemies. They were surrounded, and it was dangerous and difficult to escape. However, Major Heriberto Navarrete, the general's aide, Colonel Rodolfo Loza Márquez, and Private Jesusillo tried to escape through a small orange orchard next to the farm. All three succeeded. Gorostieta intended to follow the same path, but the siege had closed him in. A voice broke through the pounding of bullets:
>
> "Who goes there?"
>
> "Long live Christ the King!" Enrique Gorostieta replied defiantly. Those were his last words before a volley of gunshots ended his life.[27]

He who had begun the war with some doubt now died with the cry of "Long live Christ the King!" It was no mere battle cry but the reflection of an inner conviction. Much has been said about Gorostieta's "agnosticism," even in books.[28] There are conjectures that can make him a rather "cold" or not "practicing" Christian. Aurelio

---

[27] Rius Facius, 2:465–66, emphasis ours.
[28] Marta Elena Negrete, *Enrique Gorostieta Cristero Agnóstico* (El Caballito, 1981), 190.

Acevedo, who knew him personally, said that on one occasion, when riding with Gorostieta, the latter told him an experience that was decisive for him in accepting the deal with the League:

> My wife gave me a son. I took to the streets in search of a priest to baptize him and I ran all over the city in my efforts until I literally caught him: I saw him pass by in a car and I took another man and followed him until I caught up with him. But it happened that in my wanderings through the city I stumbled upon a brothel with a door to the street, where from the outside you could see the degrading and disgusting spectacle of a dance of naked ruffians and sluts. Then I made this reflection: if in my country it's a struggle just to find a minister of the Lord to impart the Sacraments to us, and on the other hand, licentiousness reigns everywhere, it means that the country is threatened with death by prostitution and crime, and it is the obligation of every Mexican to come to its defense. And I thought it through, and I accepted the proposals of the League to fight for God, for the Fatherland, and for Liberty.[29]

※ ※ ※

All reductionism is part of an ideology and, therefore, somewhat contrary to reality. In the case of the Cristeros, opinions must not fall into either a black legend, which would claim that all of them were bad, or its opposite, claiming that there was nothing reprehensible. However, examples presented over the course of innumerable pages give such impressive descriptions regarding the Catholic troops that one will be hard-pressed to find their equal in other episodes of history. This is so, even from the merely human point of view. The Cristiada provides material for archetypes, heroic figures, and even holy souls. Why not praise them? Why not publish them if they are also part of the story of the period? The cry "for God and for the Fatherland" summed up well the *forma mentis* of these medieval knights resurrected in Mexico and fighting for the same ideals.

So great was their concern to act rightly that, like Charles V and the Spanish question over the "just titles" of the Conquista, Mexico wondered whether or not it was licit to rise up in arms against an oppressive government. The answer gave rise not only to the intervention of great theologians but also ultimately defined — after several years — the position of the Church on the matter, as we will see in the next chapter.

---

[29] Acevedo, *David I*, 47.

*Main altar of the parish church in Encarnación de Díaz, Jalisco,*
*where the tabernacle reads "He is not here"*

*Three generations of Cristeros*

*Victoriano Ramírez, "El Catorce"*

*A clandestine Mass indoors*

*Clandestine Mass outdoors*

*Clandestine Mass outdoors*

*Clandestine Mass outdoors*

# 6

# Rightful Disobedience:

## DOCTRINAL JUSTIFICATION
## OF THE CRISTERO UPRISING

SHOULD NORMS HAVE BEEN OBEYED THAT WENT against not only the Church's laws but the conscience of the majority of the Mexican people? In this chapter we will analyze the doctrine on legitimate disobedience to a tyrannical regime that informed Catholic consciences in considering whether or not to obey, and the enormous consequences of this doctrine.

### RESIST OR ENDURE THE TYRANT?

There are countless pages in which wars and "rumors of war" are spoken of in the Old Testament. The people of Israel were never a submissive people. However, the Old Law does not include a clear and precise body of doctrine about countering an enemy's unjust attacks (internal or external). Perhaps one exception — because of the way it is narrated — is the aggression that the chosen people suffered from Antiochus IV Epiphanes,[1] as told in the first and second books of Maccabees.

Only a century and a half later the new teaching of Christ began to spread throughout the known world in the fullness of time (Gal 4:4), and not without certain divisions about this question. Meekness and humility of heart, turning the other cheek, and forgiveness of offenses were Christian watchwords. However, the first followers of the Crucified One were faced with a great dilemma: persecuted as rebels and fanatics by the Roman Empire, should they defend themselves or not? Was it licit to rebel against recognized authority? Had not the Master commanded respect for the authorities? Had He not submitted Himself to an unjust tribunal?

The letter kills, but the spirit gives life... The Catholic religion is not only the religion "of the Book" (Luther's *sola scripture*), but of what has always been believed, by everyone and everywhere, according to the famous maxim of St. Vincent of Lérins. This is called the

---

[1] Antiochus Epiphanes (215–164 BC) was the third son of Antiochus III the Great, who reigned in Hellenistic Syria from 175 BC.

Tradition of the Church, the second source of revelation. However, what is the Church's perennial teaching about such questions?

a. Regarding rebellion, among the first scholars who strongly opposed the use of violence were Tertullian, St. Hippolytus, Arnobius, Lactantius, and Origen, all considered respectable by the Church, but fallible guides for its teachings.

b. From another perspective, we find authors who are doctrinally more secure and considered to be the "holy fathers" of the Church, that is, those who trustworthily interpreted the teachings of Christ. Among them we find St. Athanasius, for whom "killing is not allowed, but annihilating adversaries in war is legitimate and praiseworthy. And those who fight diligently in war are rewarded with greater recompences, and funeral columns are erected to commemorate their deeds."[2] St. Ambrose, bishop of Milan, went so far as to say that "David never waged war except when provoked. In this way, he had prudence as his companion in combat, along with strength, which is used in war to defend the homeland from barbarians or to defend family or friends from thieves. It is a strength filled with justice."[3] Also, the following statement, which represents an advance in the discussion: "Those who can protect but do not protect a companion from being attacked are as guilty as the one who attacks."[4]

Nonetheless, it was certainly the great bishop of Hippo, St. Augustine, who made a qualitative leap in Christian reflection. The former Manichaean stated, when speaking of war, that, despite being a misfortune, it was still necessary in some cases: a sad necessity for good men, and a happiness for bad men. However, it would be even worse if evildoers dominated just men.[5] This type of war, in defense of the good, was aimed at restoring peace and justice. In addition, between peace and war, the former must always be preferred. In this regard, he wrote around the year 428 to Darius, governor of Africa:

> Certainly, the strongest and most faithful warriors are great
> and have their glory — which is already a title of true glory —
> to whose efforts it is due, with the help of God who protects
> them, that the indomitable enemy is defeated and peace

---

[2] St. Athanasius, *Epist. ad Amunem monachum*, in J.P. Migne, *Patrologia Graeca* 26:1173.

[3] See St. Ambrose, *De officiis*, XXXV, 177 and XXVII, 129, ed. Mauritius Testard, *Corpus Christianorum Series Latina* (Brepols, 1953), 65 and 47.

[4] Ambrose, XXXVI, 179, in CCSL 16:66.

[5] St. Augstine, *De civitate Dei*, IV, 15, ed. Bernardus Dombart and Alphonsus Kalb, CCSL 47:111.

achieved for the Republic and the provinces. But it is an object of much greater glory to kill war itself with words, rather than to kill men with the sword, and to make peace by peace, not by war. For those who fight, if they are good, they undoubtedly seek peace, even if through blood.[6]

We might summarize Augustinian thought by saying that war can be waged only for a just cause and after having exhausted the recourse of speech; its purpose always is to seek peace and use benevolence against the enemy, that is, even to seek his good. To these conditions, St. Augustine also added a final one: war must be declared by public and not by private individuals.[7]

As González Morfín rightly points out, the saintly doctor did not hesitate when it comes to the use of arms, taking a stance far from pacifism:

> Do not think that if someone fights armed with weapons of war he cannot please God. Holy David, of whom the Lord bore such great witness, was a warrior.... The centurion who said to the Lord, "I am not worthy that you should enter under my roof," was a soldier.... Cornelius, to whom an angel was sent to say to him: "Cornelius, your prayers have been accepted," bore arms.... They were also among those who came to be baptized by St. John.... When the soldiers asked him what they should do, he replied: "Rob no one by violence or by false accusation, and be content with your wages." He did not forbid them to take up arms, but he commanded them to be content with their pay.[8]

There are many other passages similar to the foregoing in which he endeavors to justify a military career and even certain types of wars. Thus, although St. Augustine does not propose a systematic doctrine about just war, he proposes a concept that encompasses, to some extent, what he says about war elsewhere: "'Just wars' are usually defined as those that are carried out to punish an injustice, for example, when a town or a city makes war to correct an evil action done against its own, or to restore to them what had been taken from them by injustice."[9] That is to say, what causes a war to be considered just or not is nothing other than the *iniquitas inimicorum* (iniquity of

---

[6] St. Augustine, *Epistulae*, 229, 2, ed. Alois Goldbacher, *Corpus Scriptorum Ecclesiasticorum Latinorum*, 57:497–98.
[7] See St. Augustine, *Contra Faustum*, XXII, 75, ed. Joseph Zycha, CSEL 25:673.
[8] St. Augustine, *Epist.* 189, 4, CSEL 57:133–34.
[9] St. Augustine, *In Heptateuchum*, VI, 10, ed. Ioannes Fraipont, CCSL 28:429.

the enemy); it will be just only to the extent that it is undertaken to avoid an evil or to repair an injustice.

In St. Augustine the thinking of the Church Fathers finds its most mature expression. War appears as an unfortunate reality that, in order to be lawful, needs to meet certain conditions. Some of these have been carried into current thought as indispensable conditions for justification of an armed response to a grave injustice. Extracted from various works, these conditions established by the bishop of Hippo are five: a) just cause; b) peace as its goal; c) rectitude of intention when fighting; d) recourse to dialogue has been exhausted, and e) a legitimate authority declares it.[10]

Undoubtedly, the convert Augustine laid the doctrinal foundations. However, the expression of the Church's teaching did not stop with him. Among the doctors of the Church, St. Thomas Aquinas has always been the surest guide throughout the centuries. In his works — mainly in the *Summa theologiae* — there are very clear elements to draw on for a doctrine of armed resistance without faltering in the effort.[11] Within the framework of the morality or immorality of war, in question 40 of the II-II of his magnum opus, he asks whether waging a military conflict is always a sin. To this he responds negatively, that is, there are cases in which war can be justly resorted to. However, for it to be considered "just": three conditions are necessary: a) that it be declared under the *authority of the prince* (for it is not for a private person to promote a war); b) that *there be a just cause*, namely, that it be done to redress an injury; and c) that *the intention of those who undertake it be correct*, that is, that they seek to obtain a great good or to avoid a great evil, but let them not be moved by ambition or cruelty.[12]

In the same sense and delving into the subject, two questions later, he deals with sedition. After explaining that it is a special sin and differs from mere war because it is not a question of attacking — or preparing to attack — a foreign enemy, but that it is two groups of the same people confronting each other, St. Thomas asks, in the second article, whether sedition is always a mortal sin, and affirms that it is. However, he clarifies that since a tyrannical regime is not just,

---

[10] González Morfín, *La guerra cristera*, 34.
[11] So authoritative is the opinion and doctrine of Aquinas that in our country, Argentina, both sides made use of it — the guerrilla movements of Catholic extraction (Montoneros), even when they ended up supporting a Marxist revolution, and the military cadres who carried out the civic-military coup of 1976 to stop its advance!
[12] See St. Thomas Aquinas, *Summa theologiae* (BAC, 1956), II-II, Q. 40, art. 1.

as it is not ordered to the common good, a rebellion against such a government would not have the nature of sedition. Moreover, a tyrant who only seeks his own good to the detriment of his people could be accused of seditiousness, because by crushing his people he encourages discord and seditions. González Morfín rightly notes: "Without being a true treatise on armed resistance, this passage from St. Thomas envisages the possibility of resisting a regime that has abandoned the search for the common good to focus only on its own benefit."[13] In the Angelic Doctor's own words: "For just as it is lawful to resist thieves, it is lawful to resist bad rulers, except if scandal is caused when such an attitude may result in a very serious disorder."[14]

In *De regimine principum* (On the Governance of Rulers), the Angelic Doctor considers the possibility of resisting a tyrannical government. There, Aquinas establishes at least three conditions for an action of armed resistance to be morally acceptable: a) the existence of a tyranny that strongly violates the rights of civil society; b) the uprising against the tyrannical government offers a chance of success; and c) the evils caused by the uprising are not likely to be greater than those that are intended to be remedied. In summary, says González Morfín:

> From what St. Thomas discusses in both the *Summa* and the *De regimine*, although scattered in different parts of his work and without the purpose of offering a concrete answer, we can say there are very valuable elements for articulating doctrine on armed resistance to an oppressive government. In the first place, he asserts that it is just, and that it must be distinguished from sedition, since a rebellion against a government which is not ordered to the good of the people does not have the characteristics of sedition. Second, he establishes four conditions that armed resistance must meet in order to be considered morally licit: a) the existence of a real tyranny; b) that the movement against tyranny has a serious chance of success; c) that worse disorders are not provoked; and d) that this attitude does not result in scandal.[15]

Scholastic thought, for its part, does not end with St. Thomas. Later (and not without certain deviations in other areas of philosophy), the Renaissance was also interested in the subject. Thus, Francisco de Vitoria, in his commentaries on the work of Aquinas, explicitly addressed the theme of resistance to a tyrannical government when

---

[13] González Morfin, *La guerra cristera*, 37.
[14] St. Thomas, *Summa theologiae*, II-II, Q. 69, art. 4.
[15] González Morfin, *La guerra cristera*, 39.

commenting on question 42 of the II-II, in which, as we said, the possibility of rebellion against an unjust government is admitted, without falling into the sin of sedition. Vitoria accepts this principle but insists on proportion (what has come to be called the principle of proportionality): "It is always advisable to foresee whether a greater evil follows from this. For example, if there are ten thousand men in the city and eight thousand die because of my sedition, it is better for the tyrant to be tolerated than for so many men to die."[16] Francisco Suárez, on the other hand, in his interpretation of Cajetan,[17] establishes that whoever undertakes a war is obliged

> to seek the maximum possible certainty in regard to victory. Moreover, he is obliged to compare the hope of victory with the danger of harm, and to see whether, when all these things are weighed, hope prevails. But if it is impossible to achieve such certainty, at least he must have a more probable hope of victory, or is equally doubtful about the country's needs and the common good.[18]

In summary, based on this brief synopsis, in the reflections developed by these classical authors we find the conditions that later predominated in the Church's teaching about when an uprising can be understood as legitimate. González Morfin summarizes the conditions:

> First, the existence of a just cause, currently explained as the existence of certain, serious, and prolonged violations of fundamental rights, or that the damage caused by the aggressor to a nation or the community of nations has been lasting, serious, and certain.
> Second, rectitude of intention. This means that the option of arms will never be the first for settling a conflict, and even less, a valid choice for asserting claims. One goes to war only out of necessity....
> Thirdly, a careful application of the principle of proportionality, which entails not resorting to military defense when it is foreseeable that the use of arms will entail more serious evils and disorders than what is intended to be eliminated....

[16] Francisco de Vitoria, *Comentarios a la Secunda Secundae de Santo Tomás*, Q. 42, art. 2, ad 3, in Francisco de Vitoria, *Comentarios a la Secunda Secundae de Santo Tomás*, vol. 2: *De caritate et prudentia (QQ. 23-56)*, ed. Vicente Beltrán de Heredia (Biblioteca de Teólogos Españoles, 1932), 300-301.
[17] The interpretation he makes of Cajetan is doubtful and, apparently, makes him say things he does not actually say.
[18] Francisco Suárez, *De bello IV*, 10, in Luciano Pereña Vicente, ed., *Teoría de la guerra en Francisco Suárez* (CSIC, 1954), vol. 2, p. 144.

The requirement that there be a well-founded probability of success. This condition was reduced by Suárez, who reduced it to the requirement that, at least, the possibility of victory was more likely than that of being defeated. This condition is included in the *Catechism*, but is omitted in some classic treatises on war.

On the other hand, it should be noted that the first condition required by St. Thomas to declare a war, that is, a competent entity makes this decision, has been left out of the doctrine received. Aquinas grants this power to the prince.... Over time, Vitoria's postulate prevailed: "Anyone, even a private individual, can undertake an action of defensive war."[19]

## THE DOCTRINE OF RESISTANCE PRIOR
## TO THE MEXICAN CONFLICT

At the time of the Cristero war, the Church did not have a complete doctrinal framework regarding this specific case. Soviet Marxism and its seizure of power was still a recent phenomenon. However, there were already some guiding documents that allow a glimpse of the crux of the matter. Thus, for example, the pontiff of social reform, Pope Leo XIII, explained the situations in which citizens should not obey those who govern unjustly. There is only one reason for men not to obey: when something is demanded of them that is obviously repugnant to natural law or divine law.

> All things in which the natural law or the will of God are violated, cannot be commanded, or executed. If then, it happens that man is forced to do one of two things, either to despise God's commands or to despise the order of rulers, we must obey Jesus Christ who commands us to give to Caesar the things that are Caesar's and to God the things that are God's (Mt 22:21)... Those who do so cannot be accused of breaking due obedience, because if the will of the rulers contradicts the will and laws of God, the rulers overstep the range of their power and pervert justice. And in this case, their authority has no value because such authority, without justice, is null.[20]

In another of his encyclicals, Leo XIII stated that when one commands "something contrary to reason, to the eternal law, to the authority of God, it is right then to disobey men in order to obey God. Thus closing the doors to tyranny, the whole state will not be captured by it."[21]

---

[19] González Morfin, *La guerra cristera*, 45–46.
[20] Leo XIII, Enc. *Diuturnum illud*, 29-VI-1881, ASS [*Acta Sanctae Sedis*] 14 (1881), 8.
[21] Leo XIII, *Libertas*, 20-VI-1888, ASS 20 (1887), 600.

Due obedience and unjustified obedience, then are clearly distinguished. Yet the pontiff who had to suffer perhaps the greatest political conflicts of the twentieth century was Pope Pius XI: the Cristiada, the confrontation with Action Française, and the Spanish Civil War, to name just a few.

After the fratricidal Mexican fight and the "Settlements" between the Church and government, there was a second revolt (called "La Segunda"), the result of discontent, uneasiness, and the intensification of persecutions. At this time Pius XI published the document entitled *Firmissimam constantiam*. There he clarified:

> Consequently, it is quite natural that when the most elementary religious and civil liberties are attacked, Catholic citizens do not resign themselves passively to renouncing those liberties. Notwithstanding, the reclaiming of these rights and liberties can be, according to the circumstances, more or less opportune, more or less energetic.

> 27. You have more than once recalled to your Faithful that the Church protects peace and order, even at the cost of grave sacrifices, and that it condemns every unjust insurrection or violence against constituted powers. On the other hand, among you it has also been said that, whenever these powers arise against justice and truth even to destroying the very foundations of authority, it is not clear how those citizens are to be condemned who united to defend themselves and the nation, by licit and appropriate means, against those who make use of public power to bring it to ruin.

> 28. While the practical solution depends on concrete circumstances, We must, however, on Our part recall to you some general principles, always to be kept in mind, and they are:
> 1) That these demands have the *ratio* [notion] of means, or of relative end, not of ultimate and absolute end;
> 2) That, as to the *ratio* of means, they must be licit actions and not intrinsically evil;
> 3) That, if they are to be means proportionate to the end, they must be used only to the extent that they serve to obtain or render possible, in whole or in part, the end, and in such manner that they do not cause to the community greater damages than those they seek to repair;
> 4) That the use of such means and the exercise of civic and political rights in their fulness, also including problems of a purely material and technical order, or any violent defense, does not enter in any manner into the task of the clergy or

of Catholic Action as such, although to both appertains the preparation of Catholics to make just use of their rights, and to defend them with all legitimate means as the common good requires;

5) The clergy and Catholic Action, being, by their mission of peace and love, consecrated to uniting all men in *vinculo pacis* (Ephesians iv. 3), must contribute to the prosperity of the nation, especially encouraging the union of those social initiatives which are not opposed to dogma or to the laws of Christian morals.[22]

The initial Cristero uprising (1926–1929) and what was called "the Second" (the aftermath of the "Settlements") ended up almost forcing the Holy See to establish a teaching on the right to insurrection that had never yet been made explicit by the Church. We have not yet seen this subject studied, namely, the historical phenomenon of the *Cristiada* as a precedent for the magisterial documents on the subject.[23]

### "GO DOWN TO THE MARKET": FROM MORALITY TO DEEDS

We read in Plato's dialogues that when his disciples were too entangled in dialectic, Plato would say: "Now let us go down to the market…" Meaning, let us get to the facts. Let's compare the principles named above with what really happened in Mexico before 1926. What did people think about it? How did events unfold? How was the doctrine conveyed to the common folk? Were the necessary conditions for the uprising met? We shall consider one idea at a time.

Just as imperial Spain of Charles V posed the moral problem of the Conquest,[24] the Cristeros also considered the legality or illegality of their uprising.

Papal magisterium had repeatedly condemned the movements of insurrection. It is enough to recall, for this purpose, the encyclical *Quod apostolici muneris* of Leo XIII, in which we read:

---

[22] Pius XI, *Firmissimam constantiam*, 28-III-1937, AAS 29 (1937), 208–9.

[23] Just as an example and as if receiving the previous teaching, the current Catechism echoes all these positions by saying in no. 2243 that "Resistance to the oppression of those who govern may not legitimately resort to arms until the following conditions are met: 1) in the event of real, serious and prolonged violations of fundamental rights, 2) after all other remedies have been exhausted, 3) without causing worse disorders, 4) with a well-founded hope of success, 5) when it is impossible to reasonably foresee better solutions."

[24] In this regard, see the beautiful work of Jean Dumont, *El amanecer de los derechos del hombre: la controversia de Valladolid* (Encuentro, 1997).

And if at any time it happen that the power of the State
is rashly and tyrannically wielded by princes, the teaching
of the Catholic church does not allow an insurrection on
private authority against them, lest public order be only the
more disturbed, and lest society take greater hurt therefrom.
And when affairs come to such a pass that there is no other
hope of safety, she teaches that relief may be hastened by the
merits of Christian patience and by earnest prayers to God.[25]

Pope Gregory XVI, shortly before this encyclical, condemned the
insurrection of the Polish Catholics against the Tsar. Further, just a
few years earlier, the Irish episcopate had condemned an insurrection
of Catholics, announcing that all who persisted in opposing the government by force of arms would be *excommunicated*, and any priest
who supported the uprising would be suspended *a divinis*.[26]

For all these reasons, Catholics wondered if what they were doing
was legitimate. In addition, apart from the Church's directive, which
they wanted to respect, there was a political problem, since the hierarchy did not want to be too direct in its statements: if the Mexican
uprising was explicitly condemned, the rebels would have to lay down
their arms with great losses and, if it was supported, there would
be more reprisals from the government, adding a global diplomatic
confrontation to an already difficult situation.

Now, what did the Cristeros have at their disposal for forming an
opinion on the legality or otherwise of armed resistance?

For understanding the thoughts and sources of those who called
for armed defense, a work published clandestinely by the National
League for the Defense of Religious Liberty[27] in 1929, just after the
"Settlements," is of capital importance. It was published by Aquiles
Moctezuma (pseudonym of the Jesuit Father Eduardo Iglesia), *The
Religious Conflict of 1926: Its Origins, Its Development, Its Solution*.[28] This
work attempts to substantiate, under the sure guidance of St. Thomas
Aquinas, the lawfulness of armed resistance against an oppressive
government; additionally, it distinguishes rebellion from revolution.

---

[25] Leo XIII, Enc. *Quod apostolici muneris*, 28-XII-1878, ASS 11 (1878/1879), 373.
As we can see, this encyclical is prior to the one previously cited, *Diuturnum illud*.
[26] Suspension *a divinis* implies that the priest is separated from his priestly
ministry, without being able to administer the sacraments in an ordinary way.
[27] The "League," as it was simply called, was the lay movement that brought together the best Catholic leaders of Mexico before and during the religious conflict.
[28] Aquiles Moctezuma (pseudonym of Eduardo Iglesias, S.J. and Rafael Martínez
del Campo, S.J.), *El conflicto religioso de 1926, sus orígenes, su desarrollo, su solución*
(no publisher, 1929).

However, as González Morfín points out,[29] the doctrine of the "right to uprising," although it had reached the Cristero leaders in a Thomistic key, had been interpreted mainly by two modern theologians: Theodor Meyer and Maurice de la Taille. The latter was, in our opinion, the one who exerted the greatest influence on the Mexican movement. In 1924, shortly before the uprising, the fourth edition of the *Dictionnaire apologétique de la foi catholique* was published in Paris. One can still read a lengthy article there regarding the term "insurrection" presenting the *status quaestionis* and contemporary thought in response to the possible afflictions by an unjust government.[30] With academic distinctions, the different types of resistance to authority are made clear:

a) *Passive resistance*, which consists of not obeying the prescriptions of a law.

b) *Active legal resistance*, which consists of demanding the revision of a law through legal means.

c) *Active armed resistance*, which consists of forcibly opposing the execution of a law.

d) *Rebellion*, which consists of going on the offensive against the authority from which the law emanates.

While the latter attitude is, it is said, in all cases *forbidden, the first is always obligatory* when it is a question of a law which prescribes actions contrary to conscience. The second, likewise, is permitted, and, in the case of the third, the question arises as to whether and in what cases it is lawful.

Yet outside of de la Taille's respectable position, there were other theologians who, looking beyond their desks, gave concrete answers to the questions that were being asked. Thus, for example, on November 4, 1926, Father Mariano Cuevas, an eminent Mexican historian then living in Rome, having consulted a notable group of moral theologians from the Gregorian University (Fathers Mostaza, Benito Oggetti, Maurice de la Taille), received the following reply: "Mexicans, civil and ecclesiastical, have the full right to exercise armed resistance in the present circumstances, if they have firm hopes of success and of not producing greater evils."[31]

Father Arthur Vermeersch, one of the most renowned Catholic moralists of the twentieth century, on various occasions spoke on behalf of the lawfulness of the armed defense undertaken by the

---

[29] González Morfin, *La guerra cristera*, 169ff.
[30] See Maurice de la Taille, "Insurrection," in *Dictionnaire Apologétique de la Foi Catholique* (Beauchesne, 1922-19244), vol. 2, coll. 1056-66.
[31] Cited by Acevedo, *David VI*, 171, emphasis ours.

Mexicans, in the first months of 1927, even going so far as to defend the Cristero movement from those who, scandalized, disapproved of it:

> Those who, believing they are defending Christian doctrine, disapprove of the armed movements of Mexican Catholics, are very wrong. For the defense of Christian morality, it is not necessary to resort to the deceptions of certain false pacifist doctrines. Mexican Catholics are using a right and fulfilling a duty.[32]

*Nota bene*: fulfilling a duty.

As we can see, several Catholic theologians gave their opinion and it reached Mexico through the normal channels of the Church. Thus, the authority of Vermeersch, cited in a letter addressed by the Episcopal Commission in Rome to the bishop of San Luis Potosí:

> As to the understanding which armed defense has caused here, we must cite the following facts: The well-known Fr. Vermeersch, S.J., professor of Morals and Sociology at the Gregorian University, insists on rejecting the arguments of those who declare the armed defense of Catholic rights illegal. These statements have caused a great sensation and have been confirmed by the declarations and comments of other and very serious theologians: Fr. Noval, a Dominican, Fr. Marotto, and other canonists and jurists. These professors and other high-ranking figures, in particular, show great interest in the success of the defenders. *The Holy See, for its part, keeps the most circumspect silence.*[33]

The Episcopate was supportive and Rome was hopeful.

It will be said that these documents are no more than the opinions of individual theologians. That may be the case. Yet this body of opinion was what allowed the uprising to be advanced in the face of official silence or, worse, the obscurity of the Catholic hierarchy's messages. What reached the future combatants through their lay leaders were these opinions, disseminated through Catholic newspapers and pamphlets published by the League, the Catholic Association of Mexican Youth (ACJM), or the Saint Joan of Arc Women's Brigades, among others.[34]

---

[32] Acevedo, 174, emphasis ours.

[33] Letter from the Commission of Bishops in Rome to Dn. Miguel de la Mora, bishop of San Luis Potosí, 11-III-1927, in Acevedo, 258, emphasis ours.

[34] Catholic groups such as the National League for Religious Defense, the Catholic Association of Mexican Youth, etc. would be the main protagonists of religious defense.

## THE MEXICAN EPISCOPATE

Mexican scholar Juan González Morfín declares that the only "official" document issued by a bishop wherein the lawfulness of recourse to arms is expressly stated was that of Mgr. José M. González y Valencia. There, as already quoted, it was said:

> We never encouraged this armed movement. But once *peaceful means were exhausted*, this movement came to be. To Our Catholic children bearing arms for the defense of their social and religious rights, after having thought it over at length before God and having consulted the wisest theologians of the city of Rome, We must say to them: be at ease in your consciences and receive Our blessing.[35]

As mentioned, the Mexican bishops, although not entirely united, had essentially taken a stance regarding the illegality of the so-called "Calles Law," by which the state interfered in the Church's inner workings: "In the present circumstances, the intervention of Catholics to bring about the freedom of the Church and its flourishing, as well as the prosperity of the nation, is not, beloved children, mere advice that we give you, but a very serious obligation that we remind you of."[36] But then...what of the lawfulness or illegality of armed war? The episcopate, while stating the above, also said, on the other hand:

> There are cases in which Catholic theologians authorize not rebellion, but armed defense against the unjust aggression of a tyrannical power, after peaceful means have been exhausted without result. The episcopate has not given any document in which it declares that this case obtains in Mexico.... If any Catholic, lay, or ecclesiastical, following the doctrine cited, believes that the case has arisen as to the lawfulness of this defense, the episcopate does not agree with this practical resolution.[37]

Among the Mexican bishops,[38] the one who stood out the most for his clarity was Mgr. José de Jesús Manríquez y Zárate, bishop of

---

[35] José María González y Valencia, *Carta pastoral*, 11-II-1927, in Barquín y Ruiz, *José María González y Valencia*, 43–44.

[36] *Pastoral Letter*, April 21, 1926, in *Cartas del episcopado Mexicano*, Biblioteca del Colegio Mexicano de Roma, quoted in González Morfín, *La guerra cristera*, 174.

[37] *Declaración del Comité Episcopal el 1 de noviembre de 1926*, cited by Barquín y Ruiz, *José María González y Valencia*, 46–47.

[38] González Morfín (*La guerra cristera*, 177) says that there were eleven prelates who were openly in favor of the armed struggle supported by the doctrine of the natural right to legitimate defense.

Huejutla. When answering an accusation of the government in which
the clergy was accused of supporting the armed uprising, he declared
from his forced exile:

> The Mexican Catholics who are on the battlefield...do
> nothing but use the inalienable right that assists them to
> prevent at all costs the ruin of the Mexican Church and the
> destruction of society.... Regarding individuals, there may
> be some cases in which passive resistance — because it is more
> perfect — is preferable. Such is the case of priests.... Such is
> also the case with innocent citizens who, for the most just
> reasons, abstain from armed struggle, and who, nevertheless,
> are sacrificed out of hatred for their faith.... But martyrdom
> is not the ordinary law; martyrs are few and it would be...
> tempting God to expect an entire people to attain the crown
> of martyrdom. Therefore, by ordinary law, the struggle must
> be actively engaged, and the aggression must be repelled in
> the form in which it occurs.... But if (a government) attacks
> the essential freedoms of citizens, if it betrays the fatherland,
> if it kills...and systematically attacks the life and honor of
> families and individuals, then armed defense is a social duty
> that is imposed on all members of the community.[39]

Here is a bishop who did not mince words!

As González Morfín rightly notes,[40] in the statement by Manríquez
y Zárate there is a conclusion that has not been studied in depth by
moral theology and that, apparently, is at odds with the common
doctrine that existed until then about armed resistance — namely,
about the "possibility of success" that the uprising should have in
order to realize its character of legality:

> This obligation [to defend by arms the essential rights tram-
> pled on by tyranny] subsists not only when the defeat of the
> tyrant is humanly possible, but also under the hypothesis
> that it is impossible, in view of the ordinary laws of war.
> The reason is because the loss of faith and of national inde-
> pendence, and the very ruin of society, are evils greater than
> the death of a large number of citizens.[41]

This is a subject that we leave to the moral theologians.

---

[39] José de Jesús Manríquez y Zárate, "Al margen de unas declaraciones," con-
testación al Subsecretario de Gobernación, 25-II-1929, in Acevedo, *David VI*,
215–17, emphasis ours.
[40] González Morfin, *La guerra cristera*, 178.
[41] Ibid., italics in the original.

## THE VATICAN'S POSITION

As we know, Rome's diplomacy is a thousand years old and more. Within the conflict we are discussing, the Holy See had to approach both sides with great care (a few years earlier it had to strike a balance in World War I) and, when pronouncing on the Mexican conflict, it did so weighing each word.

There is, however, in Rome the newspaper titled *L'Osservatore Romano*, which is responsible for disseminating—not always with complete fidelity—the positions of the Roman ecclesiastical hierarchy. Certain statements with a special resonance were published in this newspaper. To cite a well-known case, recall the news that appeared on August 11, 1926, which proved to be a godsend for the Cristero leaders in discerning the closeness of the Holy See:

> Let it not be said that Catholics could unite and organize to try to defend themselves by legal means, since any association of the faithful that seeks such an end has been strictly vetoed by the Calles Law with the most serious penalties (Arts. 10–16). So there is nothing left for the masses who do not want to live under tyranny and are no longer restrained by the peaceful preaching of the clergy other than violent rebellion.[42]

"Nothing left but violent rebellion." In this way, the idea that Rome supported in a "non-committal" way, through its semi-official newspaper, the armed effort and its justification was spreading more and more. The Vatican, in order to avoid international criticism, took almost two years to qualify this statement of the editorial with an explanatory note that read as follows:

> There are those who believe and want others to believe that rumors are circulating in Mexico and elsewhere that the Supreme Pontiff himself has given a special blessing to the armed insurrection and has even granted special indulgences to the combatants, thereby encouraging (according to their own statements) the collection of money for the combatants. It is well documented that the Holy Father has always stood by his Mexican children who are persecuted and suffering for the faith of their parents, but it is also documented that there is no truth in the aforementioned rumor.[43]

The aim was to refute claims that the papal blessing of the armed insurrection had been "documented," as well as claims that 'collections'

---

[42] *L'Osservatore Romano*, 11-VIII-1926, p. 1, emphasis ours.
[43] *L'Osservatore Romano*, 8/9-VI-1928, p. 1.

had been allowed in its favor or that "indulgences had been granted to the combatants," in the style of the ancient Crusades.

Still, not everything is so simple. It was not only *L'Osservatore Romano* that laid the foundations for an interpretation favorable to the uprising, but Pope Pius XI himself. It was a difficult time. Not only had churches been closed for worship in Mexico, but the first revolts were also taking place. In this context, the pope received a group of young Mexicans on December 30, 1926, during the celebrations for the bicentenary of the canonization of St. Aloysius Gonzaga, telling them:

> In the first place, We mention and greet you first who from the distant land of Mexico have come to Us, *children of martyrs* and strong as the martyrs themselves! Honor to you and to your land, to your bishops and your pastors, to your priests, *to all your people who bear such a glorious struggle for the honor of God*, for the Kingdom of Christ, for the honor of Holy Mother Church, for the dignity and salvation of souls, causing admiration to the whole world.[44]

After the speech, the pope called for this message to be conveyed to his children in Mexico, along with his greetings and his blessing.

Let us emphasize these words: *a glorious struggle* borne by Mexicans *for the honor of God*. As if that were not enough, on January 3, 1927, the pope received in private audience the seventeen young people who had attended the event, accompanied by Archbishop José M. González y Valencia and by some Mexican priests residing in Rome, with the following words:

> You, returning to Mexico, will tell everyone the words you have heard from our lips; you will tell them that we have greeted in you all Mexicans..., but above all and mainly, the beloved and generous Mexican youth. You will tell them that We know all that they do, we know that they fight—and how well they fight—that great war which may be called the battle for Christ.[45]

They seem to be clear words, both in their context and in their meaning.[46] However, there are those who do not believe that this

---

[44] *L'Osservatore Romano*, 4-I-1927, p. 3, emphasis ours.

[45] The full text can be read at J. Antonio López Ortega, *Las naciones extranjeras y la persecución religiosa* (no publisher, 1944), 62–64, and in Acevedo, *David VII*, 204.

[46] Furthermore, we also recall that four days after the "agreements" that ended the suspension of religious services were signed, the apostolic delegate in Mexico published a pastoral letter, written in a conciliatory tone and ambiguous terms,

papal position indicates "support" for the Cristero movement, merely giving the words a "metaphorical meaning."[47]

## WERE THE CONDITIONS MET FOR ARMED UPRISING?

It is easy, with hindsight, to see how things were. However, it is worth analyzing whether or not the circumstances for the uprising were understood to be legitimate at the time, so that it could take place in a way acceptable to the Catholic conscience. After all, as we have seen, the Cristeros themselves asked the same question. Recalling the conditions discussed, we could summarize them as follows: 1) that there are true, serious, and prolonged violations of fundamental rights; 2) all avenues of recourse have been exhausted; 3) resistance can be offered without provoking worse disorders; 4) there is a well-founded hope of success; and 5) it is impossible reasonably to foresee better solutions. Let's consider these one by one.

### 1) True, serious, and prolonged violations of fundamental rights

Since the reforms of Carranza, at the beginning of 1915, Catholics had been suffering all kinds of humiliations. From the time when Calles took office, aggression had become continuous, with the clear intention of preventing the hierarchy from fulfilling its functions without the consent and orders of the State.

To give just one example, the Cristero Aurelio Acevedo listed (not an exhaustive list) the number of priests murdered during the Calles period, comparing it with the periods that preceded and succeeded him (between 1914 and 1938). From 1914 to 1924, sixteen priests had been murdered. In the Calles period, between 1924 and 1928, fifty-six. Between 1929 and 1934, still under the aegis of Calles, nineteen, and with Cárdenas, between 1936 and 1938, another four.[48] In addition,

---

which had been previously read and approved by Portes Gil. The president, delighted with the easy success achieved, wrote in pencil in the margin of the document: "It would be good to say something condemning the use of arms," to which the prelate replied: "That he could not do it because the Pope himself had said that those who had taken up arms were within their rights." Leopoldo Ruiz y Flores, *Lo que sé del conflicto religioso*, Revista *Trento*, published in Morelia, Michoacán, corresponding to the months of April to July 1959; quoted by Rius Facius, *México Cristero*, 2:507.

[47] "This interpretation is disqualified from the very moment when the group of young people was not before the Holy Father either as combatants or on his behalf.... Finally, the full speech is not found in any official publication." Such is the position of González Morfín in his doctoral thesis (*La guerra cristera*, 182). It is worth saying that his interpretation does not convince us.

[48] See Acevedo, *David VI*, 205–9.

we must add the massacres of Catholics at church entrances, when public worship was still allowed; the proscription of all kinds of religious images and objects; the prohibition of wearing black as a sign of mourning; the beatings and harassment of Catholic activists, regardless of age or sex; the sudden deportation of hundreds of Catholics to the Islas Marías prison; the impossibility of any type of effective legal defense due to the sole fact of being Catholic. It was persecution on account of religion, thus violating a fundamental human right.

### 2) *All other avenues or recourses exhausted*

The appeals that could be filed with the Chamber of Deputies were not only arbitrarily dismissed, but some of them were not even considered. Legally speaking, there was no other recourse to be had. The attempt at an economic boycott also took place. The immediate results, in terms of negative effects for the government, were much greater than expected. The response of Catholics to the boycott in large urban areas was exemplary. Simultaneously, two million signatures were collected calling for the law to be suspended, but without any satisfactory response from the government.

In a meeting with Calles, the bishops Díaz and Ruiz proposed a diplomatic solution that would have allowed simultaneously the cessation of the boycott, the resumption of worship, and the easing of the atmosphere of discord caused by the first violent clashes: he only had to declare to the press that the registration of priests was nothing but an administrative measure, and that the State did not intend to direct the internal affairs of the Church by this means. But even that had not been amenable to President Calles. And all these vagaries were known to the multitudes who, on the other hand, experienced in their own flesh, day after day, the effects of persecution.

More than a struggle between the "religion" of disbelief and true faith, at the root of the conflict was the conviction held by the small group in power that they had to annihilate the Catholic Church in order to be master of people's consciences. The enemy to be defeated was the bishops, the priests, the teachers in Catholic schools, because they taught that when obedience to God and obedience to men are opposed, one must always obey God rather than men. In no way could this be tolerated by those who thought that a law can be issued without regard to human nature and against the most fundamental human rights, and that, because it is a law, it must be obeyed. They could not accept that the Catholic Church had spoken about social justice and had encouraged the formation of Catholic unions even before the triumph of the Revolution. They could not bear that Catholic parents educated their children in truths alien to the "positive, scientific truth" that, with a fifty year lag behind the Western world, was now trying to assert itself in Mexico as official truth. They could not tolerate that the people, 99% Catholic according to the 1910 census, came punctually to worship, day after day, a God who had been banned by the official truth. Finally, they could not bear the existence of a hierarchy claiming a divine origin and that, without having received any delegation from the revolutionary group, enjoyed greater authority throughout every stratum of the population. This, especially this, they found unendurable.[49]

Legal means had been exhausted at the very moment Calles decided to implement as many laws as necessary to subject the hierarchy of the Church to the revolutionary regulations.

*3) Not causative of worse disorder*

This requirement, as is obvious, regards the prudential sphere, that is, to the sphere of the contingent. Since the end of 1910, Mexico had been suffering an endless series of internecine wars between the different revolutionary groups, with the exception of one relative period of peace (between 1920 and 1923). The civilian population was already at the mercy of all kinds of arbitrariness from the government, so it was difficult to imagine that an even worse state of affairs would be caused than the one they were suffering. Certainly, the calamities that the war entailed, such as massacres, devastation, murders, and all kinds of reprisals, were not sought by the leaders of the Cristeros or, much less by those who rose up in arms instinctively in defense of their religion and their families.

However, as the Cristeros clearly saw, the safeguarding of the faith and the freedom to practice it and transmit it to their children was such a precious good that *no form of calamities produced were comparable to its loss*. They acted accordingly. So, while the disasters caused by the war were great, it was nevertheless unacceptable to take a passive stance when what was at stake was something so precious. They were acting, then, in good conscience.

---

[49] González Morfin, *La guerra cristera*, 199–200.

*4) A well-founded hope of success*

If an armed uprising were manifestly going to fail, it would be daring to proceed, for if it did not succeed, the situation of the oppressed would undoubtedly be worse. What can be said about the Cristeros uprising relative to this principle?

The first thing to remember, and which is often overlooked, is that throughout the war the Cristeros maintained a strong belief that they would triumph, thanks to the many victories they achieved even under disadvantageous conditions and with minimal casualties. There was an almost supernatural certainty of victory, as González Morfín states.[50]

This *morale of victory* was growing because of objective facts. The movement started by a few dozen men in a short time had twenty thousand soldiers scattered throughout a large part of the national territory and, in the month before the "Settlements" between the Church and the State, the Cristero army was composed of fifty thousand men, not counting a large number of tactical collaborators who helped them indirectly without fighting. Although the military geography had not changed substantially since the beginning of 1928, when the Cristeros clearly defined their area of influence, the governance exercised over the so-called "liberated zone" continued to increase — proof of which is that their systems for establishing and collecting taxes were increasingly effective.

On the other hand, the hope that Catholics in other countries (especially those in the United States) would decisively finance the armed movement, or that the Calles government would lose American support, was never extinguished.

In addition to this, there was enormous confidence in the military prowess of General Gorostieta, who, shortly before his death, had desisted from the attack on Guadalajara for fear that his soldiers would fall into "the delights of Capua." This decision, along with the disappearance of the caudillo, prevented the capture of the capital of Jalisco and the resolution of the problem of military supply.

---

[50] González Morfín, 202. When the Cristero general Degollado Guízar, after a resounding triumph, was congratulated by Gorostieta for his military ingenuity, he declined the praise, saying: "You are wrong in that, general: I have always believed that the triumphs of our arms in the Division under my charge are due to Christ. One cannot explain this in any other way: that without prepared leaders, inferior to those of the enemy, we always come out victorious, even when we have had to run." Degollado Guízar, *Memorias*, 213.

## 5) Impossibility of reasonably foreseeing a better solution

This condition implicitly means that the goal of armed struggle would not necessarily have to be the fall of a certain government, much less the rise of another, but only achieving a different state of affairs, wherein the rights for which the armed struggle was undertaken are guaranteed.

This possibility was always real among the Cristeros, it seems. That is why, in the perspective of the Cristero chiefs (Gorostieta and Degollado Guizar), an agreed solution was envisioned in which the government would at least grant recognition of the essential freedoms for which they were fighting. Moreover, in a letter from General Gorostieta, in which he disagreed with the League's leaders who refused to let him be the one who, when the time came, agreed to the armistice,[51] it is evident that in everyone's mind the moment of reaching an agreement with the government appeared closer and closer.

In addition, during all the time in which they bore arms, in the minds of the Cristeros there was no other objective than safeguarding their most elementary rights, then being infringed. For this very reason, they saw the motivation for fighting would come to an end the moment when the government, through the President of the Republic, admitted:

> I. That the article of the law that determines the registration of priests does not mean that the Government can register those who have not been appointed by the hierarchical superior of the respective religious creed, or in accordance with the rules of the faith itself.
>
> II. With regard to religious education, the Constitution and the laws in force strictly prohibit its teaching in primary and higher schools, whether official or private. However this does not prevent the ministers of any religion from imparting their doctrines to the elderly or their children who come for this purpose in the precincts of the Church.
>
> III. That both the Constitution and the laws of the country guarantee every inhabitant of the Republic the right of petition and, by virtue of this, the members of any church may apply to the corresponding authorities for the reform, repeal, or issuance of any law.[52]

---

[51] Acevedo, *David VII*, 231.
[52] González Morfin, *La guerra cristera*, 207.

In fact, with these declarations by President Portes Gil, the Church being granted the minimum spaces of freedom to exercise its ministry, the Cristeros decided (for the most part) to lay down their arms.

In conclusion, an opinion published by a Catholic magazine during the first year of the armed struggle can be used. In it, the motives and morality for the combatants of the need to fight the "good fight" of which St. Paul spoke are summarized:[53]

> The fighting was tough and the victory uncertain, but Mexicans have done their duty. And free men from all latitudes admire them and applaud and bless them. They are not bandits, as the government calls them, nor even rebels, as the salaried press calls them. Their real name is liberators.
>
> It is true that someone has said that injustice must not turn Catholics into unjust persons, nor dispossession into plunderers, nor banditry into bandits, nor murder into murderers, nor tyranny into anarchists. But to contend this is to ignore Catholics' right of legitimate defense.
>
> In extreme cases, when under the circumstances passive resistance is ineffective or practically impossible, it is licit to oppose the authority of the tyrant with active armed resistance....
>
> We readily concede that these groups of liberators are inferior in number and means to the Callista army. But this very thing endorses their courage and heroism in throwing themselves into an unequal struggle. We also recognize that ultimate victory, under these circumstances, will not be the work of a day. But it is a fact that the insurrection, far from being quelled, has been progressing upward, and that the throne of Callism, propped up with the gallows, has begun to totter.
>
> Anyone who has followed the Mexican question closely will have seen that the Catholics did not take up arms (only) after uselessly trying the means of peaceful resistance, or when this was practically impossible. Let us remember the boycott, which gave wonderful results, until the reds of Calles perpetrated unspeakable savagery towards its supporters. Let us remember the Memorandum presented to Congress, backed by millions of signatures of Catholics, who asked for the reform or repeal of the Law.[54]

---

[53] "I fought the good fight, I have finished the race, I have kept the faith" (2 Tim 4:7-8).
[54] Cristóbal Peón, "La situación religiosa en México y su legalidad," *Razón y Fe* 27 (1927/III): 295, 298.

\* \* \*

We have attempted to present the doctrine and the facts about the Mexican armed uprising. The episodes that concern us still have several edges to polish and investigate. Only now, entering the twenty-first century and already a hundred years after the events, we are beginning to access the sources and archives that, little by little, are more and more available to the scholar.

From the documents and testimonies, we see how the Mexican people not only applied the doctrine of the right to rise up against oppression, but even brought about, without realizing it, the Church's proclamation of a right already found in Sophocles' *Antigone* (to obey divinity before men) and already acknowledged by St. Peter and the other apostles before the Sanhedrin: "We must obey God before men."[55]

---

[55] Acts 5:29.

*Cristero banners*

# PART III
# War

\* \* \*

## PROTAGONISTS
## AND CONSEQUENCES

# 7

# The War Years

WITHOUT A DOUBT,[1] WHAT ULTIMATELY SPARKED the people's uprising was the religious discrimination that the government attempted to enforce through laws, and while it is true that in history there is never a *single* cause of events, in the case of Mexico we believe that the final trigger was the implementation of the Constitution of Querétaro.

From the moment the Episcopate announced the suspension of public worship in order to escape state interference, people began to realize what would happen: God would no longer be on the altars, therefore, "people began to go [to confession] in order to ease their consciences... In all the faces you could see paleness, in all the eyes you could see sadness," they said.[2]

At the same time, prominent bishops had initially declared themselves against the possible uprising, saying that the Church was "absolutely opposed to the use of armed force,"[3] at least as a collegial body. The government, however, insisting on "enforcing the Constitution," initiated the search and confiscation of Church property, as well as the expulsion of foreign priests and the arrest of Catholic leaders. The atmosphere was quite heated.

In the case of Calles' political (and also military) leaders, contempt for the faithful would come back to haunt them. It was almost assumed that there would be some uprisings, but they never thought that the popular revolt could be organized to fight for more than three years, as happened. Thus, when the actual application of the "Calles Law" began, little by little, various insurrections began to take place that obstructed the work of government agents.

At the beginning of 1926, especially during Holy Week, the

---

[1] It is not our objective to detail the minutiae of the war, a subject that far exceeds the proposed goal of these pages. Here we will simply cover the vicissitudes of the Cristero war in a few broad brushstrokes, following Meyer who, in our opinion, has best studied the period and provided the most extensive documentation (see, chiefly, Meyer, *La Cristiada*, vol. 1).

[2] Manuscript of Tlaltenango, anonymous, cited by Meyer, *La Cristiada*, 2:95.

[3] Pascual Díaz, *New York Times*, August 5 and 30, 1926, cited by Meyer, *La Cristiada*, 1:98.

common people called for the cessation of state violence by means of pilgrimages, processions, and prayers. The Mexican people, deeply Christian, tried to endure the hardship, but they said "they could not take it anymore," this violation of their most sacred convictions. The government tried to contain the masses but little by little, clashes with the government multiplied and "from them the war arose":

> Clashes with the government multiplied and war arose. Side by side with provocations pure and simple, all the actions by the authorities were felt as aggressions: the closure of churches, clumsily ordered by the government, even the execution of the regulations, the implementation itself, the arrest of the priest or the lay leaders, they were so many *direct causes* of the defensive uprisings of 1926.[4]

Imprisoned priests and lay people were the "direct causes." Let's keep this expression in mind.

### THE INSURRECTIONS OF 1926

The revolts began to take place almost simultaneously: on July 31 in Oaxaca there was a riot on the occasion of the surrender of the convent church of the Seven Princes of the Angels. Riots and brawls were more and more frequent and numbered in the hundreds.

We have seen, as attested by Rius Facius and Heriberto Navarrete, a representative case of the popular reaction in chapter 4, when, on August 3, in the sanctuary of the Virgin of Guadalupe (in Guadalajara), the people were attentive to guard the most precious church in the city. Children warned of the danger that was approaching and used a "password" to identify the cars that were approaching. To the question of "Who lives?," one had to answer "Long live Christ the King!" Before the defense, it happened that a vehicle passed and, when it did not answer with the watchword, one of the children threw a stone that resulted in a gunshot from inside the car. It happened that the one who was traveling there was General Muñoz, commander of the garrison. The tumult was such that the army had to intervene. After several skirmishes, the army ended up opening fire on the unarmed crowd. Even the women rushed into hand-to-hand combat against the soldiers. The incident ended in the early hours of the next day with the surrender of the civilians and almost four hundred arrested.

The month of August was marked by several disturbances: Puebla, Oaxaca, Michoacán, were some of the places where Catholics

---

[4] Meyer, *La Cristiada*, 1:103–4, emphasis ours.

spontaneously rose up against the confiscations and searches by the government. But the most important of the uprisings occurred in Zacatecas: on August 14 at night, the army arrested the mild-mannered parish priest of Chalchihuites, Luis Bátiz. The next day, Pedro Quintanar, an influential figure throughout the region and a renowned soldier, was overwhelmed by the people who begged him to do something for the freedom of their parish priest. With some men he attempted an ambush at the exit of the town but failed and had to go into hiding.

The government, aware of Quintanar's authority, mobilized the agrarian leaders and confiscated the weapons and horses of private individuals in the area in order to prevent any disturbances. Quintanar, however, accepted leadership of the movement and on August 29, with a hundred men, he managed to storm the town. He was welcomed with cries of "Long live Christ the King!"

In September, in the region of Ciudad Hidalgo, Simón Cortés, head of the "social defense," went to the countryside with his "rebel" troops. In Yuriria (Guanajuato) and Maravatío (Michoacán) the first insurgents made their appearance, setting fire to the Salvatierra station. At the end of September the government had to send reinforcements to defeat countless uprisings that were happening throughout the country.

Weeks passed and the turmoil seemed to be having an effect, so that already in "October, the army was able to realize that things were not going to be as easy as General Amaro and President Calles believed."[5] The government, moreover, tried to minimize the uprisings by saying that "no military problem affects the Republic today.... There are mobs...formed in part by fanatics who have thrown themselves into rebellious escapades."[6] Grassroots movements multiplied, but it is known that without leadership there is no success in war. This is where the key role of the Catholic lay movements came in, which supported the armed defense once it had started.

Everything had been tried: signatures, boycott, denunciations, appeals for protection, but the peaceful initiative seemed vain. The Catholic leader himself, Anacleto González Flores, having supported of peace, was now compelled to recommend armed struggle. As we have noted, at the end of December of the same year he read the following text to the Convention of the People's Union, meeting in Guadalajara: "The LNDLR orders its delegations to...immediately organize an armed movement to overthrow the government of the

[5] Meyer, 1:115.
[6] *Excélsior*, November 2, 1926.

Republic and secure by force the people's liberties."[7] The organized revolt would take place on January 1, 1927, in the face of the "irresistible popular pressure" that existed.

As we have already said, quoting Jean Meyer,[8] things were clear to the people: patience, penance, and five-month prayers had been of no use to hardened hearts. Everything possible had been done to avoid taking up arms, but there was no other way, as innumerable manifestos attest. The uprising broke out in full force and in an organized form in January 1927.

The place where the People's Union had the most influence was undoubtedly in the state of Jalisco, particularly the area called "Los Altos," where to this day the "Cristero route" can be traveled[9] (there is practically no small town that does not have its own martyrs). Aguascalientes and Colima were not left out of its influence, nor were the south of Zacatecas and part of Nayarit. The federal army's response was not long in coming and what was said to be simply a "revolt of the pious" became a guerrilla war that would not have ended without the disappointing "Settlements" of 1929, as we will see later.

While the Catholic troops rose up spontaneously to fight, often prompted by their own women, the "federals" had to recruit their men through forced conscription.[10] In many cases, this led to the desertion of the "national" troops to the "insurrectionists."

The war began with a clear imbalance and, militarily speaking, it seemed an impossible war for the Cristeros to win, if the supernatural factor had not been involved, as Meyer himself is forced to acknowledge.[11] In turn, Calles' troops were regularly benefiting from U.S. support.[12] The U.S. was a supporter of war at the beginning (*divide et impera*) and a supporter of peace later.

---

[7] Meyer, *La Cristiada*, 1:120.

[8] Meyer, 1:125.

[9] There are, in fact, several "Cristero routes" that can be explored, especially in the states of Jalisco and Colima. Such routes have not yet been explored from a historical point of view, but little by little the veil is being lifted. A good guide Silviano Hernández, *En la ruta de los mártires cristeros* (APC, 2006), which has served as a guide to us sometimes through these lands.

[10] See Meyer, *La Cristiada*, 1:149. "Underpaid, poorly fed, recruited against his will for a struggle that was not his own, the Federal soldier, who certainly did not fear death, was a potential deserter.... According to an American report, the desertion rate was as follows: in 1926, 9,421 deserters; in 1928, 28,000; in 1929, 21,214" (to give a few examples; see Meyer, 1:152).

[11] Meyer, *La Cristiada*, 3:310ff.

[12] To give an example: "In 1927 the air force received two bombers and six Bristol fighters. In November 1927, the cavalry imported 5,000 horses from the United

Regarding the method to be followed, General Amaro, the brave and "bloodthirsty" general, head of the federal troops, was inspired

> by the system invented by Weyler in Cuba, applied by the English in South Africa and . . . by the Americans in the Philippines. . . . The principle was simple: a deadline of a few days or a few weeks was set for civilian populations to evacuate a certain perimeter and take refuge in a number of planned locations. After the deadline, anyone found in the restricted zone was executed without trial. The troops seized crops and herds, set fire to pastures and forests, and slaughtered with machine guns the herds that could not be transported by train. The "roundup" (*razzia*) was one of the most successful operations practiced by the military commanders.[13]

## GENERAL GOROSTIETA AND THE ADVANCE OF THE CRISTEROS

The war continued and the uprisings throughout Mexico, mainly in its central part, continued to be outbursts of well-intentioned fervor. There were, yes, "natural caudillos" who guided the efforts of insurgence, but the vast majority of them had little experience in the art of war; their rudimentary efforts, in addition to their lack of weapons, made it almost impossible to sustain the defense. A leader was needed.

It was indeed a distinguished military officer, though not necessarily a practicing Catholic, who ended up commanding the Cristero troops on the battlefield: General Enrique Gorostieta. Belonging to a family from Monterrey and descendant of a hero of the War of Independence, he had been a brilliant officer in the Porfirian army. A cadet of the Military College of Chapultepec and a remarkable gunman, after a stay in the United States he quickly reached the rank of general, earning his stripes in the campaign with Huerta against Orozco, and then with Felipe Ángeles against Zapata. He participated in the defense of Veracruz against the Americans, until the advance of Treviño's Carranza column forced him to retreat. This exceptional soldier, remarkable for his physical strength and intellectual quality (it was said that he wrote poetry in French), had been Huerta's favorite. Unable to join the Carranza supporters, Gorostieta, a career soldier, hated the idea of having to salute a man like Obregón, who was then in power.

Already retired and detesting the dominant regime, he commented with sympathy on the Cristeros' resistance. Personally, he was a liberal

---

States, and the Mexican government acknowledged receipt of 5,000 Belgian rifles, Hotchkiss machine guns, and 75mm cannons." Meyer, *La Cristiada*, 1:157.
[13] Meyer, 1:164.

in the tradition of the nineteenth century; some said that he was a Freemason and that he had reached the 33rd degree, but apparently, this was slander. Although he would not have persecuted Christians, he was aloof from religious matters, as military men typically were.[14] Taking advantage of Gorostieta's hatred for Obregón and Calles, the League offered him a contract for three thousand gold pesos a month, in addition to a life insurance of twenty thousand pesos that, upon his death, his family would collect. A short time before, no one would have imagined that this liberal Cristero would not only join the cause but become one of the military and political mainstays of the *Cristiada*.

According to Meyer, the attraction he exercised over the combatants was exactly proportional to that which the Christian peasants exercised over him. With his sharp intelligence, the clever artilleryman understood better than anyone before him the concept of "guerrilla warfare,"[15] of which he became an outstanding theoretician and practitioner. Gorostieta, the liberal, became, in his own way, a Christian in the midst of his Cristeros, whom he admired without snobbery: "Do you think we can lose with this kind of men? No, this cause is holy, and with these defenders it is not possible for it to be lost!" He was amazed at the mettle of men and women who were unafraid of death, and of those who gave their all — as on that occasion when, after having received twenty cents from the hands of a beggar woman in San Julián, he said to his assistant, very moved: "If the cause is lost, it will be because we do not know how to defend it. But no, it cannot be lost."[16]

Under Gorostieta's leadership, the army began to consolidate its command structure, territories, and tactics. After a few months of his leadership it was possible to speak of the "Cristero army" in July 1927. With his vision of the war, he was able to extend rapidly the Cristero zone of control to six states: Jalisco, Nayarit, Aguascalientes, Zacatecas, Querétaro, and Guanajuato (June 1928). In this way, he naturally became the supreme leader of the insurrection. In October and November 1927, the Cristeros became so strong in Jalisco that

---

[14] See Meyer 1:199–206. To get an idea of his temperament, consult the book of Navarrete, *Por Dios y por la Patria*, 162–68. At the time of writing (May 2012), the Gorostieta family has donated to the state of Jalisco about twenty letters from Gorostieta to his family demonstrating his Catholicism, which sweep away his supposed "agnosticism."

[15] "The whole technique of the Liberators lies in their mobility: rapid strikes against infrastructure [bridges, viaducts, tunnels, causeways, culverts, etc.], on military trains, on official supplies, and then an immediate retreat to those tortuous mountains that form the best of fortresses for a guerrilla." Acevedo, *David V*, 380.

[16] Gorostieta's words to Luis Alcorta, cited by Meyer, *La Cristiada*, 1:203.

the federals could not take it back. Some say that, if the Cristeros had had a unified command from the beginning, success could have been achieved very easily. After a year of fighting, the guerrilla troops numbered twenty-five thousand in Sinaloa, Nayarit, Jalisco, Michoacán, Guanajuato, Aguascalientes, Mexico, Zacatecas, Puebla, Oaxaca, Morelos, and Veracruz.

The insurgents had already transitioned from fierce but amorphous hordes into a serious threat: "Our struggle is on a very good path," said Gorostieta, "so good that the Callista no longer sleeps because they are thinking about us, and I am convinced that the loss of their sleep is justified, since they are already flying very low."[17] However, the main problem was not the troops but the lack of weapons and ammunition. It was always the greatest limitation throughout the war. In a large number of battles, the Cristeros had to retreat due to lack of bullets. They made grenades and cannons themselves and the ammunition was transported from one place to another by the Women's Brigades of Saint Joan of Arc. "They even used wooden cannons, bound with iron. When bombs dropped by airplanes failed to detonate, in Colima and Los Altos, bomb-makers filled hundreds, even thousands of cartridges from them; from one bomb they made 270 grenades."[18] The best source of supplies were victories against the enemy throughout the war.

In terms of the methods of warfare, there were different styles, and each region had its own: in Durango, the Cristeros prowled in the mountains with their entire families, in more or less provisional camps and living on migratory agriculture. The rugged terrain allowed these foot soldiers to lay deadly ambushes for the federals, who could not operate for more than a few days in a mountain range where all provisioning was impossible. Their baggage trains, and in particular the supply convoys, were the Cristeros' favorite prey. In Zacatecas and Jalisco, the cavalry reigned, indispensable in these areas of extensive plateaus. In the volcanoes of Colima, combatants and families lived in fortified camps, and war was waged using trenches, barbed wire, and mines. In the mountains of the Coalcomán district, the Cristeros never offered a pitched battle against the large federal columns, but harassed them night and day, the groups of each region being relieved as the enemy progressed.[19]

---

[17] Letter from Gorostieta to Acevedo, Meyer, 1:248.
[18] González Morfín, *La guerra cristera*, 136–37.
[19] See Meyer, *La Cristiada*, 3:246.

The struggle was not easy and, as Meyer recalled, the Mexican federal army had never before possessed such heavy weaponry or such firm support, in financial, military, and political aid, as the United States lavished on it at that time for the fight. On the other hand, never had an insurrectionary movement had, with so few means, so many supporters and so much resilience in combat.[20]

Although the fight was unequal, the guerrilla warfare tactics employed by the Cristero troops weakened the army more and more, and by mid-1928, the fact that the "rebels" had not been defeated was a real embarrassment, almost a quasi-victory. In addition, the loyalty of the Cristero fighters made the struggle a tough moral bastion to overcome. In January and February 1929, for example, more than two hundred important battles were fought in Los Altos de Jalisco. There, thousands of Cristeros were imprisoned. The government's offers of amnesty yielded no more result than the surrender of some twenty Cristeros in two months![21]

---

[20] See Meyer, 3:259.

[21] Such was the fear that arose among the federal troops that circulars such as those cited below were often published to soften the combatants little by little, without much success. In a letter addressed to the Cristeros by the municipal president of La Barca, Jalisco, it read: "Two years have passed, during which a good number of neighbors and children of our beloved native state, carried away by concerns, have been developing a hostile action towards the constituted authorities that, although they have caused serious damage to the general interests, to the extent of causing in many cases reductions in regional production and weakening of the manufacturing sector, it is also true that its effects have been felt in the business and personal interests of the same people who have caused this state of affairs. As this abnormal situation must not be allowed to continue, the authorities have decided to use all means of persuasion to bring about the rapprochement of the hitherto disaffected elements, to whom it offers full amnesty, providing that all those who, understanding the serious damage they bring to their people by their hostile attitude, wish to exchange their weapons for farming or workshop implements, thus returning to a quiet and honest life, at the same time to cooperate in the progress and growth of our country. They must lay down their arms and present themselves to the authorities, who, in addition to giving them assurances of their persons and interests, will provide them with the necessary means to move to where it is best for them and return to their homes with every guarantee. With such dispositions our government intends to bring back to the bosom of society all the sons and daughters of the country, so that they may cooperate in its growth and progress, forgetting useless grievances that only lead to misery in homes and the stagnation of the various national enterprises. Now in the mind of the authorities there is the desire that a complete and definitive tranquility be established in the country, for which it magnanimously offers this opportunity as a demonstration of its good purposes and best intentions so that in the shadow of its protection all may enjoy the benefits of an honest, upright administration eager to see all the

However, let's go back a little. By the end of 1928, General Gorostieta was already the undisputed leader of the movement, although the League did not always look favorably on him.[22] The war was in the balance and was beginning to tilt in favor of the counterrevolutionaries. From mid-August 1928, as noted by U.S. military observers, "the initiative passed into the hands of the Cristeros."[23] At the same time, in November of that year, federal officials acknowledged that the situation was "very difficult for their troops, who are continuously on the defensive and often defeated."[24] On the other hand, Dwight Morrow, ambassador of the United States and architect of the future "settlements," believed that a peace process without the solution of the religious question was unlikely at that point.[25]

There was an additional factor that influenced the war's end: the rebellion of Generals Manzo and Escobar against the government of Calles-Portes Gil, at the beginning of March 1929. The attempted rebellion — which did not amount to much — was condemned by the United States and, therefore, had no chance of success. From then on, the insurgents tried to win over the Catholics by abolishing the Calles Law in their areas (Sonora, Chihuahua, Coahuila, Durango, and Veracruz) and sought to make a pact with Gorostieta. Gorostieta

---

children of our beloved Mexico united fraternally and on the path of progress. Convinced that it is not in vain that this invitation will be favourably received by the individuals now distant from the public administration and that they will know how to interpret these acts of nobility and disinterestedness that in no way could be taken as acts of weakness, since militarily the towns of the state are controlled, and mainly with the preferential aim of AVOIDING USELESS SHEDDING OF FRATERNAL BLOOD, since our government intends to preserve it intact for the growth of our race, which the future seems to indicate that it has an important role to fill." Archivo del Gobierno de Jalisco, January 4, 1929, quoted in Meyer, *La Cristiada*, 1:271–72.

[22] Perhaps because of his supposed coldness in matters of the Faith. We have already considered Gorostieta's alleged "agnosticism." Without pausing too long, we repeat that he was no agnostic — especially after his life among the Cristeros: "Forward and with the Cross. We must finish as men what we have undertaken as men. We must not be discouraged by anything and by anyone. You can rest assured that I will see this through to the end with you, and that I will lead you only to places that are worthy. *God has been giving me light* to overcome all kinds of difficulties and now that success is on the horizon. *He will not abandon me. At least that is what I ask daily in my prayers."* Luis Luna's private archives, quoted in Meyer, *La Cristiada*, 1:281, emphasis ours.

[23] *Departament of State Records*, 812.00/Jalisco 23, August 30, 1928, quoted by Meyer, *La Cristiada*, 1:282.

[24] Meyer, 1:282.

[25] See *Departament of State Records*, 812.00/Jalisco 40, January 17, 1929, quote by Meyer, *La Cristiada*, 1:285.

analyzed the situation: Manzo and Escobar were nothing more than unscrupulous generals and corrupt politicians, whose improbable victory would not change the situation in the Mexican Republic at all. A tactical alliance did not risk anything, however, and might finally make it possible to obtain the ammunition so desired for three years. Escobar's people, on the other hand, wanted to use the Cristeros to their own benefit in order to mobilize the masses. In the end, the alliance did not prosper.

On the part of the government, the imminent revolt provoked a rapid response from Calles (then former president), who had left the command in the hands of Portes Gil. Gil, after having himself appointed Secretary of War and abandoning the entire center-west to the Cristeros, "gathered thirty-five thousand men that he threw on the northwest to crush, in the battle of Jiménez, Manzo's armies, betrayed as they were by the high command; his trains were bombed by the American air force."[26] Clearly, Escobar's rebellion could not succeed without the permission of the northern "friend."

This fortuitous situation gave the Cristero army the opportunity for a strong offensive that took place in March and April 1929. From March 3 to May 15, the Cristeros crushed the auxiliary troops abandoned by the federals and took over all of western Mexico, from Durango to Coalcomán, with the exception of the largest cities. The arrival of the troops of General Cedillo, head of the First Division of the Center, was not enough to restore the situation, and "General Amaro despaired for the first time, making President Portes Gil say that the entire west was in arms and that *it was vital to make a compromise with the Church.*"[27]

The United States began to doubt and was unhappy with the Cristero positions in the north, especially when American mines were threatened, and the train tracks were blown up in search of wagons with ammunition. Thus, through constant efforts, the federal forces "were engulfed by a large-scale, organized, coordinated, and remarkably executed offensive, which continued victoriously, until the peace of June 1929."[28] Things were "golden," as they say in Mexico.[29]

---

[26]  Meyer, 1:288, emphasis ours.
[27]  Meyer, 1:290, emphasis ours.
[28]  Meyer, 1:292.
[29]  "Things are looking up, as they say, and now we can say with complete frankness, and very strongly, that the arms of the Cristeros will triumph, and very soon," Cristero Acevedo told Santiago Martínez, March 5, 1929 (Meyer, 1:293).

The "liberators" were received with open arms in the towns when they arrived, such as in Huejúcar, where ten thousand people gave them an ecstatic welcome. The same happened in Colotlán, Santa María, Tepetongo, Valparaíso, and Chalchihuites. Reinforcements were obtained, food was obtained, and progress continued. The popularity of the Cristeros was such that Gorostieta himself feared women, observing "we had a dread of the cities, because the girls immediately came out to flirt with the soldiers."[30]

On May 20, the government began a counterattack to finish off the seven thousand Cristeros of Los Altos. Calles had decided to destroy them by combining the regular army, aviation, artillery, and permanent occupation by General Cedillo's irregular troops. Jalisco alone received thirty-five thousand men. A skillful strategist, Gorostieta, in order to save ammunition, ordered a general dispersal while waiting for the storm to pass. At the same time, he was concerned about the extremely precise information he received concerning the progress of the negotiations led by Ambassador Morrow. He ordered everyone to remain on the defensive, waiting for the results and taking advantage of the passage of time in hopes that the assault would soften.

It was at this very moment when, passing through Michoacán, Gorostieta was accidentally killed by a patrol—the victim of a series of curious coincidences, such that those who killed him could not believe it. Although we have already referred to this, we must quote here, *in extenso*, a long paragraph on the death of General Enrique Gorostieta. Perhaps the history of the Cristiada would have been different without this sad episode. As recounted by Rius Facius:[31]

> General Gorostieta demonstrated, with his own extraordinary activity and courage, the justice of the cause he defended. There was no moment's rest. He traveled constantly from one place to another to organize his forces, to arrange new and more decisive attacks, and to attend to innumerable matters of a civil and administrative nature.
>
> In the Michoacán region, Callista General Lázaro Cárdenas received reinforcements. Gorostieta, in anticipation of some disaster, appointed General Alfonso Carrillo Galindo as military head of the state and ordered him to march there to avert the danger.
>
> For him to take possession of his new position, General Gorostieta and a small group of his most devoted officers

[30] Meyer, 1:300.
[31] Rius Facius, *México Cristero*, 2:464–66.

accompanied General Carrillo to Michoacán. At the same
time, without any prior agreement having been reached,
ten Cristeros under the command of Colonel Rodolfo Loza
Márquez left the Las Cuestas ranch, among them his brother,
the civilian chief Ildefonso Loza Márquez, from Los Altos,
where he had organized several civilian headquarters. On
the night of May 19, 1929, they arrived at the Barranquillas
ranch and, minutes later, General Gorostieta's group arrived
at the same place. The next day, to avoid any encounter with
government forces, they all climbed a nearby mountain, while
a federal detachment crossed the ranch. Once the danger
was over, the Cristeros returned to Barranquillas and there
General Gorostieta dictated to Major Heriberto Navarrete
a letter addressed to Chihuahuan General Marcelo Caraveo,
inviting him to join the movement.

The dust on the road caused the head of the National
Guard an extremely uncomfortable eye infection and, to
avoid the sun's rays, they chose to walk at night and hide
during the day. Thus, with various incidents, they arrived
on May 28 at Los Sauces, a place near Ocotlán, Jal., where
the engineer Alfonso Garmendia joined them.

On May 31, the group left for Pitahayo, Jal., and the next
day, faced with federal soldiers in Tototlán and the Carrozas
hacienda, they continued their route to arrive at nine o'clock
in the morning of Sunday, June 2, at the El Valle hacienda,
about 18 miles from Atotonilco.

The twenty Cristeros entered the courtyard of the farm.
The journey had been long and tiring. They tended to their
horses, loosened their saddles, and removed their bridles so
that they could eat and drink. Then they ate their own food:
a jug of milk and bread. General Gorostieta felt a stabbing
pain in his eyes. He lay down in a room next to the hallway
to rest for a bit.

In front of the farm there were some poor adobe houses,
behind it a ravine through which a path cut.

The Cristeros had breakfast. Some went to a small shop
whose doors faced the hacienda, others went up to the roof,
to observe the plain from there. They unknowingly left
the hidden path of the ravine unguarded. It was there that,
surprisingly, the first soldiers of the 42nd Cavalry Regiment
appeared. They climbed slowly, carelessly, keeping their weapons in dustcovers. A fat, dark-skinned captain led the way.
One of General Gorostieta's men noticed, from the door of
the small shop, the presence of the soldiers, and fired his

pistol at them. Colonel Loza Márquez ran to hide inside the farm. He wore a pitch helmet, as usual among the military, and this detail confused the cavalry soldiers, who shouted not to shoot, that they are on the same side—until a cry of "Long live Christ the King!" roused them out of their mistake, and they prepared to attack.

General Gorostieta rose quickly, gauged the danger that threatened them, and gave the order: "We have to get out of here any way we can. Mount your horses, all of you, and let us get out before they surround us."

But the horses, with the sound of the gunshots, reared up, and only General Gorostieta managed to mount his. He took the crucifix on his chest in his hands for a moment, looked at it and rushed towards the exit. A volley of gunfire received him outside, and his horse fell. He returned inside the mansion.

"These filthy men killed my horse and took my files," he said indignantly.

One of his men asked him: "What should we do, general?"

"Fight with bravery and die like men," he replied.

The Cristeros boldly repulsed their enemies. They were surrounded and it would be dangerous and difficult to escape. However, Major Heriberto Navarrete, the general's aide, Colonel Rodolfo Loza Márquez and Private Jesusillo tried to make it through a small orange orchard next to the farm. All three succeeded.

Gorostieta intended to follow the same path, but the siege had already closed. A voice broke through the pounding of gunfire:

"Who lives?"

"Long live Christ the King!" answered Enrique Gorostieta defiantly. They were his last words: a shower of bullets ended his life.[32]

Gorostieta's death was very important, no doubt, but did not negate the Cristeros' position of strength. The government could not continue to pay for the troops because the soldiers, fatigued and frightened

---

[32] "Engraved on his tombstone, at the foot of a crucified Christ, this epitaph was engraved, a complete synthesis of his life: 'Long live Christ the King! In memory of Major General Enrique Gorostieta Velarde, his wife and children. He was born in Monterrey, N. L., on September 18, 1890. God called him to his bosom on June 2, 1929. He was a Christian, a patriot, and a gentleman. He had an ideal in his life and for it he knew how to die: God, Fatherland, and Freedom'" (Rius Facius, 2:468). About Gorostieta's death, there are other versions: see Víctor Ceja Reyes, *Los Cristeros: Crónica de los que perdieron* (Grijalbo, 1982), 2:311-48.

by the war's duration, deserted *en masse*, as we have already seen.[33]

After Gorostieta's death, Father Aristeo Pedroza became the supreme leader of Los Altos, while General Degollado, head of the National Guard, and José Gutiérrez y Gutiérrez succeeded him as the head of the South Division. The government's inaction increasingly emboldened the Cristeros, who were uneasy about the negotiations that were developing behind the scenes between the episcopate and the government.

The Cristero movement was at its peak: in the west alone, there were more than 25,000 armed and organized men, with 2,000 civil authorities and about 300 schools. In the rest of the country, there were between 25,000 and 30,000 Cristeros, some organized better, some worse. The engagements were accelerating and the political factor was also in play: with a weakened government and with José Vasconcelos campaigning for the presidency (he had the support of the conservatives), the government had to hasten the end of the war to show that it had "pacified the country" (this was, in large part, the reason why Ambassador Morrow, Portes Gil, and Calles hurried to make peace, fearing the Catholic vote for the new candidate).[34]

Gorostieta himself, before he died, was anxious about the peace negotiations. He knew that, once peace was made, he would have no choice but to submit. "As soon as the churches open, they will all leave me. I know you. I did not come to fight for religious freedom only, but for everyone. I have no choice but to continue fighting"[35]; and so he did. What would have happened without his early death? We do not know, but things would most likely not have been so easy for the government (and for the Church). Santiago Dueñas, one of his lieutenants, a day before his death, told him: "They are saying that the churches are going to open, and the priests will stop us going into the countryside... if you want, we can shoot at the priests,"[36] to

---

[33] See Meyer, *La Cristiada*, 1:306.
[34] "Gorostieta thought of the presidential elections as a possible way out. In January he sent Navarrete to talk to Vasconcelos, passing through Guadalajara, to establish an alliance. Vasconcelos gave him an appointment for the day after the elections, which gave Gorostieta a lot to think about. He would have wanted Vasconcelos to join the movement immediately, since he was convinced in advance of the result of the electoral fraud and feared that the government would stage a coup. Reason was on his side, for Morrow, Portes Gil, and Calles hastened to make peace, to deprive him [Vasconcelos], at the decisive moment of the vote rigging, of the battle-hardened element of Catholic dissent." Meyer, *La Cristiada*, 1:315.
[35] Meyer, 1:318–19.
[36] Navarrete, *Por Dios y por la Patria*, 231.

which Gorostieta, laughing, replied that he would be the first to lay down his arms at the ringing of the bells. He understood his men, and the profound reason for their fight, which is why he expected nothing more from the moment the Church made peace with the State.

※ ※ ※

The terrible war that could only be won "at the expense of the Mexican people," as Don Porfirio Díaz prophesied, took a horrifying toll: a recent[37] investigation affirms that there were at least 35,000 Cristeros killed during the conflict while 1,500 were killed after the "Settlements" to prevent "any resumption of the movement."[38]

According to the latest census, the total population of Mexico is about 112,000,000[39] inhabitants. However, at the time of the Cristiada, it was not more than 15,000,000. Can the number of losses be calculated with certainty? We realize this is not completely possible. Some believe that Mexico lost, on both sides combined, more than 80,000 Mexicans,[40] distributed as follows: 25,000 to 30,000 Cristero combatants and 50,000 federal troops. Others mention a higher number of federal casualties, bringing them to 90,000.[41] Be that as it may, the number of Cristeros was always smaller than that of the national troops but, as in any fratricidal war, the losses were the country's. It was Mexican blood that was spilled—and at the cost of great suffering that continues to this day.

---

[37] See Juan González Morfín, *Murieron por sus creencias* (Panorama, 2012), 122. Perhaps the "feeling" of a greater number of deaths after the Settlements comes from the statement of General Degollado Guízar, who said he was "sure that after the negotiations the number of deaths of the Cristero army was greater than during the three years of the struggle" (ibid., 117). The reality is that the number of Cristero *leaders* killed after the negotiations was greater, not the number of *soldiers*.

[38] Meyer, *La Cristiada*, 1:34.

[39] The last Mexican census is from 2010. At present (2013) some estimate that the figure amounts to more than 130,000,000.

[40] Meyer, *La Cristiada*, 3:271. President Portes Gil arrives at a lower figure in his *Memoirs*, saying that only about a thousand died per month, counting both sides (see Rius Facius, *México Cristero*, 2:502). In 1986, then-president of Mexico, Miguel de la Madrid, declared on an official visit to France that the total number of dead on both sides, including the civilian population, was 250,000. See Jean Meyer, *Pro domo mea: "La Cristiada" a la distancia* (CIDE, 2004), 13.

[41] See Héctor Aguilar Camín and Lorenzo Meyer, *A la sombra de la Revolución Mexicana* (Cal y Arena, 19904), 103.

*Francisco Orozco y Jiménez and Blessed Anacleto González Flores*

*General Enrique Gorostieta*

# 8

# Freemasonry in the Cristiada

*The struggle is eternal. The struggle began twenty centuries ago.
In Mexico, the government and Freemasonry have been one and
the same in recent years.*
— Emilio Portes Gil, President of Mexico

L ITTLE IS KNOWN ABOUT THIS ASPECT OF THE
Cristiada. As Freemasonry is a subject difficult to research,
little or nothing exists on this question.[1] However, throughout our research the subject has come up frequently in the people,
statements, and governors of Mexico. We will not dwell on this topic
much but rather offer a brief overview of the influence that this
organization had on the events that concern us.

## FREEMASONRY AND ITS IDEAS

There are many concepts and opinions about Freemasonry, either
because of the complexity of the movement or because the definitions
that Freemasonry gives of itself are usually vague and do not reveal
its true and ultimate aims.[2]

According to the English and Scottish rites, Freemasonry is "a
beautiful system of morality clothed with allegory and illustrated with
symbols" or "a cosmopolitan and continually progressing institution,
which has for its object the investigation of truth and the perfection
of humanity. It is founded on freedom and tolerance, it does not formulate any dogma, nor does it rest on any." Some followers define it
this way: "it is a universal, philanthropic, philosophical and forward-
thinking association, which seeks to inculcate in its followers the love
of truth, the study of universal morality, the sciences and the arts, the
sentiments of self-denial and philanthropy and religious tolerance;

---

[1] Alejandro Gutiérrez Hernández, "La masonería mexicana, un caso de estudio
pendiente para la historia," in Franco Savarino and Andrea Mutolo, eds., *El
anticlericalismo en México* (Cámara de Diputados-Porrúa-ITESM, 2008), 227–51.
Sadly, this work is weak; its greatest merit is to show how in Mexico, even today,
the subject has not been seriously studied.
[2] We are inspired here by the article by Luis P. Conde, "Freemasonry," in *Enci-
clopedia RIAL*. Statements in quotation marks are from the same article.

it aims to eliminate racial hatred, conflicts of nationality, opinions, beliefs and interests, uniting all men by the bonds of solidarity and blending them in a mutual affection of fond reciprocity."

Freemasonry accepts belief in God as Supreme Being or Great Architect, but under this vague deism a deeper reality can be perceived. Leo XIII in his encyclical *Humanum genus* showed how the religious, philosophical, and moral doctrines that inspire Freemasonry lead to the denial of the God's existence, the denial of morality itself and open the way to atheism, pantheism, enlightenment, spiritualism, etc.

However, the Masonic agenda has not always been the same. As Freemasonry spread throughout Europe, the philanthropic and humanitarian purpose that Freemasonry proposed in its beginnings was not maintained. Alongside Freemasonry proper, which was conventional, traditional and mainstream, numerous sects emerged, some particularly secretive, Kabbalistic, eclectic, and pseudo-mystical (French Martinists, German Pietists) and others purely political (Bavarian Illuminati), and even regular Freemasonry over the years began to divide into numerous branches and rites.

The final step in this split was taken by the Grand Orient of France in 1877 when it erased from its statutes the obligation, hitherto required, of belief in the Supreme Being to whom they gave the name of Great Architect of the Universe. This led to the Grand Lodge of England condemning that of France. The position adopted by French Freemasonry was consistent with the anti-clerical, secularist, and rationalist attitude its members advocated. The French step was followed by many Orients and Lodges, both European and Latin American.

Freemasonry, then, cannot be spoken of in a univocal sense, since there is not just one form of it. There are many "Freemasonries" independent of each other (English, American, German, Austrian, Scandinavian, Dutch, Grand Orient of France, the French National Grand Lodge, Italian Freemasonry, Latin American Freemasonry, etc.) and within these there is an extraordinary variety of rites (Ancient and Accepted Scottish Rite, York Rite, Rectified Scottish Rite, Universal Mixed Rite, etc.). Each of them, as naturally results from not having a visible political head, has different features. In the case of Mexico, the one that had the most influence was dependent on the French Grand Orient, which is presented as more atheist, sectarian, and avowedly anti-Catholic.

As for its doctrine, it can be analyzed from the religious, moral, and philosophical point of view. First of all, Freemasonry proclaims as a basic and incontrovertible principle the absolute independence of human reason from any authority or teaching. Naturalism and rationalism are its starting points. The consequence of this radical decision is the denial of most of our duties to God, and religious indifferentism. All the teachings of the Church, therefore, are nothing more than myths from which modern and cultured man must free himself. In the reception of the supreme degrees, apostasy is de rigueur, that is, the denial of the faith: explicitly or through the performance of sacrilegious actions that presume apostasy. Since the Catholic Church claims to be in charge of transmitting the Christ's teachings, Freemasonry is compelled to oppose it.

Religious truths knowable by the natural light of reason soon become for Masons the product of superstition and religious fanaticism and, although they usually speak of a Supreme Being, this is quite different from the God of Christian revelation, transcendent to the world, provident, personal. For Freemasonry, God becomes a word in the vocabulary of juvenile peoples, which is repudiated when civilization reaches maturity. Such maturity presupposes the emancipation of humanity from any kind of "slavery," especially religious slavery.

As for morality, Freemasonry preaches universal morality, which leads to the negation of all objective moral norms (eternal law, divine law, etc.), that is, moral relativism, which can uphold, in theory and in practice, the Machiavellian principle that the end justifies the means.

Pope Leo XIII, in the encyclical *Humanum genus*, quoted above, denounces the lack of true moral or religious tolerance when the lodge promulgates various anti-Christian laws, prohibiting religious orders, confiscating Church property, actively promoting divorce, suppressing religious teaching from schools, removing Christian emblems from hospitals, classrooms, courts of justice, etc.

The summary of activities of the Lodge Union of the Peoples (France), in 1891, proclaimed that "all the great laws that have been passed in France for twenty years, and those that will be approved in the future, have been elaborated in our Workshops and have been the object of our labor."

From the philosophical point of view, all philosophical systems fit in Freemasonry as long as they do not have Catholic content. Their religion is that of Humanity. Its gospel is Science, its god is reason. Philosophically, it can be described as a skepticism and relativism of a practical and a somewhat speculative type. The lodge accepts and sponsors all theories that do not claim the exclusivity of truth. It is an eclectic system in which, rejecting any openness to the supernatural, there is room for atheism, pantheism, illuminism, or spiritualism.

### FREEMASONRY IN MEXICO

In Mexico,[3] as elsewhere, it is very difficult to precisely pinpoint the year in which Freemasonry began to operate. According to Félix Navarrete,[4] in 1785 an Italian painter named Felipe Fabris was prosecuted for being a Freemason. In 1793, the priest of Molango denounced a Frenchman, a street vendor, for his acceptance of and regard for the sect of the Freemasons, so it could be deduced that already at the end of the eighteenth century or the beginning of the nineteenth there were Freemasons in Mexico, most likely as a result of the first immigrations in the middle of that same century from Italy, France, and Spain.

Amid these imprecisions and lack of data, there is a book that is very illuminating because it was written by an initiate. It is entitled *Historia de la masonería en México desde 1806 hasta 1884*, by José María Mateos, founder of the Mexican National Rite, published with the authorization of the Supreme Grand Orient of the same rite in the official newspaper *La Tolerancia* in 1884. In it is the following paragraph:

> Since when was it [Freemasonry] introduced among us?.... Since 1806. Freemasonry in Mexico dates back to that time, as there is no evidence that any Lodge had been established before it. The vigilance established by the government and the absolute prohibition of any meeting that could instill suspicion kept the Mexicans in a state of complete inertia.[5]

---

[3] Of great value is Meyer's "El anticlerical revolucionario. 1910-1940. Un ensayo de empatía histórica," in Ricardo Ávila Palafox, Carlos Martínez Assad, and Jean Meyer, eds., *Las formas y las políticas del dominio agrario* (Universidad de Guadalajara, 1992), 284-304. It is especially worth considering the fourth proposition, where the French author dares to say: "Freemasonry is to the Mexican political elite what the gymnasium or the baths were to the Greek and Roman" (ibid., 288-90).

[4] See Félix Navarrete, *La masonería en la Historia y en las Leyes de Méjico* (JUS, 1957), 28. For more information on its origins, see María Eugenia Vázquez Samadeni, "Masonería, papeles públicos y cultura política en el primer México independiente, 1821-1828," in *Estudios de Historia Moderna y Contemporánea de México* 28 (2009): 35-83.

[5] José María Mateos, *Historia de la masonería en México desde 1806 hasta 1884*, ch. I, p. 8, quoted in F. Navarrete, *La masonería*, 29-30.

Navarrete affirms in his substantial work on Freemasonry in Mexico that the movement that ended up settling in Mexican lands was not the English (apparently more tolerant) but the Scottish,[6] with French roots and under the name of the Ancient and Accepted Scottish Rite. It is the most radical and anticlerical of all.[7]

## FREEMASONRY AND ITS INFLUENCE ON THE CRISTIADA

While revolutions can develop quickly, they are not organized in one day. The work of Freemasonry, in the case of the so-called Mexican Revolution, came long before it. Thus we can see how the famous Constitution of 1857, the "jewel of Mexican liberalism," was the fruit of efforts by the Freemason brethren. Zalce y Rodríguez highlighted this in the middle of the last century: "The constitution of 1857 still in force in the Republic with few modifications, was the work of the Masonic Order and especially of the Mexican National Rite, the one that crowned its work, begun in 1833 and was brought to a triumphant conclusion in 1857."[8]

As we will see later, most of Mexico's political leaders belonged to the "fraternity," even those of the most disparate leanings, such as "the Indian" Benito Juárez and the Emperor Maximilian I. It did not matter then whether someone leaned more to the left or to the right, in modern terms, for the ship would always have a rudder obedient to the "brethren."

It is true, we recognize, that as soon as one dives into the literature of the history of Freemasonry, it is common to find exaggerated views for or against it. The truth is that its influence in the Mexican situation examined here cannot be avoided without opening up an historical lacuna. Mexico would not have been what it is, for better or worse, without Freemasonry and, consequently, the same holds for the history of the Cristero counterrevolution. As we have said, it was the ruling class who spearheaded the modernization of Mexico, and they had no qualms about showing their support for or simply becoming members of the lodge. This was the case with Porfirio Díaz, who, although he declared himself a Catholic, became a Grand Master Mason between 1861 and 1895.[9]

---

[6]  See Sara A. Frahm, "La Cruz y el compás, compromiso y conflicto," *Secuencia* 22 (1992): 67–102.

[7]  See F. Navarrete, *La masonería*, 31.

[8]  Luis Zalce y Rodríguez, *Apuntes para la historia de la masonería en México* (Talleres Tipográficos de la Penitenciaría del Distrito Federal, 1950), 1:197.

[9]  He used to say: "Like Porfirio Díaz, in particular and as head of a family, I am a Catholic, a Roman Apostolic Catholic. As head of state, I do not profess any

Catholicism was the soul of Mexico and therefore Freemasonry, with its apparent doctrine of total tolerance of all kinds of creeds and abolition of religious "sectarianism," was an enemy difficult to avoid. In 1914, for example, a group of Catholics rose up in defense of religion in the states of Jalisco and Colima with the following anti-Carranza proclamation that foreshadowed what would come from the "tolerant" Constitution of Querétaro:

> Gentlemen of Carranza: by persecuting the Catholic religion to death, you have provoked us. You are the only ones to blame. *Your sectarianism is a danger to the fatherland,* an outrage to civilization, an embarrassment to the same group of honest liberals. We have the right to live in our fatherland freely, to exist as a political group and to claim all rights, because we are citizens, and to be Catholics because we are free. And if we are attacked, we have the right to repel barbaric and unjust aggression. *You have gone back twenty centuries,* uttering, in various forms, that savage cry: Christians, *to the lions!* We will not retreat, *we will gladly die for Christ, but not in the arena and with our hands raised to heaven like our primitive brothers; we will die with faith in our hearts and holding our guns.* Honest compatriots: whatever your creed, before God, before you, and before the whole world, we solemnly declare that the fight has been forced by the sectarianism of Carranza and that we fight for the Roman Catholic Apostolic Religion and for our political ideals that are perfectly expressed in two words: true democracy. Death to Carranza! Death to Masonry![10]

However, it should not be thought that Catholics "imagined" or "felt" themselves to be persecuted; looking at the situation from a Christian point of view, it would be too simplistic to reach this conclusion. No, it was the Freemasons who openly declared themselves the antagonists of Church doctrine. Thus, one of the many societies with less than innocent names, "Mexican Anti-Clerical Federation," openly Masonic, was among the first to protest against its "common enemy" (the Church) in the face of the imminent reconstruction of

---

religion, because the law does not allow me to do so." Moisés González Navarro, *Masones y cristeros en Jalisco* (El colegio de México, 2000), 17.

[10] Meyer, *La Cristiada,* 2:98, emphasis ours. And at the same time, Anacleto González Flores said: "The Revolution, which is a faithful ally of both Protestantism and Freemasonry, continues its tenacious march towards the demolition of Catholicism.... We are in the presence of a threefold immense conspiracy against the sacred principles of the Church." Sáenz, *La nave y las tempestades,* 150.

a monument dedicated to Christ the King. Among this Federation's
statutes published in April 1923, we read:

> It is considered as the center and bond of union of all
> those who recognize the Catholic clergy as the *common
> enemy*... The bloody struggle that we had to endure during
> the last ten years... seeking the implantation of a true democ-
> racy, the reign of justice and the solution of hidden social
> problems, made us lose sight of the reactionary work of the
> *eternal enemies of freedom.*[11]

The "eternal enemies of freedom" had to be weakened, but it would
be difficult to destroy them one by one, hence the creation of a
"national church" in order to deceive unsuspecting Catholics and have
them accept an easily controllable creed. This was what was attempted
with the "pope" Pérez in 1924, as described above. With the support
of Swiss Freemasonry and the local government, an attempt was
made to divide Mexican Catholics. The failure was blatantly obvious.

Rius Facius points out that the Masonic Supreme Council held in
Geneva in 1924[12] was one of those that endorsed the election of the
party that had Pérez as a pawn and Obregón as king:

> His name was Joaquín Pérez y Budar. He was born in Juxt-
> lahuaca, Oax., on August 16, 1851. When he turned eighteen,
> he dedicated himself to commerce and, in 1872, he rebelled
> against the presidential reelection of Lerdo de Tejada. He
> retired with the rank of captain to return to commerce. He
> married and thirteen months later he was widowed. He
> entered the seminary. In 1881 he sang his first Mass in the
> diocese of Veracruz. He returned to his fatherland and, with
> great shamelessness, entered the Masonic lodge "Friends of
> the Light" without ceasing to exercise his priestly ministry.[13]

Next we turn to the conflict's more direct protagonists and the
link they had with the lodge.

### THE CASE OF CALLES

The French diplomat Ernest Lagarde, an invaluable source used
by Meyer, managed to meet with President Calles during the years
of the Cristiada. Following these conversations, as a good diplomat,

---

[11] *Estatutos de la Federación Anticlerical Mexicana*, April 1923, 33 pp., pp. 7 and
3, cited by Meyer, *La Cristiada*, 2:126, emphasis ours.
[12] See Sáenz, *La nave y las tempestades*, 153–54.
[13] Rius Facius, *México Cristero*, 1:245.

he sent his summaries to France. In these, he presented his vision of the interviewee:

> "Every week that passes without religious exercises (said Calles) will cause the Catholic religion to lose 2 percent of its faithful..." He was determined to put an end to the Church and to rid his country of it once and for all. At times, *President Calles, despite his realism and coldness, gave me the impression of approaching the religious question with an apocalyptic and mystical spirit.*[14]

To which Lagarde added:

> The easing of tensions that, thanks to the political spirit of Obregón and the desire for peace with the Holy See, occurred in relations with the Holy See did not survive the arrival of the new president... Born in Mexico, but of Levantine descent, Protestant by education,[15] and totally irreligious (Calles is a Freemason, and has recently received the insignia of the 33rd degree), Calles is a spiteful and bitter adversary of the Roman Church, not because he wants to prevent it from extending its authority and power, but because he is *determined to extirpate the Catholic faith from Mexico...* What is particularly serious about him is that he is a man of principles, with an energy that reaches obstinacy and cruelty, ready to attack not only people, but principles and the institution itself, and the system of government to which he adheres in virtue of philosophical convictions condemns as economically and politically evil *the Church's very existence.*[16]

Regarding Calles' affiliation to Freemasonry and his merits to be honored, Rius Facius tells us:

> Plutarco Elías Calles was a 33rd degree Freemason and, as a reward for his relentless campaign of national persecution against Catholicism, the medal of Masonic Merit was granted to him on May 28, 1926, by the hands of the supreme grand commander of the Scottish Rite, Luis Manuel Rojas. The ceremony was held in the green room of the national palace. The commander said in his suggestive speech: "The order over which I have the honor to preside

---

[14] Ernest Lagarde, *Chargé d'affaires de la République Française au Mexique, à son Excellence M. Aristide Briand, ministre des Affaires Étrangères,* quoted in Meyer, *La Cristiada,* 2:8, emphasis ours.

[15] Meyer says that this claim has not been substantiated.

[16] Lagarde, *Chargé d'affaires,* quoted in Meyer, *La Cristiada,* 2:238–39, emphasis ours.

has never granted this high distinction. It has been ordered for the extraordinary merit of which you have earned as President of the Republic, solving, in such a short time, the most serious problems."[17]

To tell the truth, he had not only deep political convictions, but also firmly anti-Catholic principles. Although he had a high rank in Freemasonry, it seems that it was only because of his anti-religion policy.

It was an Italian journalist who, in Meyer's opinion and without much scruple, crudely defined the Calles of yesteryear:

> Calles does not have a precise ideology, like Obregón, to achieve his goals, which are "order and progress"; he is ready for anything, he has decided to be "the master of his own house"... Perhaps it was an Italian journalist, invited by Calles, as part of his international propaganda campaign, who best defined the character: "In Mexico there is no Bolshevism...! [Mexico] is at this moment a fiefdom of the Second Masonic Social International, governed by a Herriot[18] in a Mexican general's riding boots and by a certain group of feudal barons in "comrade's" jackets, who are sometimes called governors of the states, sometimes divisional generals with command of operations, sometimes senators or deputies.[19]

There can be no doubt, then, as to why international Freemasonry supported his government as soon as the armed conflict began and throughout its course.[20] The lodge attempted, even after the war, as it says, "to modernize the country and get it out of its economic and ideological backwardness. In this context, the Masonic organization

---

[17] Aquiles Moctezuma, *El conflicto religioso*, cited by Rius Facius, *México Cristero*, 2:7. About Calles' Freemasonry in 1926, the Sovereign Grand Master of the Scottish Rite of Mexico affirmed: "Freemasonry is spreading very rapidly in Mexico. Especially in officialdom and in the military: President Calles and three members of his cabinet—Aarón Sáenz, Secretary of Foreign Affairs, Luis Montes de Oca, Secretary of Finance, and Adalberto Tejada, Secretary of the Interior—are members of the brotherhood." *The New Age* XXVI (July 1927): 445, cited by Joseph H. L. Schlarman, *México tierra de volcanes* (Porrúa, 1973), 597.
[18] Herriot was a radical socialist politician in France during the Third Republic.
[19] Marco Appelius, *El águila de Chapultepec* (no publisher, Barcelona, 1928), 286, quoted by Rius Facius, *México Cristero*, 2:169.
[20] "From August to October 1926, Calles received the support of several Masonic lodges in Argentina, Brazil, Morocco, and the United States, including Nebraska City, Knights of the Ku Klux Klan, American Indian Wig-Wam Inc., Chief White Eagle Great High Priest (the latter granted Calles the degree of Gray Eagle), Cuba, Spain, and Puerto Rico." González Navarro, *Masones y cristeros en Jalisco*, 64.

emerged as a new moral power, capable of replacing religion and offering...schools of precedence for the exercise of power."[21] Calles was not, however, the only ruler associated with these ideas.

## THE CASE OF PORTES GIL

After the tyrannicide perpetrated by José de León Toral[22] against the elected president, Álvaro Obregón (July 1928), Obregon's people asked Calles to eliminate from the cabinet those ministers who had demonstrated they were enemies of Obregonism. The changes that were made allowed Portes Gil to take the position of Secretary of the Interior. Until then he had been governor of the state of Tamaulipas and of little political significance, but with "a brilliant Masonic career" according to Rius Facius.[23]

The affiliation of Portes Gil cannot be questioned, especially since he tried to flaunt it. In fact, after the "Settlements," the then-president of Mexico began to be branded as a coward or a collaborator with the enemy (the Church) by his own anticlerical supporters. They said that, by brokering the "settlements," he had triggered a setback in the revolutionary process.

As the accusation became more and more serious and might make him lose popularity among those closest to him, he was forced to make a public statement on July 27, 1929, at the celebration of the summer solstice before more than two hundred 33rd-degree Masons. At the banquet, raising his voice, he declared:

> Most Venerable Grand Master, Venerable Brothers... The clergy have fully recognized the State and have openly declared that they are strictly subject to the laws. And I could not deny Catholics the right to submit to the laws, because that is the categorical imperative that, as a governor,

---

[21] Beatriz Urías Horcasitas, "De moral y regeneración: el programa de 'ingeniería social' posrevolucionario a través de las revistas masónicas, 1939–1945," *Cuicuilco* 32 (2004): 87–119. Cited by Alejandro Gutiérrez Hernández, "La masonería mexicana, un caso de estudio pendiente para la historia," in Savarino and Mutolo, *El anticlericalismo en México*, 248.

[22] José de León Toral (Matehuala, San Luis Potosí, December 23, 1900–Mexico City, February 9, 1929) was the young Catholic who assassinated the elected president, Álvaro Obregón, on July 17, 1928. Toral was then tortured and shot. Obregón's autopsy, apparently, revealed that not all shots were fired with Toral's pistol, thus casting his guilt into doubt and raising the question of whether there might have been an internal plot to assassinate him, using the young Catholic as a scapegoat.

[23] Rius Facius, *México Cristero*, 2:424, emphasis ours.

obliges me to be respectful of the law. *The struggle is not beginning. The struggle is eternal. The struggle began twenty centuries ago.* Hence, there is no need to be frightened. What we must do is to remain at our post. Not to fall into the vice into which previous governments fell, and especially those of forty years ago, where one concession after another and one tolerance after another led to the absolute annulment of our legislation.

What we have to do, then, is be vigilant, each one in his place. Governors and public officials, zealous in complying with the law and ensuring that it is complied with. And as long as I am in the government, before the Freemasons I swear that I will be zealous that the laws of Mexico, the constitutional laws which fully guarantee free conscience, but which subject the religious ministers to a certain system: I proclaim, I say, before Freemasonry, that while I am in government, this legislation will be strictly observed... In Mexico, the State and Freemasonry in recent years have been one and the same: two entities marching in lockstep, because the men who in recent years have been in power have always known how to show solidarity with Freemasonry's revolutionary principles.[24]

Let us highlight these words: "the State and Freemasonry in recent years have been one and the same." To support this statement by Portes Gil, we present a summary of the meticulous list that Félix Navarrete prepared on the Masonic affiliation of Mexican leaders until the religious conflict:[25]

General Guadalupe Victoria (President 1824–1829).

General Vicente Guerrero (President April-December 1829).

General Anastasio Bustamante (President 1830–1832).

General Manuel Gómez Pedraza (President 1832–1833).

General Antonio López de Santa Anna (President nine times. The first in 1833, the last in 1853).

Dr. Valentín Gómez Farías (Vice-President acting as president, always in union with Santa Anna, four times in 1833–34).

General Nicolás Bravo (occupied the government with various titles four times, from 1824–1842).

---

[24] Ruiz y Flores, *Lo que sé del conflicto religioso*, quoted in Rius Facius, *México Cristero*, 2:509-11. The same is found in the magazine *Crisol*, September 10, 1929, pp. 116-22; emphasis ours.
[25] See F. Navarrete, *La masonería*, 239-46.

General Mariano Paredes y Arrillaga (President in 1846).

General Mariano Arista (President 1851–1853).

Juan B. Ceballos (President 1853).

General Manuel María Lombardini (President in 1853).

General Ignacio Comonfort (President three times, in 1856, 1857 and 1858).

Benito Juárez (President 1858–1872).

General Juan N. Almonte (he was in 1863 a member of the Regency of the empire and in 1864 Lieutenant of the empire).

Maximilian I (emperor from 1864 to 1867).

General Porfirio Díaz (President 1876–1880 and from 1884 to 1911).

General Manuel González (President 1880–1884).

Francisco I. Madero (President 1911–1913).

General Plutarco Elías Calles (President 1924–1928).

Emilio Portes Gil (President 1928–1930).

### FREEMASONRY: ONE OF THE CAUSES OF WAR

Without oversimplifying, we must say that the Masonic lodge and order played an important role in the religious conflict. To ignore this would be to ignore the very nature of Mexican politics, even to this day. A long but quite helpful paragraph by Meyer, quoted already, clarifies the matter:

> In fact, *Freemasonry and government were closely related*, to such an extent that it was necessary to be a brother Mason to occupy a position of importance; governors, ministers, senators, congressmen, and generals were closely or distantly related to the lodges. The governor and general Heriberto Jara, President Ortiz Rubio, General Urquizo and General Roberto Cruz were Freemasons. As for Portes Gil, he was Grand Master in 1933–1934.[26] General Cárdenas, also a Freemason, tried to nationalize Freemasonry when he became president.
>
> If the politician was necessarily a Freemason, it can be said that, in practice, all public officials were brothers: "The great majority of the officers belong to the Masonic order and are therefore resentful against the Roman Church for having condemned that order...." Freemasonry, controlled

---

[26] Zalce y Rodríguez, *Apuntes para la historia de la masonería en México*, 2:90, 92, 102, 130, 131.

and restricted by Porfirio Díaz, recovered from 1914 on the active role it had played during the Reform, and provided the government with an organization and with leadership: city mayors, presidents of agrarian communities, union leaders and teachers were very often Freemasons. Under such conditions, it was only natural that *the order would publicly give its unconditional support to the government's religious policy. Freemasonry had a nightmare: the Roman clergy, the cause of evil in the world.* Freemasonry therefore gave Calles the Medal of Merit for his educational work, and the lodge of Valley of Mexico organized a "public demonstration in support of the policy of religious intolerance, and the members of the regular and irregular lodges in the capital paraded with their own banners"[27]... Catholics had, as a basis for their fears and allegations of conspiracy the minutes of the 1906 Masonic Congress of Buenos Aires, which proclaimed the urgency of fighting Catholics, and a very curious text by Dr. Robert A. Greenfield, published in New York on December 20, 1927 and quoted by International Civic Organization, on the occasion of the VI Pan-American Conference, meeting in Cuba:[28] *"As a Protestant I am a supporter of Freemasonry....* Leaving Catholicism to enter the very broad field of Protestantism was, without a doubt, an advance, and besides, we Americans have always believed, since the previous century, that *the Catholic religion is an insurmountable obstacle to the union of all the countries of America."*[29]

A certain Jesuit priest, summarizing near the end of the war the "whys" of this fratricidal struggle (June 1, 1929), explained to Rome the causes of the problem:

The causes of the religious conflict.

1) Remote cause, the North American inclination to de-Catholicize Mexico, which includes: a) the influence of Protestant sects; b) influence of Freemasonry; c) the influence of North American liberalism; d) North American expansionism; e) exclusion of European elements and influence; f) US hegemony (imperialism); g) world predominance of American finance.

---

[27] Zalce y Rodríguez, 92–93.
[28] Comité Central de la International Civic Organisation, *La querella de México ante la VI Conferencia Panamericana en Cuba* (San Antonio, 1928), 21.
[29] The quotations in this great paragraph all correspond to Meyer, *La Cristiada*, 2:197–99, emphasis ours.

2) Proximate cause: a) the trend of the revolution; b) Constitution of 1917; c) Calles' insolence and politics. 3) Occasional cause: enforcing article 130. 4) Prelude: the declarations of the Archbishop of Mexico, deliberately prompted by our own people or even by our enemies.[30]

Finally, and in order to see the influence that Freemasonry in the northern country had on the Mexican situation, we must mention an article that appeared in 1928 in the Vatican newspaper *L'Osservatore Romano*. It is the supposed "protest" of Freemasonry and North American Protestantism against Calles' policy of persecuting Catholicism, but this protest is nothing more than a diplomatic masquerade that, like it or not, indicates the intentions of the lodge and of international policy regarding Mexico. Thus, on June 26, the section "The Mexican Persecution" reappeared, occupying the first two columns of the main page. Immediately afterwards, with a large heading: "Masonic and Protestant documentation," it was followed by two articles, of which we cite only the first.

These stories, under the title "The Religious Question in Mexico," had recently been published by the *International Civic Organization*, a group that boasted of being Masonic and Protestant (!). We reproduce below most of the first article, signed by Robert A. Greenfield, with an initial epigraph that read: "Condemnation of the barbarity of the Mexican government":

> As a Protestant and supporter of Freemasonry, I condemn the anti-Catholic events in Mexico to defend my country, the United States, rather than to denounce injustices against Catholicism. However, first of all I must declare that, with the exception of some leaders of Protestant sects and some eminent Freemasons, we all condemn the barbaric way in which the government of General Plutarco Elías Calles has opposed the faithful of the Catholic religion.
>
> The government derived from the Mexican Revolution and presided over by Venustiano Carranza devised a program of radical action. The revolutionary movements of Europe, as well as that of Russia, immediately aligned themselves with the dominant group in Mexico, and *first General Obregón and then General Calles adapted this program with the greatest thoroughness from that of the worldwide revolution.*

---

[30] *El actual conflicto religioso,* memorandum written by a prelate at the request of Rome, 27 pp., June 1, 1929, in Meyer, 2:347.

> *This program consists of several steps and the first is the destruction of all religions.*
>
> Since Mexico is a country in which Catholicism dominates, it is natural that the strongest hostility of the government is precisely against this religion. The Mexican radicals soon realized that some elements of Protestantism and Freemasonry in the United States were sympathetic to the idea of destroying Catholicism and, *believing that by this tactic they would win American support* for the realization of their entire revolutionary program, the Mexican politicians came to an agreement with the most powerful anti-Catholic institutions.[31]

Greenfield's explanation continued with the heading: "The obvious reasons for agreement with the persecutor," the contents of which read:

> It is true, however, that *in the struggle for extermination against Catholicism we are necessarily in agreement, Freemasons and Protestants*, and that *we have given loyal* and sufficiently broad support *to the Calles regime* in this field. The reason is obvious: Catholicism is an overly absorbing religion.
>
> In a very few years, it has won over 15 percent of the population of our country and threatens to invade the upper echelons of our government. While Protestant churches have very few parishioners, although they offer them clothing, food, and entertainment to attract people, Catholic churches, where offerings are collected *from* believers, are full of faithful. This absurdity goes against the grain of Protestant leaders, whose intentions are excellent and in good faith: if American civilization has favored the whole world in the material order, it is natural that we should now also want to exercise a spiritual dominion.
>
> *We think that Protestantism is more in line with modern culture than Catholicism, which is a medieval religion:* Spanish America should be grateful for the effort we put into investing millions of dollars in propagating the Gospel through useful institutions such as the Y.M.C.A., the Rotary Club, and the Missions.

With unusual sincerity, Dr. Greenfield's argument, in a heading *L'Osservatore Romano* entitled "A curious 'fault' of Catholicism and a very curious 'merit' of Protestantism," reads:

---

[31] *L'Osservatore Romano*, 26-VI-1928, translation and emphasis ours.

*To leave Catholicism to enter the vast field of Protestantism is truly progress.* We Americans have always believed, since the last century, that *the Catholic religion is an insurmountable obstacle to the union of all the countries of America.* I believe that no one will condemn us for our noble purpose of Americanizing the continent, nor will anyone believe that it is possible to achieve this ideal as long as the Latin superstition that has always hindered it remains in force.

The main fault that we Anglo-Saxons rightly blame on Spanish Catholicism is that it produced a hybrid race that has prevented us from achieving the annexation of rich territories populated with people whom we regard as living on a lower level of culture. *Protestantism, on the other hand, more practical and more conscious of freedoms, admitted as a necessity the extermination of the natives, or their confinement on reservations, to prevent the mixing of the two races....* If Spanish America has enjoyed the benefit of our civilizing influence, if it is progressing in reflection of our material civilization, it is natural that it should strive to prepare itself for its complete spiritual identification with us, convinced that riches and progress will be achieved with our religious institutions, not with Catholicism. It is true that their ancient religion has created architecture, sculpture, painting, music, and literature, but these treasures do not serve to ensure the well-being of peoples.[32]

Freemasonry, together with North American Protestantism, was in agreement about the cultural and political domination of their neighboring country. Once again, Don Porfirio Díaz's sarcastic statement was confirmed: "Poor Mexico: so far from God and so close to the United States."

✳ ✳ ✳

In light of the foregoing analysis, it is strange that, to this day, some still insist on pretending that Freemasonry was merely an imaginary threat to Mexican Catholicism.[33]

---

[32] Ibid.

[33] This is the thought, among others, of several liberal historians who try to minimize the Masonic role as if it had not existed, as can be seen here: "The interpretation of political reality made by these groups is characterized by maintaining that there is a sinister plan orchestrated by the 'enemies' of Christ: Jews, Freemasons and Communists, to destroy the Christian social structure. It is a 'paranoid' vision of history." David B. Castillo Murillo, *La extrema derecha del conservadurismo mexicano: El caso de Salvador Abascal y Salvador Borrego* (Universidad Autónoma Metropolitana, 2012), 12; see also p. 51.

*Calles the Mason*

*The tyrant Plutarco Elías Calles*

# 9

# Religious Hatred

**M**EXICO WAS AND CONTINUES TO BE A DEEPLY religious country; it is difficult to change a people's roots. During the period known as the "Porfiriato" (1876 to 1911), relations between Church and State remained relatively calm. It is true that the Constitution of 1857, prior to Don Porfirio's rise to power, had laid the foundations of the subsequent religious persecution, but the so-called "new Constantine," without being a man of faith, had enough good sense not to exacerbate the situation, following a policy that, unlike his predecessors, tolerated religion by turning a deaf ear to anti-Catholic sectarianism:

> There is not much wealth in the hands of the Church, and there are no popular uprisings except when the people feel wounded in their inalienable traditions and in their legitimate freedom of conscience. *The persecution of the Church, whether the clergy are involved or not, means war, and such a war the government can win only against its own people,* by means of the humiliating, despotic, costly, and dangerous support of the United States. *Without its religion, Mexico is hopelessly lost.*[1]

A "war against its own people," said the Mexican president himself. Declarations such as this make further evidence unnecessary. If the most elementary rules of Aristotelian logic had been followed, this war — this entirely avoidable genocide, which took an enormous number of lives from both federal and Cristero forces — could have been avoided.

What was the guiding spirit behind the struggle? What was the reason for so much religious hatred? The grassroots movement, without direct guidance from the Church, as we have seen, did not fit into the mental schemes of the government leaders, who, faithful to radical principles, saw in religion the "opium of the people" assisted by tonsured men in cassocks. The confusion was such that those who persecuted the people gave the following reasons for doing so: "1) because they belong to the old guard of the right wing, 2) because they are Catholics, 3) because they were able to act on their own

---

[1] Paul Murray, *The Catholic Church in Mexico* (EPM, 1965), 1:301, quoted by Meyer, *La Cristiada*, 2:44, emphasis ours.

initiative."[2] The last point was particularly important: for them it was impossible to understand how the Cristeros could be a *Catholic* and *people's* movement simultaneously.

In this chapter, we attempt to summarize that passion, that recurring idea, that acted as the driving force behind the conflict.

## THE BATTLE OVER CULTURE: NAMES AND SYMBOLS

We have already noted above the undeniable kinship between the Mexican Revolution and the French Revolution, or more accurately, between the Cristero counterrevolution and the French counterrevolution. The latter are first cousins: both were thoroughly grassroots— and both were completely silenced. In both cases, all the methods of a true cultural revolution were used: it was not just a matter of fighting with bayonets to defeat bodies, it was a matter of fighting against culture to conquer minds.

In the early years of the *La République*, the cumbersome method of changing "old" names to new ones was used in France. Nothing was to be allowed to recall the *ancien régime*: the months, the years, the days, and even the Lord's Prayer were changed—to "Thermidor," "the First Year of the Revolution," or the *adveniat republicam tuam* said in place of *adveniat regnum tuum*. The Mexican revolutionaries did not shun this pre-Gramsci method of changing the people's "common sense." Thus, phrases such as those that the governor of Jalisco telegraphed to General Amaro became more and more common: "your [letter]-of the fourth of May— concerning instructions about changing the names of towns and ranches bearing holy names, I have already given orders to city mayors to begin the process of changing names before Congress, so that people with revolutionary merit are recognized."[3]

Not even Spain, "retrograde Spain," conquering Spain, had dared to do so much. If there is one thing that still amazes the traveler when he sets foot in the lands conquered by Cortés, it is the enormous respect they had for the indigenous names of the inhabitants: far from naming the new cities with names of Spaniards, the traditional name was respected[4] or a Christian appellation was added. But it was not the same policy in the period that concerns us. All relations with Catholicism had to be banished and, as was the case in the

---

[2] Meyer, *La Cristiada*, 1:386.
[3] Archive of the Government of Jalisco, May 9, 1927, telegram to General Joaquín Amaro, quoted by Meyer, *La Cristiada*, 1:178.
[4] For those who wish to test this claim, try to pronounce the following populations: Izhuatepec, Huejotzingo, Huaxtepec, Ixtacamaxtitlán, Tepatitlán.

Soviet Union, prayer was forbidden along with teaching one's children to pray. In the state of Durango, for example, as early as 1926, the authorities "distributed a manifesto that imposed the penalty of fine and imprisonment on anyone who taught their children to pray, had images in their home, or who wore medals or relics."[5]

For the government, the meaning of popular symbols was a sign of loyalty to the old country, the "anti-revolutionary" fatherland. It was necessary to banish the symbols of Catholicism engraved in popular piety. Thus, the Armed Forces of the Federation, as the official forces were called, becoming the "active agent of anticlericalism and of the anti-religion struggle waged its own war, its religious war."[6] Wearing a rosary around one's neck, a scapular, or an image of Christ the King, were sufficient evidence of potential insurrection. Decree 71 of 1926, for example, even decreed on the tolling of bells and religious images that together with the "sacred objects had to be placed and enclosed more than two meters from the ground, so that no one could kiss them."[7]

Such was the hatred that these enemies of the people tried to ridicule the Catholic faith in every possible way. Evidence of this is the famous Cristero magazine, *David*, directed by General Aurelio Acevedo, who echoed the revolutionary fury commenting in the first person:

> The first Callista who entered San Julián (Jalisco), was General Tranquilino Mendoza, alias "El Tigre." He arrived at the Hacienda de Jalpa to rescue about twenty federals who were going from San Juan de los Lagos and whom we had besieged in a hut at the Rancho del Capulín, just under 4 miles from San Julián, owned by Don Nicario Jiménez. The Callista General, Tranquilino Mendoza...brought with him a bull dog with a Franciscan Rosary around its neck, thus displaying his contempt and mockery for the Holy Rosary.[8]

Another similar episode happened on January 15, 1928, in Huejuquilla, a town in Jalisco. There, Carmelita Robles, a pious young lady, had an oratory in her house, with a tabernacle and the Blessed Sacrament. Upon entering her house, the soldiers broke in, looting as much as they could. López Beltrán recounts that one of them

---

[5] Rius Facius, *México Cristero*, 2:120.

[6] "The general Eulogio Ortiz ordered the execution of a soldier on whose neck he saw a scapular; some officers led their troops into battle shouting 'Long live Satan!'; and the colonel 'Black Hand,' executioner of Cocula, died exclaiming: 'Long live the Devil.'" Meyer, *La Cristiada*, 1:146.

[7] Meyer, *La Cristiada*, 2:248.

[8] Lauro López Beltrán, *La persecución religiosa en México* (Tradición, 1991), 63.

looked at the devout image of Our Lord Jesus Christ, who was
venerated there with the title and avocation of the "Divine
Prisoner" and took off the image's hair and tunic, and left the
oratory dressed like Jesus, shouting, amidst laughter and blasphemies from his comrades: "Adore Christ the King." Other
villains forced the door of the nearby church of St. Anthony
and filled the empty tabernacle with filth. They did the same
in the glass case that contained another image of Jesus Christ,
called in the town "The Lord of the Wounds of the Passion."[9]

Never had the title been better confirmed than in this incident.

But where this hatred could be most verified was not so much in
the rank-and-file combatants who, in the end, carried out orders and
not infrequently went over to the Cristero army, as we mentioned; it
was mainly the federal leaders who used violence from above.

### THE RULERS' HATRED FOR CATHOLICS

We have seen that it was not the common people who were behind the
struggle against the Church. On the contrary, the political caudillos were
the main promoters of the persecution and social division of Mexico.
To understand this, it is not necessary to delve into obscure unofficial
biographies. The intolerance was so massive that many of the leaders
left an unforgettable imprint on their writings and official speeches.

Once he became president, the people understood that Calles
would not change. He could not change because his anti-Christian
ideas were so fervent that they were set in stone. It was almost an
"obsession," as the French diplomat Ernest Lagarde called it:

> At certain moments, President Calles, in spite of his realism
> and coldness, *gave me the impression of being obsessed* by the
> idea of the moral obligation imposed on him by the oath he
> took to be faithful to the Constitution, and to *approach the
> religious question with an apocalyptic and mystical spirit*: the
> current conflict was not, in his opinion, a localized battle
> between Church and State, such as those that almost all
> countries have seen.... Here there was an all-out battle
> between the religious idea and the secular idea, between
> reaction and progress, between light and darkness.[10]

A "fight to the death," said Calles. These were harsh words, heartfelt
to the core. The Irish writer Francis McCullagh, speaking of Calles,
also sensed it:

---

[9] López Beltrán, 90.
[10] Lagarde, *Chargé d'affaires*, quoted in Meyer, *La Cristiada*, 2:273–74, emphasis ours.

For one reason or another Calles feels an intense hatred against the Catholic Church, a hatred that is almost as great as that of Cromwell." An American journalist who was in Mexico once had the opportunity to discuss the religious question at length with Calles, or rather, to listen to what Calles told him about the matter for an hour and a half. This correspondent was a Protestant, and was not particularly interested in religious subjects, but he came out of that interview in a cold sweat and declared to me (when he was able to regain the use of words) that he had been dismayed by the abyss opened by the dictator's words. "I saw at the bottom of them," he told me, "not the hatred of one life, but many generations of hatred."[11]

The case of Calles is paradigmatic, but it was not singular. Religion and especially the clergy were the "syphilis" that the State had to fight because "the curse of the friars brings glorification,"[12] said Obregón.

### AGAINST THE HEART OF CATHOLICISM

Catholicism is not simply a religion of signs, images, or prayers: it is a *worldview* that, over the centuries, has taken on a universal character, into which rich and poor, men and women, commoners and nobles enter. An illiterate old woman believes the same as a learned theologian from the Sorbonne, as St. Thomas Aquinas says. This spiritual "structure" is transmitted in its application by two fundamental pillars: fidelity to the pope (and to his authentic magisterium) and the administration of the sacraments.

In the time of the Cristiada, the Church's enemies knew that a priest was more dangerous from a pulpit than with a carbine in his hands. But not only that: confession was also dangerous, since it was something the State could not interfere with, no matter how much it wanted to. To confess, to ask forgiveness for sins and to receive absolution, was seen as "seditious" because a priest is more powerful in the internal forum of conscience than the State can ever be in the external forum.[13] Confession, then, also had to be forbidden. Believe it or not, the question was even debated when drafting the Constitution of Querétaro of 1917. The representative Alonzo Romero described confession and priestly celibacy as follows:

---

[11] Pereyra, *México falsificado*, 2:250, emphasis ours.
[12] Meyer, *La Cristiada*, 2:80.
[13] When the Catholic faithful confess to a priest who acts *in persona Christi*, the priest is solemnly bound to keep the sacramental seal (i.e., the secrecy of the content of the confession), under pain of excommunication.

I am going to demonstrate that *each of these points constitutes a great immorality* .... The poor in spirit who consciously, in a submissive way, in a degrading way allow their wives, the women they love most, all those people who are related to their most intimate feelings, to empty into the lewd ears of those nefarious and degraded men everything that takes place in the home, all those secrets that should not leave the home .... *Every woman who confesses is an adulteress* and every husband who allows it is a pimp and condoner of such immoral practices [*applause*].... As for clerical marriage, not performing a natural act...what would happen, gentlemen, when a man endowed with flesh and blood, a man who has a nervous system capable of developing reproductive functions, cannot carry them out because a dam has been placed on its development? What happens? He has to prosper in someone else's domain. That is why there are so many homes in a disastrous state.... if we do not take steps to prevent these assaults on morality, we will never reach a satisfactory conclusion and we will leave room for every home to be a disaster, for every woman to be an adulteress...and every priest a satyr loose in the bosom of society [*more applause*].[14]

This now seems unthinkable — that in a nation's fundamental charter, such as a national constitution, that there would be a debate over confession. But it happened in Mexico at the beginning of the century. Politicians were not the only skeptics. Among military men there were also such opinions: General Múgica, for example, was convinced that "confession is where the danger lies, it is where all the secret of the all-embracing power that resides in these black and truly retrograde men throughout their institutional existence in Mexico." It was "one of the great immoralities, a great crime being committed, and we must demand vigorously, and once and for all, that it be abolished completely."[15]

Confession was not the only symbol of Catholicism to be attacked. Mexico, which declares itself 99% Catholic and 100% Guadalupean, would suffer enormously if something happened to the tilma left by the miraculous apparition of Tepeyac: the image of the Virgin of Guadalupe. On November 14, 1921, Juan M. Esponda, an official of the private secretariat of the Mexican President, went to the Shrine of the Virgin of Guadalupe, in the Federal District, and deposited a stick of dynamite at the foot of the revered image in the middle of a bouquet

---

[14] *Journal of the Debates of the Constituent Congress*, 2:1031-32, quoted by Meyer, *La Cristiada*, 2:86–87, emphasis ours.
[15] *Journal of the Debates*, 1059 and 1040, in Meyer, *La Cristiada*, 2:87.

of flowers. After the explosion, the unfortunate Esponda tried to flee and avoided lynching and saved his life thanks to a group of soldiers. According to contemporary photos, the damage was considerable. The glass that covered the image was broken and the bronze crucifix on the altar of the Virgin was bent over, melted, as if it had defended the Lord's Mother from the explosion.[16] Yet the image was unharmed.

The frustrated terrorist was subjected to a mock trial and, finally, declared innocent. As always, the government not only wanted to ignore the attack, but once again blamed popular "fanaticism." Governor Eduardo Neri declared: "The damage caused to the church in question was of little consideration and the act itself only serves to benefit the clergy."[17] The victims were cast as victimizers. Be that as it may, all the religious hatred shown on the part of the government only increased the devotion and anger of the common people, who saw in much of it the hand of the enemy.

Nevertheless, it was not limited to images or scapulars. There were certain phenomena that might be characterized as symptomatic or pathological. That in a war people kill and die is not new; what was new were certain attitudes that are rarely seen except in religious wars. The following paragraph is hard to ignore, as it may strike many readers as particularly powerful. Those who have read the history of the French Revolution, especially in the so-called "terror" years or, closer to home, the religious persecution that occurred in Spain in the 1930s, will feel as though they are looking at the same picture with a different background. Meyer, who is not exactly a man "of the Church," recounted from his youth, not without amazement:

> Secularization, secularism, anticlericalism, vandalism, sacrilege, iconoclasm, blasphemies—all tendencies were to be found, from tolerance to the black religiosity those who celebrate Mass backwards.... There was no lack of cases of elaborate perversion, of inversion, of a "world upside down." This obsession with "fanatically turning this world upside down" went far. The priests recognized the devil in the soldiers who officiated by putting their vestments on backwards, who read books upside down, with opaque glasses, and in those soldiers who indulged in feasts and dances in the churches, organizing covens, dancing with the Virgins [i.e., statues of Our Lady], stripping the saints, shooting the Christs [i.e., statues of

---

[16] The same was told to us in the Basilica of Guadalupe, where the crucifix is kept for the veneration of the faithful.

[17] *Excélsior*, November 15, 1921, and *La Nación*, January 18, 1947, quoted in Meyer, *La Cristiada*, 2:119.

Christ], fornicating, urinating, and defecating on the altars. This explains the astonishing testimony of a woman who swore to us that, having entered to make up General Ortiz's room and surprising him in his shirt, she saw a cloven tail and hooves. "Calles' rabble ... when they arrive in a village ... renew the scenes of 1793 in France .... They have turned our churches into barracks and stables, destroyed the holy images, desecrated the tabernacles .... In the Immaculate Conception church they held a dance. One of the farmers took the image of the Blessed Virgin, danced with it ...." Governor Ambrosio Puente decreed in Morelos: "Anyone who asks priests for any sacrament will be put to death," and General R. González, in Michoacán: "Any person who provides food and money to the rebels, as well as presenting children to be baptized or presenting themselves to verify marriages or hearing their preaching, will be put to death, with no recourse." And General Daniel Sánchez forbade dressing in mourning without authorization, under penalty of death.[18]

One of the hostages in Valparaíso, J. Rodríguez's father, was forced to hang on display the body of his dead son, who had attacked the prison to free the hostages. Before shooting Fr. Daniel Pérez, his executioners flayed his cheeks with a knife. The corpse of the vicar of Cuquío was dragged by a horse, while the soldiers shouted at the town's residents: "Here's goat meat!" The Cristero leader Doroteo Dimas, killed in the capture of Jalpa in 1927, was buried in Huejotitlán. Colonel Quiñones had the corpse dug up and hung out to view. On January 24, 1928, the federal soldiers who had surprised Nicho Hernández's troops asleep in Cartagena, killing their leader and several soldiers, returned to hang and shoot the civilians whom they found burying the corpses. Then they exhumed the bodies of Don Nicho and eleven others, which they stripped naked and crucified.

Similarly, the executions of priests and sacrileges were surrounded by a horror *consciously felt* and shared by the perpetrators and spectators. Execution squads often refused to fire, and one soldier had to be shot to move the others to obey, but not without first asking for the priest's forgiveness. The tale is brief: the churches were desecrated, the officers entered them on horseback, made their horses eat hosts, transformed the altars into tables or beds, set fire to the buildings or used them as barracks and stables. The images were shot, or virgins were stripped naked to dance with them. They dressed up in vestments and took "the hosts with coffee and

---

[18] Meyer, *La Cristiada*, 2:210–11, emphasis ours.

milk in the chalice." General Ignacio Leal took the trouble
to burn the crosses scattered around the field and the church
pulpits, despite the protests of his colleague Ubaldo Garza.
Z. Martínez also furiously hunted down images.[19]

Even the language used in the struggle revealed the inner spirit of
those men who, while fighting, would say: "If you don't surrender, we'll
take your women to f——"; "If you let them get away with it, you're
not men! And long live Christ the King, sons of b ——"; "Death to
Christ and his Mother, the great wh——"! "Long live the Devil, long
live the great demon!"[20]

It is said that atheists often have more faith in supernatural things
than believers do. The invocation of the devil was, in the federal army,
one of the many "rites" to be performed:

> There were infamous orgies where Christ was horribly blas-
> phemed. In Guanajuato — as the press reported — an Army
> general, after dirty and profane ranting, as only a demoniac
> could do and after shouting against Christ and against the
> Immaculate Virgin, with unclean words, he began to acclaim
> *Lucifer* whom he toasted amid shouts of approval of many:
> *Death to Christ! Down with Christ! Let's crush Christ forever!*
> *Lucifer be our God! He is our chief! Up Lucifer! Long live Lucifer!*
> That was the satanic cry, amid the fumes of alcoholic bev-
> erages, chanted by his fellow believers, of the man who has
> now been judged by God: two years later he was defeated by
> the Cristeros at the barracks of El Borbollón, at the foot of
> the Colima Volcano, about whom it was said — eyewitnesses
> described it — that he had tattooed, on his back and legs, a
> demon that embraced his body with its tail. It was Eulogio
> Ortiz, on whom, in his final moments, may God, who is
> goodness and mercy, have shown mercy.[21]

In this war of religion, the federal troops indulged in the most
atrocious crimes to humiliate the people:

> The violence that characterized the behavior of the govern-
> ment forces, violence carried to an extreme degree, was due
> as much to the *nature of the war* as to that of the federal army:
> from the practical point of view, because it was a people's
> war, an insurrection that the regular army was to crush;
> ideologically, *because it was a religious war.*[22]

---

[19] Meyer, 3:255–56.
[20] Meyer, 3:247.
[21] Spectator, *Los cristeros del volcán de Colima*, 1:83, emphasis ours.
[22] Meyer, *La Cristiada*, 3:249.

In addition to harassing peaceful citizens and robbing them, the third objective was "dishonoring families. There are the fathers of families who ceaselessly mourn the rape of their daughters and even their wives, since nights in places where federal forces were present were nights of diabolical assault."[23]

The fury, sadism, and cruelty of the stories never cease to cause amazement. We have limited ourselves to including only a few to illustrate the situation, but pages and pages could be filled with them, as López Beltrán has done.[24] There was a hatred of the supernatural, of the religious, that had never been seen before — especially when fighting against these values was equivalent to fighting against what the people wanted and loved.

It would be unfair to conclude by recounting only what men did with the things of God without telling what God did with the things of men. And if we understand that history is the study of transcendent facts, we believe it is worth mentioning that certain events in the Cristiada were also transcendent, that is, they went beyond what is normal in wars.

As early as the 1960s, Meyer recorded some astonishing events that, despite their extraordinary nature, are nonetheless true. The interesting thing is that his accounts are based on interviews with the troops *opposed* to the Cristeros, who observed evidence of divine aid in favor of their opponents. Consider only one paragraph:

> The images resisted the sacrilegious arsonists and gunmen (the Christ of Pegueros). The Cristeros received supernatural help in combat: Saint James and the Virgin intervened at their side, without their ever seeing them. Most notably, it was *federal soldiers* who report seeing a woman on a white horse, an invincible rider on a gray horse, alongside the Cristeros or in the clouds. Countless acts of divine providence occurred, such as a rising river that swept away federal troops and that dragged them into the hands of the Cristeros of Santiago Bayacora, or a fog that saved the people of Cocula, Colima, Valparaíso from defeat. The cry of "Long live Christ the King!" made the enemy tremble and paralyzed the horses. The animals showed their respect, bowing to receive the blessing, like the horses of the Cristeros of San Julián, or by refusing to enter a church, like the cow that Colonel Quiñones wanted to slaughter on the altar of Tlacuitapan.[25]

---

[23] Quoted in Meyer, 3:250.
[24] López Beltrán, *La persecución religiosa en México*, 620.
[25] Meyer, *La Cristiada*, 3:311, emphasis ours. Meyer, not much inclined to relate these points, is forced to deal with them in the section entitled "De lo sociológico a lo sobrenatural" (*La Cristiada*, 3:310-15).

*Desecration by federal troops*

*Father Zedano, priest in Zapotlán*

*Turning a church into a mess hall; note hats placed on altar*

*A chapel ransacked by federals*

# 10

# The Blood of a People:

## FOR THE CHURCH AND FOR MEXICO

*When it is not possible to rule from within the government, with
a sense of duty, then one rules from outside, from society, with
the law. And when you can't..., because power doesn't recognize
it? You appeal to force to maintain the law and impose it. And
when there is no force? Compromise and give in? No, no, then
you go...to the catacombs and to the arena, but you don't fall to
your knees, because the idols are in the Capitol.*[1]
                                        —Juan Vázquez de Mella

T HE CRISTERO WAR, AS WE HAVE ALREADY SAID,
was hushed up for years by the government and the church
hierarchy. A controversial silence, certainly, but a silence
nonetheless. The first news received about those who had offered their
lives "for God and for the Fatherland"—as the leaders of the "League"
said—came to light thanks to flyers, pamphlets, and booklets that,
immediately after the conflict, began to circulate under pseudonyms
or clandestinely, as such publications were not allowed. From the start
and ignoring this ban, there were those who denounced the persecutions and martyrdoms perpetrated by the state apparatus. Thanks to
this documentation, in 1988, the heroic virtues of some who had died
from hatred for the Faith could at last be recognized. This was the case
of Jesuit Father Miguel Agustín Pro Juárez, the first Mexican priest
beatified by the Church. Later, several more were raised to the glory
of the altars, but always taking care to ensure one detail: they had not
acted violently in the war years. A prudential reason was offered for
this: the Church, it was said, should not be able to be seen as endorsing
"violent" saints. That's too politically incorrect for our times! Be that as
it may, nearly all of the beatified were "peaceful" priests and lay people.

Not all, however.

First, a clarification: What did it mean for the Church to declare
them "martyrs," and how far does that statement go? It is worth pausing over this question. A "martyr" in the Catholic sphere is someone

---

[1] Quoted in Meyer, *La Cristiada*, 1:382, emphasis ours.

who has been a "witness": a witness of Christ to the point of giving his life for Him. In the Cristero conflict, there were many who offered themselves for God; but there were others whose motives were not always clear. Were they fighting for Christ or for their country? In other words, not all of them died in defense of the faith and due to someone else's hatred of it, at least not directly. Could they also be considered "martyrs" as the Church understands it? We consult the great doctor of the Church, St. Thomas Aquinas:

> "Martyrs" is the same as "witnesses," that is, insofar as by their bodily sufferings they bear witness to the truth unto death. Not just any truth, but the truth that accords with godliness (Titus 1:1), which is revealed to us through Christ. Hence the martyrs of Christ are as it were witnesses of his truth. But it is the truth of the faith which is at stake, which is therefore the cause of all martyrdom. Now, to the truth of faith belongs not only the belief of the heart, but also the external confession, which is manifested not only by words by which the faith is confessed, but also by works by which the possession of that faith is demonstrated, according to the text of James 2:18: *I, by my works, will show you my faith*. In this sense St. Paul says (Titus 1:16) concerning some: "They profess to know God, but they deny him by their deeds." Therefore, the practice of all the virtues, as far as they refer to God, are manifestations of faith, by means of which it is evident to us that God demands these works of us and rewards us for them. And in this respect, they can be the cause of martyrdom. That is why the Church celebrates the martyrdom of St. John the Baptist, who suffered death not for defending the faith, but for rebuking adultery.[2]

There will be, then, among those who died in defense of their country, many *martyrs* who died in defense of the faith, if they ordered that love for earthly things in accordance with divine love. This distinction has not been made — as far as we know — in the beatifications or canonizations of Mexican martyrs, but it would be appropriate.

Here we intend only to provide an overview of those cases of martyrdom we consider most significant; to this end, we will divide them into groups.

### THE MARTYRDOM OF THE FAITHFUL

Martyrdom and persecution, far from what one might think, were never the exclusive preserve of the clergy or nuns. In the history

---

[2] St. Thomas Aquinas, *Summa theologiae*, II-II, Q. 124, art. 5.

of the Cristiada we find testimonies ranging from highly educated intellectuals to unassuming merchants, from bishops to simple priests, because, as Cardoso rightly said, "there was no social class, age, profession, or sex in our Mexican society that did not receive a baptism of honor and glory, because one of their own had offered his blood and his life in homage to Jesus Christ the King."[3]

The counterrevolution, as discussed, happened mainly in the form of guerrilla warfare, and the Catholic guerrillas were forced to live in the mountains. This caused the federal army to carry out again and again the so-called "mass roundups": anyone who was not in the cities was potentially an enemy. We have previously seen reports of the "roundups," among them one of the first in the twentieth century. It was apparently General Amaro, in charge of the federal troops, who, contrary to all war tactics, instead of winning the sympathy of the ranchers and the common people, frightened the peasants with these frequent raids. Inspired by the system invented by General Valeriano Weyler in Cuba and following the advice of the American military attaché, who recommended using the methods employed by their northern brothers in the Philippines, he decided to organize "roundups" as a necessary prelude to raids by the federal troops. The principle was simple: a deadline of a few days or a few weeks was set for civilian populations to evacuate a certain perimeter and take refuge in a series of planned locations. After the deadline, anyone found in the forbidden zone was executed without trial. The soldiers then seized crops and herds, set fire to pastures and forests, and slaughtered with machine guns the livestock that could not be moved by train.

The "roundup" was one of the most common practices of the military commanders. In Jalisco, Michoacán, Colima, Durango and some areas of Guanajuato, Querétaro, Zacatecas, and Guerrero they caused untold suffering for the affected populations. Still, beyond the huge immediate profits they obtained, this method was counterproductive for the federal forces in a certain way, as proved by the testimony of the politician José Guadalupe de Anda:

> More than half of the people who didn't get involved in anything and lived peacefully on their ranch, when the roundup came... left and went to the mountains to join the others

---

[3] Joaquín Cardoso, *Los mártires mexicanos. El martirologio católico de nuestros días* (Buena Prensa, 1958), 364. Cardoso's book, together with Blanco Gil's *El clamor de la sangre*, attempt to provide a local martyrology of the Cristero persecution — and they more than succeed.

[the Cristeros]...and now they are fighting with more deter-
mination, like fierce dogs, seeking revenge, because they
took their women and children away to die of hunger and
disease in the villages....[4]

The people of Colima still have memories of the excesses...
torture in filthy mud baths, forcing victims to eat manure...
cattle theft...loading the fruits of their theft onto trains...a
mercenary attitude toward the rebel movement, demanding
money in exchange for allowing the surrender of some of the
rebels, with which the work of peacekeeping was reduced
to a simple operation of commercial arithmetic and business that should not be disrupted.... Burning ranches and
towns, rapes, massacres, looting, the federal troops behaved
like the big companies, and the brutalities attributed to
General Amaro are indescribable. Generals Jaime Carrillo,
Waldo Garza, and Rivas Guillén used gas against the Cristero chief Domingo Anaya and the civilians of the Rancho
de San Isidro (San Francisco del Rincón, Guanajuato). The
summary executions, the refinements in torture, the venality
of the executioners who enriched themselves with their victims' blood, made Portes Gil see the need to "repress very
harshly the countless and scandalous abuses committed by
the police agents of the Federal District and of the Interior...
unforgivable murders, staged as suicides." "What some bad
military elements and many corrupt authorities are doing
is fomenting more revolt with their abuses and excesses.
Because for every peaceful peasant they hang, many who
remained quiet tilling their land now rise up.... They do not
know the quality of these rough ranchers, who are like the
purebred bulls that become emboldened under punishment."[5]

When it came to eliminating opponents, death by hanging was
widely regarded as furnishing an example to others and as a form of
counterpropaganda—and was sometimes carried too far. As American tourists decried in the press the spectacle of men hanging from
telegraph poles along the railroad between Guadalajara and La Barca,
the Minister of War ordered that when hangings were carried out
they should be done more diplomatically, that is, in places away from
railways and highways.[6] Torture

---

[4] José Guadalupe de Anda, *Los cristeros* (Compañía general editora, 1941), 256,
quoted in Meyer, *La Cristiada*, 1:164–65.
[5] Meyer, *La Cristiada*, 1:167–68.
[6] The photograph that illustrates this episode is very famous: see p. 226.

was practiced systematically, not only to obtain information, but also to prolong torment, to force Catholics to deny their faith, to punish them more effectively, since *death was not enough to frighten them*. To walk on the soles of flayed feet, to be skinned, burned, have bones broken, be quartered alive, hung by the thumbs, strangled, electrocuted, burned piecemeal with a blowtorch, subjected to the torture on the rack, with combat boots, with water through a funnel, with a rope, to be dragged by horses.... All this awaited those who fell into the hands of the federal soldier. No one was forgiven: General Pablo Rodríguez had several civilians hanged in La Tinaja (San Miguel el Alto) to get the catechist Cecilio Gómez, who surrendered to obtain pardon for the other hostages. He was hanged in front of his sons, who were then forced to serve food to the general. In broad daylight, in Colima, in the Independence Garden, Francisco Santillán, 14, and Manuel Hernández, 17, were shot after being tortured. When the federal troops took Zapotitlán, they entered the city and pillaged it, raping the women, desecrating the church, and taking everything. When they surprised the Telcruz camp, they raped the women in the presence of their husbands and children, after which they killed the men and smashed the children against the rocks.[7]

Let's look at some specific examples.

## A SIMPLE MERCHANT: JOSÉ GARCÍA FARFÁN, THE FIRST MARTYR OF THE WAR

The city of Puebla, as Rius Facius,[8] a great historian of the ACJM, points out, had the glory of receiving the first fruits of that generous sacrifice that would redeem Mexico:

> Two days before the suppression of worship throughout the Republic decreed by the episcopate, an old and modest merchant from that city, José García Farfán, a native of Tlaxco, state of Tlaxcala, 66 years old at the time, fell ill. With an energetic character, he was widely known and esteemed in his neighborhood for his frequent acts of charity and his unwavering piety. He had promoted Catholic publications in his small general store. With the purpose of settling some pending matter with the magazine *El Mensajero del Corazón*

---

[7] Meyer, *La Cristiada*, 3:252–53, emphasis ours.
[8] While we were writing these lines (January 2013), this great author of the Cristero counterrevolution and historian of the ACJM died in the state of Mexico. We owe him a great deal, including some information obtained through his daughter, Amalia.

*de Jesús* and to pay a visit to the Virgin of Guadalupe, he was in Mexico City for a few days in June 1926. On his return to Puebla he took with him several signs provided by the League for the Defense of Religious Liberty, to which he had belonged from the beginning.

He put in his shop window those signs that said: "Long live Christ the King! Long live the Virgin of Guadalupe!, Only God does not die!," etc.

On July 28 he went to Communion, as if he foresaw the imminent end of his life. In the middle of the morning, the assistant to General Juan Guadalupe Amaya, who was accompanied by General Daniel Sánchez and another soldier, entered the dry goods store in a car that stopped outside. The assistant ordered Farfán to go out to see General Amaya who was calling him.

"Where is he?"

"In his car, right there at the door."

"Well, tell your general that there is the same distance from your car to my counter as from my counter to your car. And if he wants to speak to me, let him come here, where I am at his command."

Both generals entered the store and showered the old owner with expletives, ordering him to remove the signs from the shop window. José García Farfán refused, because in his house only God and then himself were in charge, and if anyone dared to remove those signs from there, they would have to face the consequences. Amaya took out his pistol and shot the old man at point-blank range, who luckily was not injured, and began to tear the signs from the window.

García Farfán could not resist attacking him and, full of anger, took a glass jar containing pickled chiles and threw it at the soldier. General Sánchez stopped the improvised projectile with his arm and received a wound in the wrist. That was enough for García Farfán to calm down and apologize to his opponent. And while he treated the wounded man with Franciscan humility, Amaya continued to destroy the contents of the shop window. He left, through carelessness, a sign that said: "God does not die!"

García Farfán was arrested by the military and taken to the San Francisco barracks, heedless of neighbors that tried to rescue him and the intervention of a lawyer who filed an appeal for protection that was not taken into account by his captors.

On the morning of July 29, Amaya formed the squad to shoot the elderly Catholic and, moments before giving the order to fire, with merciless sarcasm he told García Farfán:

"Let's see now how Catholics die…"
"Like this," replied the martyr as he pressed the crucifix of his
rosary to his breast, while shouting: "Long live Christ the King!"
The bullets went through his body. But there, on the
window of his shop, a sign proclaimed: "God does not die!"[9]

Common people but with an unwavering faith. They did not fear
those who could kill the body but could not kill the soul.[10]

## YOUNG MARTYRS: TOMÁS DE LA MORA
## AND JOSÉ SÁNCHEZ DEL RÍO

Young people and children were not exempt from armed combat
and although they did not always fight with guns in hand, they were
a valuable help when it came to giving logistical support to the insurgents for Christ the King, which earned them government persecution.

In the days of the boycott, when several cities were paralyzed, the
European press published the following incident taken from a letter:
"Near Guadalajara they arrested *a twelve-year-old boy* because he was
handing out boycott leaflets. To make him say who had given them to
him, after not getting a word out of him, they began to whip him cruelly.
And that was not enough. The brutes waited for his mother to come and
bring him food, and then, in front of her, they began to whip him again.
Amid the boy's broken cries resounded the anguished ones of the mother:
*Don't talk, son, don't talk!* The scene was repeated several times, until seeing
themselves defeated by a child and a woman, *they broke his arms.*"[11]

It was common to hear phrases such as: "I'm going to heaven," "Let's
go for it now," "It's worth it," etc. For, as they said, heaven "was cheap":

> We have to win heaven now that it is cheaply won. Our
> grandparents, how much they would have wanted to earn
> glory like this and now God gives it to us, I'm leaving…. To
> his mother, the young Honorio Lamas, executed in the com-
> pany of his father Manuel, left this consolation: "How easy
> heaven is right now, Mama!"[12]

Statements like this gave courage to those who heard and agreed
with them.

---

[9] Rius Facius, *México Cristero*, 2:69–71.
[10] Meyer added (*La Cristiada*, 3:280n21) that "the government gave great importance to the Rosary: the baker of Valle de Guadalupe was hanged for praying
it, as well as the catechist of San Miguel el Alto."
[11] Constantino Bayle, "Méjico, La era de los mártires," *Razón y fe* 26 (1926/IV):
430, cited by González Morfín, *Murieron por sus creencias*, 26–27, emphasis ours.
[12] Meyer, *La Cristiada*, 3:298–99.

*Tomás de la Mora and the first time he was hanged...*

There were some young people and children who acted as intermediaries between groups of Cristeros. Among them was Tomás de la Mora, a young man of barely 17 years old, whose priest and uncle, Father Miguel de la Mora, had been martyred a few days earlier.

Tomás was a young man with a very pure heart, ardent piety, and great enthusiasm for the cause of Christ. He was 17 years old and studied at the Conciliar Seminary of the Diocese of Colima, where he was a model of piety and dedication.

Tomás, though one of the youngest, was always the mentor to his companions and friends, and even to his older brothers. He wanted to be a saint and one of his most fervent dreams was to die a martyr, as he once wrote to his sister, then living in Mexico City, where public worship had not yet been suspended:[13]

> Colima, May 31, 1926.
>
> Dear Sister,
>
> I'm writing to you in a hurry, because I've just had dinner and because I have to go to a meeting....
>
> Despite being so lukewarm and so unvirtuous... I believe this persecution will make Mexico shine for the heroism of its Martyrs.
>
> You who are close to the Blessed Sacrament, ask Him to give all Catholics courage not to falter. We don't have to ask anymore that the persecution should end, but that in every Catholic there should be a hero, as in the time of Nero.
>
> Do not cease to strive to advance in virtue. For if you do not advance, you will surely go backwards.
>
> The paper has run out.
>
> Your brother.
> Tomás de la Mora[14]

Tomás knew, since he had been taught it from childhood, that whoever died for Christ went to Heaven, as he had discussed more than once with Father Ochoa, chaplain of the Cristeros of Colima:

"Martyrs are Saints, right?"
"Yes," he was answered.
"And if we are killed for Jesus Christ, will we be martyrs?"

---

[13] Let us remember that Colima had suspended worship before the rest of the dioceses due to the abuses committed by the government there.

[14] Spectator, *Los cristeros del volcán de Colima*, 1:320–21, emphasis ours.

"He who gives his life for the cause of Jesus Christ is a
martyr," the priest answered.

"Oh," he said, and his eyes shone with rejoicing, "when
we are hanged for the sake of Christ the King, then we shall
be martyrs, then we shall be holy!"[15]

On August 27, 1927, "Tomasito," as he was called, was arrested,
while playing with his younger brothers, because it had been discovered that he had some dealings with the Cristeros. It is true that
due to his weak health and his age, he had not yet been able to bear
arms, but he was content to support them through his friends, communicate news, and encourage those who came to Colima in search
of food or clothing.

Upon arriving at the house, he exclaimed nobly:

"If you are looking for me," he told the soldiers, "here I am.
I am the only one responsible for everything. Don't seek to
hurt my papa."

When he saw his mother arrive, her face reflecting the
anguish of her anxiety and alarm at what was happening, he
said in a broken voice:

"Mama, they're going to kill me...!" She took him by
the hand and accompanied him in the midst of the soldiers
in the search they made of the house. When he arrived at
his bedside, he took his religious medal and hung it on his
chest. Tomás was a boy of unwavering piety. His fervent
devotion had earned him the rank of prefect in the Marian
Congregation.

He was then taken to the seminary building where he
had been an exemplary student and which had been com-
mandeered by the oppressors and turned into barracks. The
general was there, Flores, gloating in his post as chief. They
led him to into his presence and the following dialogue
ensued between the general and the Acejotaemero:

"You're a little boy," says the soldier, "you're not capable of
anything. You have to tell us who is advising you."

"Don't say," replied Tomás de la Mora, "that I am a child,
because I know very well what I am doing: no one advises me."

"Look," he replied, "if you tell us what you know about
who are those committed to the Cristeros, we will spare
your life, we will free you."

"It will be in vain," replied Thomas with holy resignation,
"for if I am released today, tomorrow I shall continue to work

---

[15] Spectator, 1:321.

and fight for Christ in union with my companions: to fight for religious liberty is the duty of every true Catholic.

"You're a snot-nosed kid, you don't know what death is," said the general irritably. "Tell us what we ask you, *now*."

"If you, General, say that I don't know what death is because I haven't died, you don't know either, because you've never died either."[16]

The last moments of life were recounted by a spectator who was not far away:

"Don't waste your time, boy."

"Don't you lose your time, General," the holy young man replied. "I have already told you that I will say nothing. I am willing to suffer death rather than be a traitor to the cause of those who fight for Christ. I die gladly. I love my religion, and I offer my life for it. You don't know what religion is, and that is why you persecute it. But I know it and I love it. If you knew it, you would love it too."

"Think carefully about what you say."

"I've already thought about everything..."

"Well," General Flores finished, "since you reject everything, I will have you hanged this very night."

"Very well," replies Tomás de la Mora, "just give me an hour to prepare for death..."

Only God knows what the hero prayed and the feelings of his heart. But the struggle did not cease. Several times, when he was on his knees, one of the officers approached him to make more proposals in the General's name. But he rejected them immediately, saying:

"Be so kind as to leave me. Don't waste my time. Don't you see that I have very little life left? Do me the favor of retiring and leaving me alone. *I am preparing myself for death*."

It was already close to midnight when he was taken out of the barracks. The soldiers who drove were silent, they did not speak a word; they were sleepy and annoyed. Tomás, however, was happy, his soul alert: it was the hour of his triumph. It was the great day so longed for, which he had so begged God for....

"Why are you all so quiet?" he said to the soldiers. "Say something. *It's not me who's going to die!*"...

At last they came to the Galván causeway, or Piedra Lisa, as it is more commonly called by the town. At the

---

[16] Rius Facius, *México Cristero*, 2:306–8.

foot of one of the trees, the escort halted. This tree was located where Zaragoza Street ended on the eastern side of the road.[17]

When they reached the Galván road, the tragic procession stopped and hung the rope from a tree, with a noose at one end.

"Put it on!" one of the executioners ordered his victim.

Tomás, almost smiling, with his characteristic joviality, replied: *I don't know how to do it: it's the first time I've been hanged. Tell me how.*

The executioner roughly passed the rope around his neck and Tomás, with the strength of his undefeated reason and his absolute faith, cried: "Long live Christ the King! Long live Holy Mary of Guadalupe!"

Like an ominous pendulum, his slender form swung back and forth in the shadows of the night.

The next day, Sunday, the body of the martyr was collected by his parents and deposited in his home, through which the people processed, restraining their helpless rage and bearing witness to their admiration for another of the Cristero martyrs.[18]

## José Sánchez del Río

As a result of the endless defeats they suffered, the Callistas took revenge on all those who had the misfortune to fall into their hands. Such was the case, known throughout the civilized world, of the boy José Sánchez del Río, who belonged to the vanguard of the Local Group of the ACJM of Sahuayo, Michoacán. Being only 13 years old when he joined the Cristero forces, he was accepted as an adjutant and not as a soldier because of his tender age.[19]

---

[17] Spectator, *Los cristeros del volcán de Colima*, 1:324–26, emphasis ours. It was at his request that he was hanged from that tree. "He stopped in front of a historic tree, revered by liberals as a kind of sacred place. Under him, on a stone that is still preserved, Benito Juárez had once sat to rest, the very embodiment of Mexican liberalism and one of the Church's most bitter enemies. In that precise place that Tomasito stopped, saying to the soldiers: 'This is a place of ignominy. Here hang me so that this place of curse may be changed into a blessing.' Then a soldier approached him to put the noose around his neck. 'Don't touch me,' Tomás told him, 'because it stains me.' 'Why?' the soldier asked. 'Because you are soldiers of the devil and we are of Christ the King.'" Sáenz, *La nave y las tempestades*, 442.

[18] Rius Facius, *México Cristero*, 2:306–9.

[19] He was to carry the Cristeros flag.

In a battle fought near Cotija, Mich., on February 5, 1928, when his commander's horse was killed, he gave him his horse, saying:

"My general, here is my horse. Save yourself even if they kill me. I am not needed, but you are."

And joining action to speech, he took a rifle and began to shoot at the enemy before him until he ran out of bullets. Then he was captured and taken to the enemy leader, whom he faced and said:

"They caught me because I ran out of ammunition, but I didn't give up."

Such audacity in a child surprised the soldier, who wanted to flatter him to join the Revolution and include him in the list of his soldiers. However, when he was asked, José protested:

"I'm not a Callista," he said, "I'm a prisoner."

From Cotija he wrote to his mother this simple epistle:

"Mama: They have already arrested me, and they are going to kill me, I am happy. All I regret is that you will grieve. Don't cry, we'll see each other in heaven. José, killed for Christ the King."

From Jiquilpan he was transferred to his hometown, Sahuayo, and his father, learning what was happening, returned from exile and offered as much money as he could collect in exchange for José's freedom. But José, imprisoned in the parish church used by the federal troops as a barracks, did not waste any opportunity to rebuke his jailers for the irreverence they committed in desecrating the church and, on one occasion, he hanged two fine fighting cocks, owned by the local congressman who used the sacristy as a pen. At 11 p.m. on February 10, that is, five days after his arrest, without a trial to condemn him, they cut off the soles of his feet and took him barefoot to the village cemetery. Throughout the ordeal, José was shouting and cheering Christ the King and the Virgin of Guadalupe. One of his executioners, Rafael Gil Martínez, asked him:

"What do you want us to tell your parents?"

And José, with great effort, said once more:

"Long live Christ the King, and we will see each other in heaven!"

These were his last words. The dagger and a shot to the temple did the rest.[20]

---

[20] José Sánchez del Río was beatified along with eleven other Mexican martyrs

The blood of these young martyrs would be the seed of new Christians for Mexico.

## WOMEN: HUMILIATION AND RAPE

There are those who maintain that the war against the Cristero revolution could not have taken place without the help of Mexican women. We think they are right. Women, as discussed above, had a preeminent role in communications, ammunition transport, and logistical tasks. All of which was done in the utmost secrecy—in fact, so much was concealed that even after the armed conflict, few on the enemy side knew of the existence of organized women's groups. In any case, the supporting roles they played meant that they, too, were not exempt from punishment.

There are numerous examples we could list, but a few will suffice.[21] Zenaida Llerenas, a young militant from Colima who provided the Cristeros with food, medicine, and supplies, fell into an ambush and was locked up in the local jail:

> Her youth and beauty from the first moment provoked the low instincts of her jailers, who tore her clothes. She was subjected to uninterrupted interrogation. They wanted to know what the mechanism of her organization was, the names of her superiors, their meeting places, but she kept an obstinate silence. The young girl pressed her lips tightly together and only the color of her face and the brightness of her eyes showed her feelings of indignation, shame, or terror.
>
> "Your pride," said the general, "is that you are a virgin, but if you insist on your silence I will hand you over to the soldiers at this very moment."
>
> The men applauded the proposal with foul comments and loud laughter. The young woman muttered a prayer, raising her eyes to heaven, and nodded no, to the repeated question of whether she was willing to betray her own.
>
> Then the commander, full of anger, cried out to his soldiers:
>
> "Take her! She's yours."
>
> And that poor girl perished, a victim of the sadism of her executioners.[22]

---

in 2005 and canonized in 2016.

[21] For further reading on this, consult the book by Reynoso de Alba, *La actuación de la mujer*, 65–82.

[22] Luis Rivero del Val, *Entre las patas de los caballos* (JUS, 1953), quoted by Rius Facius, *México Cristero*, 2:262.

Father Ochoa, always discreetly guarding the women's names, relates what happened in Colima in this way: in Colima, General Ávila Camacho was one of the main chiefs

> under whose command there were a great multitude of Callistas cursing with infernal language. The viciousness of those soldiers was completely diabolical. Many families who were taking refuge in the ravines fell into the clutches of the impious soldiery, who unleashed their degenerate and bestial fury against them. In a cave where persecuted families took refuge, several people were found by soldiers, and in a horror that beggars belief, women were raped in front of their husbands and children. The men were murdered. Two little girls wept in terror as they embraced their parents; the soldiers killed them by smashing them against the cave walls.[23]

Young boys and girls were willing to give everything for Christ. They did not fear death. On the contrary, there were even cases when they joked about it. In Colima, for example, the young Francisco Santillán and Manuel Hernández were arrested in 1928 in that city on charges of supporting the Cristeros. The day after their arrest, on June 25, they were summarily executed along with some young women of the Women's Brigades of Saint Joan of Arc:

> Manuel and Francisco were placed behind the cathedral, and next to them Candelaria and María, who had Benedicto's corpse and the supplies in front of them. People crowded to watch this sinister spectacle.
> "Look," Francisco remarked to his companion with manifest joy, "we are going to die at the feet of the Virgin of Guadalupe. We are under the window where, inside, her image is."
> Manuel smiled and asked the firing squad for permission to speak, but his request was denied three times. Then he told Francisco to take off his hat:
> "In a few moments we will be in the presence of God, we must not die with our heads covered."
> With painful effort, Francisco obeyed and, as he did, a thick stream of blood flowed from the wounds on his temple and neck. He crossed himself and was imitated by Manuel. When the executioners aimed at their chests, he shouted:

---

[23] Spectator, *Los cristeros del volcán de Colima*, 1:304.

"Long live Christ the King!"
Francis seconded this oath and prayer:
"And Holy Mary of Guadalupe!"[24]

Another case was that of Carmen Robles Ibarra, murdered in
the state of Zacatecas. Carmen had an oratory in her house in Huejuquilla where the Blessed Sacrament was kept after the closure of
the churches. When the federal soldiers arrived in the city, they burst
in with blows and blasphemies, shooting anyone who claimed to be
a Catholic. Carmen, anticipating what might happen, consumed the
consecrated hosts to avoid any kind of desecration. When they arrived
at her home, the soldiers began to loot the house and took Carmen
prisoner because they considered her the head of the Catholic women.
Dragging her into the street, they threw her to the ground with all
kinds of insults. Then they tore off her clothes and raped her while
mocking her purity.

They arrested Carmen and several young ladies, and after harassing and beating them, threw a rope around their necks and dragged
them on foot to San Antonio. Arriving there, to provoke them, they
undressed the statue of Christ the Prisoner; and a soldier, putting
on the statue's clothes, went out into the street as if in procession
so that they could "adore Christ the King." Then, they burned the
statue and converted the tabernacle into a toilet.

Carmen, in fact, was the president of the People's Union: a young
lady educated in moral and religious matters. Her days on earth soon
came to an end:

> In the middle of a dark night in Mezquitic, in a deep ravine,
> a girl was riding a donkey, and a soldier was pulling the
> animal's saddle, while another was beating the donkey with
> sticks. The next girl came, and so on. It is not known if she
> was one of the prisoners. A girl heard one of the soldiers
> say, "How barbaric! Why did you throw dirt in the woman's
> mouth? The bitch didn't want to die."[25]

### INTELLECTUALS AND LEADERS: ANACLETO GONZÁLEZ FLORES

Anacleto González Flores was born in Tepatitlán, Jalisco, a small
town very close to Guadalajara, on July 13, 1888. After spending five
years at the Seminary of San Juan de los Lagos, he decided that his

[24] Rius Facius, *México Cristero*, 2:264.
[25] Reynoso del Alba, *La actuación de la mujer*, 74.

vocation would not be the altar — at least, not the altar for perpetuating Christ's sacrifice. After leaving the seminary he did not let those years of preparation go to waste and took advantage of his humanist education to become a lawyer. In the years that followed, he would take on various roles: catechist, literature professor, journalist, writer, politician, guild leader, etc. It was, without a doubt, in his role as an orator where he stood out the most, being a passionate and skilled orator.

In 1925, and once the conflicts had begun, he moved to Guadalajara and assumed the leadership of the People's Union at the same time as that of the ACJM and the League, as mentioned above. As a Catholic leader, he left a unique mark on the ranks of the people of Jalisco, impressions that were reflected in writing in the magazine *Gladium* that he directed and that earned him the award from Pope Benedict XV, the *Pro Ecclesia et Pontifice* Cross.

He was one of the main organizers of the boycott against the government that almost paralyzed Guadalajara. Initially a supporter of peaceful resistance, some saw him as a "Mexican Gandhi." Nothing could be further from the truth. His peaceful fight was the beginning of the uprising and González Flores was simply following the legitimate path to combat government oppression: from peaceful struggle to armed struggle (in fact, when he had to bear arms, he did so without scruples).

During the armed conflict he was named First Civil Head of Jalisco, which made him an attractive target for the police. This is not the place to eulogize González Flores,[26] but we have no hesitation in saying that he was the soul of the Cristero uprising in the state of Jalisco. During the most difficult times, he had to hide in various houses, until it was the turn of the home of the brothers Jorge and Ramón Vargas González. Luis Padilla Gómez, another of his comrades,[27] was also there.

At three o'clock in the morning of April 1, 1927, the Callista soldiers surrounded the house at 405 Mezquitán Street. The secret police jumped down from the roof while others knocked on the door,

---

[26] The bibliography regarding his life is extensive. We believe that one of the best works is that of Alfredo Sáenz, *Anacleto González Flores y la Epopeya Cristera* (APC, 2002). Among extant works of his, there are more than seven or eight books in his own handwriting, all referring to the political-religious question of his convulsed Mexico.

[27] We had the joy of being in that very house, in an exciting interview with the Vargas's sister, who was just 11 years old at the time of the events but remembered special details despite her age.

raided it and arrested the four mentioned above, taking them to the "Colorado Barracks" where they were tortured.

One of his best biographers describes the succeeding events:

> When the men arrived at their destination, the interrogation began immediately. What they were looking for was for Anacleto to admit his role in the Cristero struggle and denounce those who were part of the armed movement in Jalisco. They also wanted him to reveal the place where Bishop Orozco y Jiménez was hiding.... He therefore fully acknowledged his role in the movement within the city but said nothing about his comrades or the whereabouts of the prelate....
>
> "Tell us, miserable fanatic, where is Orozco y Jiménez hiding?"
>
> "I don't know."
>
> The blade tore his feet apart. In the words of Gómez Robledo, "the man who lived by his words would die by his silence."
>
> "Tell us, who are the leaders of that damned League that intends to overthrow our leader and lord General Calles?"
>
> "There is only one Lord of heaven and earth. I don't know what you are asking me..."
>
> After taking him down, they delivered a powerful blow to his shoulder with the butt of a rifle. With his mouth dripping with blood from the blows, he began to exhort them with that eloquence of his, so vibrant and passionate.... The torture was suspended. A "summary court-martial" was then simulated, which sentenced the prisoners to the death penalty.[28]

On hearing the sentence, Anacleto replied with these bold words:

> "I will say only one thing, and that is: I have worked with all my strength to defend the cause of Jesus Christ and his Church. You will kill me but know that the cause will not die with me."
>
> The soldiers separated Florencio Vargas González from those sentenced, because they believed, erroneously, that he had not yet reached the age of majority.
>
> Anacleto was bleeding profusely and the general ordered that the execution squad be formed, but he asked that the Vargas brothers and Luis Padilla be shot first so that he could comfort them until the last moment.
>
> Overcoming his physical pains, he exhorted his martyr brothers to suffer for their eternal liberation with fortitude,

---

[28] Sáenz, *La nave y las tempestades*, 314–15.

and when Luis expressed his desire to confess, Anacleto replied:

> "No, brother, it is no longer time to go to confession, but to ask for forgiveness and to forgive. It is a Father, and not a Judge, who awaits you. Your very blood will purify you."
>
> The four of them prayed, aloud, the Act of Contrition.
>
> As soon as they had finished doing so, Jorge and Ramón Vargas González were shot.[29]

Anacleto's words at the time of his death were widely known and strengthened the spirits of those who were in the fight:

> General, I forgive you from my heart. Very soon we will see each other before the divine tribunal. The same Judge who is going to judge me will be your Judge, and then you will have in me an intercessor with God.... You will kill me but know that the cause will not die with me. Many are behind me ready to defend it to the point of martyrdom. I am leaving, but with the certainty that I will soon see, from Heaven, the triumph of Religion and of my country.... For the second time let the Americas hear this holy cry: I die, but God does not die![30]

### PRIESTS AND RELIGIOUS: MATEO CORREA MAGALLANES, RODRIGO AGUILAR ALEMÁN, MIGUEL AGUSTÍN PRO

The Mexican Revolution, as we have seen, had an intensely anticlerical component and one of the favorite targets were the priests, who were accused of being the "ideologues" of the people. To be part of the clergy in those times was risky and the honor that had once been recognized by the state changed now into the honor of martyrdom. It meant embracing the priesthood as one would embrace the most gruesome cross, and seminarians were aware of this, as well as those in charge of their formation. This is demonstrated in the speech Bishop Lara gave to some young seminarians four years before the beginning of the Cristero War:

> What can I offer them but a prospect of prolonged sorrows and privations, of toil and suffering, of persecution and martyrdom? What is the Catholic priest today in the face of the

---

[29] Rius Facius, *México Cristero*, 2:183–84, emphasis ours.
[30] Joaquín Blanco Gil, *El clamor de la sangre*, 138. This "second life" of the cry "God does not die!" harked back to the martyrdom and the last words of the Catholic president of Ecuador Gabriel García Moreno, uttered 50 years earlier, when he was assassinated by Freemasons on August 6, 1875.

> iniquitous laws that govern us if not an outlaw from whom
> the most sacred rights of citizenship are taken away?... Have
> we not seen... the Catholic priests, and only them, slapped
> and mocked by any scoundrel who carried a carbine?... In
> cages like pigs... shot at like dogs, by the side of the road?
> Well, that is the prospect that awaits you... the humiliation,
> sacrifice, death, and ignominy of the Cross. I don't want to,
> I must not deceive you.[31]

With great realism and without mincing words, this great pastor of
the Mexican episcopate dotted the i's and crossed the t's. It wasn't easy
to be a priest in those times. The greatest persecution had just begun
and there were still more to come in a century that would make the
most Catholic martyrs of any century in the history of the Church.[32]

The hierarchy of the Church, faced with the first conflicts, tried
to call them only "regrettable accidents,"[33] but little by little, it had
to change its stance in the face of the regularity of the martyrdoms.
In fact, of the 4,593 priests in Mexico in 1925, at the end of the war
several hundred of them had been killed.[34]

Here are a few examples to illustrate.

*Father Mateo Correa Magallanes, martyred for keeping the seal of confession*

Father Mateo Correa Magallanes was born in Tepechitlán, Zacatecas, on July 23, 1866. After entering the seminary and completing
the relevant studies, he was ordained a priest and eventually became
parish priest of Valparaíso where he exercised his ministry.

When the persecution began, he, like numerous priests, did not
want to abandon his flock; he had to take refuge in the hacienda
of San José de Sauceda. He was there when on January 30, 1927, a
rancher went to ask for confession for his mother, who was seriously
ill. Ignoring the danger he risked when leaving the hideout, he communicated his desire to José María Miranda, owner of the hacienda,

---

[31] Lara y Torres, "Speech on the Reconstruction of the Fatherland," delivered
October 30, 1922, in *Documents for History*, 54–55, quoted by Meyer, *La Cristiada*, 2:123.

[32] The first priest martyred and later canonized was Fr. Luis Batis Sainz, executed on August 15, 1926.

[33] Meyer, *La Cristiada*, 2:383.

[34] The number of those martyred, according to Rius Facius (*México Cristero*,
2:309), amounts to two hundred, while Meyer (*La Cristiada*, 1:49) specifies
one hundred and twenty-five, divided as follows: "59 from the archdiocese of
Guadalajara, 35 in Jalisco, 6 in Zacatecas and 18 in Guanajuato, diocese of León,
and 7 from the small diocese of Colima."

who offered to accompany him. When they started down the road and reached an old warehouse in San Pedro, they met Major Contreras who had been brooding over a defeat by the Cristero troops.

Someone identified the casual passers-by and after being arrested they were transferred to the town of Fresnillo, Zacatecas, where they were locked in the prison infirmary. Their time had come.

> On the night of February 5, Father Correa was taken out of his prison, bade farewell to his friend José María Miranda, and blessed his fellow inmates. Brought into the presence of General Eulogio Ortiz, the latter said to him:
> "First you are going to confess those rebellious bandits you see there and who are going to be shot immediately, then we will see what we'll do with you."
> The good priest confessed and encouraged those brave Catholics to die; they had been taken prisoner during armed fighting in defense of their faith.
> "Now," said the soldier to the priest, "you are going to reveal to me what those bandits have just told you."
> "I never will," the parish priest replied indignantly.
> "What do you mean, never?," replied the general, irritated. "I'm going to order you to be shot right away."
> "You can do it," concluded the martyr, "but don't forget that a priest must keep the secret of confession. I am willing to die."
> Hours later, at the beginning of February 6, 1927, between four and five in the morning, he was taken out of his prison in a car without the people realizing and, less than a mile away from the cemetery, they killed him.
> Thus he died, a martyr for the seal of confession — that elderly priest who had been decorated, on July 17, 1926, with the ACJM badge by the local chapter of Valparaíso.[35]

*Father Rodrigo Aguilar Alemán, killed for not shouting "Long Live Calles"*

Father Aguilar was serving in 1927 as interim chaplain of the Union chapter of Tula, Jalisco. Faced with persecution, he had been forced to leave the parish church to move to a humble ranch in the town of Ejutla from where he attended to his faithful, administered the sacraments, and even directed the preaching of spiritual exercises. Meanwhile, the Cristero troops had achieved important victories in Jalisco, which had been alarming the government.

President Calles had given orders to mobilize a powerful convoy

---

[35] Meyer, 1:150–52. Father Correa was canonized along with twenty-four other Mexican martyrs by John Paul II on May 21, 2000.

under the command of the ferocious General Juan B. Izaguirre to
finish pulverizing the insurgents. It was thus that on October 27 of
that year, the eve of the newly-instituted feast of Christ the King,
several soldiers and farmers entered the city of Ejutla and began to
commit sacrileges: they burned images of saints and sacred vestments,
drank from the chalice and ate the consecrated hosts from a cibo-
rium, making a parody of the Mass. Since General Izaguirre was a
government representative, he arrogated to himself the right to do
whatever he wanted: "He raided homes, his troops assaulted many
women and took prisoner the priest Aguilar, whom he took to the
town square; in the presence of all the people, he offered freedom if
he would shout 'Long live Calles!,'"[36] as Rius Facius recounts.

> The priest, powerless to resist, was taken to the local jail,
> where he spent the night. The next day, the feast of Christ the
> King, they took him out of prison at dawn and brought him
> to the foot of a thick mango tree, which is still preserved in
> the square of Ejutla. Then they threw a rope over one of the
> larger branches and put it around the priest's neck. A soldier,
> wanting to test the priest's courage, asked him haughtily:
> "Who lives?," to which the Father replied:
> "Christ the King and Holy Mary of Guadalupe!"
> Then they pulled the rope, and the priest was hung. After
> a little while they took him down and with annoyance the
> soldier repeated his question:
> "Who lives?," to which the priest, without hesitation,
> exclaimed:
> "Christ the King and Holy Mary of Guadalupe!"
> Then the rope was pulled tightly, and the priest was left
> hanging again. It was taken down again, and for the third
> time the insolent soldier asked him:
> "Who lives?"
> The saint, with his dying breath, cried out for the last time:
> "Long live Christ the King and Holy Mary of Guadalupe!"
> He was strung up again, and his soul flew to heaven.[37]

---

[36] Meyer, 1:284.
[37] Sáenz, *La nave y las tempestades*, 427–28. Meyer, in his observations, has
questioned the last moments of the martyr. Almost in the same way as Father
Sáenz narrates them are they found on the official Vatican website: www.vatican.
va/news_services/liturgy/saints/ns_lit_doc_20000521_aguilar-aleman_sp.html.
For our part, we have not accessed the records of his canonization.

*Father Miguel Agustín Pro*

The dynamic father Miguel Agustín Pro Juárez[38] was born on January 13, 1891, in Guadalupe, Zacatecas. When he reached adolescence, his great love for his neighbor, especially for the manual workers, made him visit the miners who worked for his father and, ultimately, he entered the Society of Jesus, on August 10, 1911, at the age of twenty. Once in religious life and as a result of the persecution that had already begun, he and his companions had to leave Mexico and go into exile. After a few months in Baja California del Norte, they embarked for Granada (Spain) where they continued their studies. He also had the joy of continuing his studies in Belgium, where he received priestly ordination in August 1925.

His eagerness to work with laborers and the neediest was enormous, but his poor health made his superiors send him to Mexico, thinking that he did not have much longer to live.

From then on his priestly life comprised a treasure-trove of anecdotes that would be difficult to summarize. The idea was for him to rest, but he remained extremely active. In the biographies that can be consulted there are endless daring adventures and laughter. He was filled with a spirit both combative and joyful: living incognito in order to exercise his ministry, Father Pro was forced to go around as an ice cream maker, nurse, postal delivery man, rancher, and playboy (on more than one occasion being arm in arm with a woman saved his life).

His function in the Federal District was to comfort and administer the sacraments to those who were deprived of them because of the suspension of worship. Father Pro knew the danger he was in, but this did not intimidate him. On the contrary, every day he asked for and encouraged others to ask for the crown of martyrdom, to the point that he offered his life for the conversion of President Calles. Whenever he heard that a priest or layman had been martyred, he saw a missed opportunity and lamented, saying jokingly: "It seems

---

[38] There is a huge bibliography for Fr. Miguel Agustín Pro Juárez, whose case is one of the most well-documented, not only because of the international significance that was given to it in the media, but also because of the work of dissemination carried out by the Jesuits, as Fr. Cardoso recounts (*Los mártires mexicanos*, 363): "Your brothers in religion, we have believed it an urgent duty to do everything in our power for the glorification of that brother of ours whom we loved so much in life." The best biographies we have consulted on Fr. Pro are by two Jesuits: Antonio Dragón, *El Padre Pro* (Editorial Vasca, 1934) and Rafael Ramírez Torres, *Miguel Agustín Pro* (Tradición, 1976). We include here a summary of Fr. Pro's last moments.

that this treat was not meant for Miguel," meaning that it was not yet his time to die in this way.

Meanwhile, in some Catholic circles, there was talk of plotting Calles's assassination. Opinion was divided because not everyone saw it as morally licit or practically viable. At that time, moreover, the presidential succession of Calles to Obregón (shortly before this re-elected for 1928–1932) was about to take place. On November 13, 1927, in the Federal District, a group of determined Catholics, according to plans made by the League, carried out an attack on the car in which the future president was traveling. The attack failed and the vehicle in which the Catholics were traveling was seized, but one of the main masterminds and perpetrators attempted to create the perfect alibi. It was Segura Vilchis, who, dressed very correctly, managed to approach General Obregón brazenly and asked him:

> "What's the matter, General?"
> "An attack by the fanatics," he replied, still dazed by the noise.
> "What these clerics do is unspeakable," added the supposed rescuer. "Please accept my protest, General. Here is my card in case I can provide you with any service.[39]

The card read: *Luis Segura Vilchis, engineer*. He was none other than the ringleader of the attack. He had personally launched the bombs while his colleagues were shooting with pistols. Segura Vilchis knew that Obregón was great at remembering faces, so by being present to him at the moment he would achieve the best alibi in case of a summons.

While this was happening, the Pro brothers, completely oblivious to the situation, were enjoying a family meal in a house in the Colonia Anáhuac.

The engineer Luis Segura Vilchis was affiliated with the League in a unit called "direct action" while he was an employee of the Light and Power Company, and was therefore knowledgeable about chemistry and mechanics. The League had planned Obregón's death on other occasions that had not yet succeeded. Perhaps for this reason, and perhaps also tired of the indecisiveness, Segura Vilchis did not hesitate to carry out the attack.

How did they get to the Pro brothers? Around that time, Humberto, the priest's brother, had been appointed regional head of the

---

[39] Cardoso, *Los mártires mexicanos*, 373. Regarding this book, Meyer has observed that the meeting did not take place in the street, but in the bullring where Obregón went after the attack.

League in Mexico City, and the Essex car used in the attack was registered under his pseudonym (Daniel García).

When investigations began and the real ownership of the car was realized, Father Pro and his brothers were immediately implicated as the perpetrators of the failed assassination. This was a major coup for the police, as the federal forces had for some time been seeking out a cleric to accuse of "seditious" activity. Meanwhile Segura Vilchis, although initially detained, had been released because of his cunning alibi, but when he learned of the investigations, he asked for a new audience with the general Roberto Cruz and confessed everything to exonerate the innocent. It was too late.

The Pro brothers were arrested at the house of Señora Valdés, Federal District, where they were hiding. Someone, as was usual in these cases, had denounced them. At three o'clock in the morning on Friday, November 18, 1927, the barking of some dogs woke up the occupants of the house. Several agents, followed by a group of about twenty soldiers, banged on the street door while others jumped over the rooftops until they reached the door of the room where the Pro brothers slept.

"Don't move!" shouted the agents.

Father Pro, without being intimidated, turned to his brothers, and said to them: "Repent of your sins, as if you were in the presence of God. I'm going to give the absolution: *Ego vos absolvo a peccatis vestris, in nomine Patris et Filii et Spiritus Sancti. Amen.* Let us offer our lives to God for religious freedom in Mexico and make the offering together, so that the Lord may accept them together."

And turning to Basail, the chief of the agents, he said to him:

"This lady—Señora Valdés—is not to blame. Leave her alone and do with us what you will."

He went to a cupboard, from which he took a crucifix and a rosary. He was ready. Basail showed some humanity and advised Pro that he should put on his coat, because it was very cold. It was November and early in the morning, but the padre answered quite naturally:

"I don't have a coat. Yesterday I found someone more impoverished than I was, and I gave it to him."

Then Señora Valdés took a cotton blanket from a bed and threw it over him. Immediately, the landlady and the servants knelt down. They were sure that they had had a saint in their house and wanted to pay tribute to him, while the Pros exclaimed in chorus:

"Long live Christ the King! Long live the Virgin of Guadalupe!"

And the entourage departed for the Inspector's office.[40]

Once arrested, all kinds of influential people were mobilized so that the worst would not happen. The Minister of Argentina, Manuel Malbrán (some name Eduardo Labettgle), had once had the priest in his home and had influence over General Calles. When he learned that his friend the priest was in prison, he went to the President, who replied that nothing could be done because it was a matter of "high politics." Even so, he managed to get a false promise that nothing serious would happen to the Pros, other than exile.

On the morning of November 23, 1927, it was said that the Pro brothers were to be committed to the judicial authorities to be examined in a formal trial. None of this was done.

A lawyer, Luis E. MacGregor, completely oblivious to the bloody plot, learned that everything was ready for the execution by firing squad, because near the Inspector's office he saw empty ambulances arrive to transport the future corpses. In a fit of righteous indignation, he went to the First Supernumerary District Court, headed by Julio López Masse:

> "I've come to file a plea for an injunction for the Pro brothers," MacGregor told Mariano Azuela.
> "Have you drafted your plea, counselor?" Azuela asked.[41]

MacGregor did not even know the full names of the alleged victims. From a newspaper of that same day, he obtained the necessary data and filed the injunction. It was immediately admitted, and the judge ordered the provisional suspension, instructing the court clerk, Fausto Pérez Nieto, to run to the Inspectorate to notify Roberto Cruz of his finding. Both went to the scene of the drama, but found that the gatekeepers, so solicitous to admit spectators who wanted to witness the executions, delayed the clerk's entrance. When, at last, the attorney MacGregor managed to enter with Pérez Nieto, the deed was already done.

Those moments had been intensely tragic for the detainees. On their knees, Father Pro and his brother Roberto had prayed fervently. In one of the last prayers, the priest addressed God and prayed for

---

[40] Cardoso, 380–81.

[41] With respect to the details of the appeal for protection, see the enlightening chapter by Raúl González Schmal, "Un amparo insólito y el conflicto religioso de 1926-1927," in Manuel González Oropeza and Eduardo Ferrer Mac-Gregor, eds., *El juicio de Amparo a 160 años de la primera sentencia* (Universidad Nacional Autónoma de México, 2011), 559–86.

General Calles. Suddenly, at exactly twenty minutes past ten in the morning, Lieutenant Colonel Mazcorro appeared in the cell and ordered Father Miguel to follow him. Clinging to a hope that only he retained, Roberto told his older brother:

"We'll see you outside, Miguel. They are going to release us."
The priest, smiling as usual, shook his hand and said:
"No, Roberto, we'll see you in heaven. They're going to shoot me," and left.

After taking him out of his cell, Detective Quintana approached Father Miguel and whispered in his ear: "Father, forgive me."

With the greatest naturalness in the world, Pro bowed his head, as if he were in confession, and answered: "Not only do I forgive you, brother, but I thank you."

Major Torres, head of the execution squad, asked the priest what his last wish was, to which he replied laconically: "To pray."

He knelt down, bowed his head as he crossed himself, slowly kissed the small crucifix he carried in one hand and the rosary he carried in the other, and rising he cried out loudly: "Long live Christ the King!"

A volley of bullets sealed the triumphant words. It was 10:30 on the morning of November 23, 1927.

## AN EXEMPLARY BISHOP: MGR. FRANCISCO OROZCO Y JIMÉNEZ

From among the bishops,[42] there were no martyrs strictly speaking, but there were several candidates for martyrdom. Among those who lived at the time of the Cristiada, some, after the exile decreed by the government, had chosen the United States or Rome, while a few, with the toleration of the local governments, had hidden in cities. Only two remained on the battlefield comforting and encouraging the Cristeros, even if they did not agree with the armed uprising: Mgr. Velasco, bishop of Colima and Mgr. Orozco y Jiménez, bishop of Guadalajara. We will discuss only the second because his was an exemplary case.

Born in Zamora, Michoacán, on November 19, 1864, and after a privileged education in Rome at a minor seminary with twelve other boys, Francisco Orozco y Jiménez, showed promise of a bright future.

---

[42] We make use here of some sections of Fidel González Fernández's book, *Sangre y corazón de un pueblo. Historia de la persecución anticatólica en México y sus mártires*, 2 vols. (Arzobispado de Guadalajara, 2008). Both volumes were then summarized by Miguel Romano Gómez, *Titanes de la Evangelización* (Arquidiócesis de Guadalajara, 2012).

The four years studying the humanities were a great joy for the young seminarian. After completing his studies in theology, he was ordained a priest in 1888. From there he returned to Mexico and then, under the protective wing of Don Antonio Plancarte y Labastida, he became a professor of various subjects and vice-rector of the Conciliar Seminary of Mexico City. There he taught, among other subjects, Latin, Hebrew, History, Hermeneutics, Philosophy and Theology.

Seeing his excellent leadership skills and the training he had received since childhood, the pope did not hesitate to appoint him bishop of Chiapas, at the age of thirty-eight. There he tried to make up for what Fray Bartolomé de las Casas had neglected centuries before in evangelizing the Indians; this caused some conflicts with the local authorities who accused him of conspiring with the natives against the government. He spent ten years in southern Mexico, and then went to the archdiocese of Guadalajara, where he took possession of the diocese in February 1913.

There he began his great work. First he divided the enormous diocese into twenty-five *foranías* (tributary districts), which resembled the current post-conciliar deaneries (subzones for better administration). The direction of the "Center for Catholic Social Studies," the Association of Catholic Ladies, the "Clothing Bank for the Poor," visits throughout the diocese, pastoral letters, edicts, are just some of the activities that can be mentioned.

Undoubtedly, what most caught the government's attention about the young archbishop was his courageous stance on the proclamation of Christ as King of Mexico, which took place on January 11, 1914. There, the people of Jalisco were also able to show their bravery in the civic parade that started at the cathedral and went to the sanctuary of Guadalupe. Let us remember that these were difficult times for Catholicism, where this type of public display was considered contrary to the national reform. It was enough to connect a few dots for Mgr. Orozco y Jiménez to earn himself a reputation as a rebel.

The rebellion was in its infancy and as a result of some discussions with the government, the activists from the north decided to descend like a bloody wave on the south, in the direction of Guadalajara. It was July 8, 1914. Unprepared, trusting, and inexperienced, priests did not know that they were guilty for the mere fact of wearing cassocks; more than a hundred went to prison. Foreign clergy were forced to leave the country, and bishops were ordered into exile. Needless to say, the looting of churches, convents, and parishes was the order of the day.

Thus Archbishop Orozco y Jiménez suffered the first of his exiles. He spent two long years in his old home, the Pontifical Latin American College in Rome. From there he issued messages full of love and anguish. But he wasn't someone to remain locked up: without authorization and incognito, he planned his return to his fatherland under the name of Jesús Quiroz. Once there, it was nearly two years of a wandering and hidden life. A long, gray beard was his permanent disguise. As best he could, he fulfilled his duties as a bishop. He improvised a cathedral amongst the hills and valleys between Huitzila and El Salvador, in Zacatecas, confessed, administered confirmation, and even ordained priests in the midst of persecution.

Little by little, the government became aware of his disobedience and began to offer a bounty to anyone who would betray him. He was, they said, a threat to the country, and they even deployed a special brigade of three hundred men to catch him, under the command of Lieutenant Colonel Flores. Finally, in the parish of Lagos de Moreno he was found ministering to souls, which earned him not only mistreatment but also his second exile, on July 6, 1918.

This time he took refuge for a little more than a year in the north. From Chicago, between anguish and hope, he had his eyes and his heart fixed on his distant and beloved flock. He blessed, prayed, and encouraged Catholic life in his diocese. It was from there that he blessed the first Regional Catholic Congress of Workers from afar.

After various diplomatic procedures, the Carranza government allowed him to enter, which he did with a tremendous welcome, on October 14, 1919. His third residence was the longest of all, more than four years, with joys and sorrows, and glories. But he would once again have to leave his country.

On June 4, 1921, a series of attacks led to a bomb exploding in his house in Guadalajara. Continually attacked by the press and in the face of a continuous siege, he saw that the most prudent thing was exile, so he announced his departure for an *ad limina*[43] visit and left on May 29, 1924, to stay in Rome for a whole year.

He returned in May 1925. Back in his homeland, an order from the Ministry of the Interior notified him to present himself voluntarily "so as not to be taken by force." Knowing what would happen if he presented

---

[43] This is the name given to the visit that the bishops periodically make to the Holy Father in Rome; it is short for "*ad limina apostolorum*," that is, to the threshold of the apostles, because of the relics found in Rome, especially those of Saints Peter and Paul.

himself and as an example for his priests, he preferred to go into hiding.

The Cristero struggle and the closure of the churches began and while the country shuddered, the elusive archbishop went up and down ravines and hills, eluding the reach of his persecutors. The ranches at La Flecha, La Lobera, El Cedral, and El Carrizo were temporary hiding places and improvised cathedrals for preaching, administering the sacraments, and sending or receiving communications. He spent three years shepherding on horseback, in continuous anxiety and with unrelenting dangers. He was, as he has been called, "the Athanasius of the twentieth century," because although he did not achieve martyrdom, exile and a wandering life made him resemble that holy Church father of the third century. He only wanted peace but was blamed for the war.

His courage was unmatched by any other prelate, and although he was not in favor of armed struggle (not in principle, but for tactical reasons), he never condemned or restrained it.

The "Settlements" came on June 21, 1929, and he came out of hiding to appear before President Emilio Portes Gil at the request of the conciliatory bishops. Here is the painful account of Rius Facius:

> Following his instructions, Mgr. Orozco y Jiménez delivered to the Ministry of the Interior the list of priests, which amounted to more than five hundred, who would minister in his diocese.
>
> "A few days later—wrote the Archbishop of Guadalajara himself after some time—on the feast of St. Peter the Apostle, public worship was solemnly opened in Guadalajara, at the same time as in the capital. On the same day I had an audience with President Portes Gil, accompanied, at my direction, by the most illustrious Apostolic Delegate and the Archbishop of Mexico: I had the floor for one hour, pointing out that, although there had been differences of opinion up to that date, on how to act in relations with the civil authorities, from then on, given the new norms of the Holy See, which I, like the other prelates, would respectfully obey, I hoped there would be no fear of misunderstandings. I was received with undue severity, or rather coldness on the part of the president. And in conclusion to all that I said, the only thing he said was, that having agreed that I would leave the country, I should leave the Republic on the day I wanted, but not go into hiding. That is the reason why I

find myself in this exile, which I naturally describe as unjust and illogical. God allows it. Blessed be He!"[44]

Thus, he began his fourth exile that would end only in May 1930, when he returned to consecrate his successor Don José Garibi y Rivera, and Don Vicente Camacho bishop of Tabasco. He was allowed to remain in residence for less than two years (even after several years had passed since the "Settlements"), because on January 24, 1932, he was once again arrested as a criminal and expelled from the country.

From the United States, he left for the Eternal City. There he lived under the protection of the Vatican, which recognized him as a true hero. It was he that Pope Pius XI appointed to celebrate the solemnity that, on December 12, 1933, crowned the Virgin of Guadalupe sovereign over Latin America and the Philippine Islands. He was sixty-nine years old, and some thought he would quickly become a cardinal. "*Guarda, guarda, quale figura di Cardenale. Egli è più cardinale di tutti noi,*" Cardinal Dominioni would say: "Look, look at that figure of a cardinal. He is more cardinal than all of us."

However, he could not bring himself to live outside of Mexico. His eagerness to return together with his peculiar audacity made him (once again!) return on August 18, 1934. To his enemies, he was an outlaw whom they would not leave alone. The old pastor emeritus of Guadalajara would sometimes function as the old gardener of the hospital of San José, and at other times as a magnificent mitered prelate who appeared unexpectedly, in grandeur, in the cathedral or in the basilica of Zapopan. There, he was the sign of the struggle, and the crowds were captivated by his words. After so turbulent a life, he was able to escape from this earthly exile on February 18, 1936.

---

[44] Rius Facius, *México Cristero*, 2:503.

Lic. MIGUEL GOMEZ LOZA
Confesor de la Fé de Cristo
† 21 de Marzo de 1928.

"La sangre de los mártires es semilla
de cristianos".—(Tertuliano).

Pío XI a los Confesores de la fé en México

Guadalajara, Jal., marzo 21 de 1948.

*Blessed Anacleto González Flores and Miguel Gómez Loza*

*Blessed Miguel Pro, in disguise*          *Leaders of the Cristeros*

*Execution of Father Francisco Vera in 1927*

*Martyrdom of Father Miguel Pro*

*Cristeros hanged along the railroad tracks*

*Mgr. Francisco Orozco y Jiménez, wearing a beard to help his disguise*

# II

# The Settlements

T HE FRATRICIDAL WAR THAT HAD BEEN BLEEDING Mexico could not last forever. The revolution had awakened within the Mexican people a resurgence of religious sentiment that united it with its ancestors and constituted it as a nation. The struggle, although long, was to end in a truce—a painful one, to be sure. The well-known historian of the Cristiada, Jean Meyer, when writing his thesis on the war's outcome, summed up the position of the Catholic hierarchy with the following phrase: "from the Church of silence to the silence of the Church."[1] And no wonder, as we will see.

What was happening politically that ultimately led both sides to reach this kind of agreement? Here is a brief outline.

*On the part of the ecclesiastical hierarchy:*

The lack of sacraments (about two or three years without confession, communion, baptisms, marriages, etc.), made the faithful gradually begin to forget religion.[2]

The fear of never achieving peace because the Cristeros were, if not winning the war, at least creating serious difficulties of victory for the national army.

The concern about the enormous independence from the hierarchy, which the insurgent Catholics were acquiring.

*On the part of the government:*

The United States was pressing for an end to the religious conflict as soon as possible since each day that passed was detrimental to its economic interests in Mexico.

The slow but steady rise of a possible national leader, José Vasconcelos, worried the government because of the popularity he was achieving in the opposition camps.

---

[1] Meyer, *La Cristiada*, 1:323.
[2] It was argued that the Mexican people, after a few years without sacraments, were declining morally. The Cristero leader, Heriberto Navarrete (*Por Dios y por la Patria*, 252–53), says that after consulting with a dignitary, he heard that the arrangements were made "due to the lack of spiritual attention, the morals of the people [were] declining alarmingly... gradually becoming a complacent conformism."

The uprising of Generals Manzo and Escobar raised fears of a definitive alliance between the Cristeros and the rebel military.

Without resorting to oversimplified Marxist explanations, it must be taken into account that the Mexican well-to-do classes were also harmed by the long religious conflict.[3]

Starting July 1927, at the behest of Calles and Obregón, the government had initiated contacts with the exiled bishops mainly in the United States to put an end to the conflict. In these circumstances, diplomacy had failed as a result of certain newspaper leaks; however, a "protocol" signed by the interested parties remained that would be the basis for the future agreement of 1929.

Although a couple of bishops served as diplomats on behalf of the Church, in the event of an arrangement it was clear that the final decision was the Pope's, as can be read in various statements.[4] Let us keep the following in mind: the same Supreme Pontiff who shortly before had asked for the repeal of the laws, would now request peaceful settlement on certain conditions.[5] In this regard, Mgr. González y Valencia wrote:

> In nothing is the Holy Father so explicit and so insistent, as in teaching that in Mexico there is no other remedy than to persevere until the reform of the law is achieved. And Cardinal Boggiani [apostolic nuncio] repeated to me a few days ago that we cannot and should not admit any arrangement other than one based on the repeal of the law. That is why I was surprised that the statements of the Committee conclude by supposing the possibility of an agreement between the Holy See and the Government, even if the latter does not repeal the laws...[6]

With the Mexican government, the new attempts at peacemaking had the future president of Mexico as an actor (Obregón, in 1928) with the United States ambassador, Morrow, as his advisor.

For its part, the League begged to be heard. Any compromise

---

[3] As Meyer says (*La Cristiada*, 2:324): "There were in all these social classes, especially the well-to-do, people for whom, unfortunately, religious conflict and bitter persecution meant nothing but inconvenience and loss."
[4] See Acevedo, *David V*, 194.
[5] Apparently, the change of position happened chronologically after the assassination of Obregón. See Mutolo, *Gli "arreglos" tra l'episcopato e il governo*, 87.
[6] Archive of the Curia of the Archbishopric of Mexico, in *Unpublished Sources*, doc. 17, cited by Mutolo, 70.

appeared to be a mistake, since given the tenor of the government's public statements, everything suggested that it would quickly fail to comply with the negotiations. It was this that motivated the League to send, in May 1928,[7] a "memorandum" that, although recognizing papal authority, opposed the possible compromise in harsh terms:

> To His Holiness, the Sovereign Pontiff, Pius XI: Those of us who sign this representation ... dare to state the following points:
>
> 1) We are going to address an extremely serious matter, and we confess that we continue to experience a certain unease ....
>
> 2) That ... more or less well-founded rumors have been circulating that certain individuals of the persecuting sectarian government have been attempting to enter into talks with some of the Most Reverend Prelates in order to reach an agreement which is substantially based on these two points: a) Immediate resumption of public worship, b) a promise on the part of the persecutors to gradually repeal the persecutory laws. At this time it is certain that these negotiations are being conducted with particular activity with some prelates.
>
> 3) That ... we are in a position to know what is wanted and felt in the various social classes in relation to the issue of religious conflict ....
>
> 4) That there are in all these social classes, especially in the well-to-do, people for whom, unfortunately, religious conflict and bitter persecution mean nothing but the inconvenience and loss that are caused by the fight, and for this reason they would like it to cease in any way as soon as possible and return to peace, even if this peace were the one that reigns in tombs. These people have never fought for their faith and will never fight for it.
>
> 5) That, thank God, it is not the dominant opinion among those who feel the conflict in their souls. Those who have devoted themselves ... manifest ... a deep concern, a deep fear, a grave bewilderment every time there is talk of an end to the conflict by means of a provisional settlement, such as the one we have stated. They are aware of the very serious consequences that will follow from it:

---

[7] In September of that same year, the newspaper *Excélsior* stated that "Monsignor Ruiz y Flores, before leaving Rome, had declared that *the pope was willing to negotiate, through the delegates, without demanding (as before) a reform of the laws.*" Meyer, *La Cristiada*, 2:332, emphasis ours.

a) a feeling of discouragement....

b) From such an impression it is to be feared that hence-forth the most self-sacrificing would retire disappointed to their homes and would not want to cooperate afterwards in the work of reconquering their liberties and maintaining those that they might have obtained.

c) The certainty that this example would be followed by Catholic youth and by new generations, in view of the failure suffered...because it would be considered that *negotiations and compromises had been entered into prematurely.*

d) As a consequence, the impossibility to formally attempt to regain things of the utmost importance: freedom of edu-cation, social restructuring according to the doctrines of the Church, etc.

e) The well-founded fear that the idea that the people, and in general Catholic society, will form of the Church is not precisely what is needed to save the Church and the Mexican fatherland: *the Church would become in their eyes a society of prisoners confined to temples and sacristies,* without influence or means to face the great social problems.

f) The decrease and perhaps the loss of the feeling of respect, veneration, and loyalty, characteristic of the Mexi-can Catholic people and society, towards their prelates....

g) The confusion it would cause in many because they would find inconsistent the conduct followed by the Epis-copate in suspending services and strongly condemning the Calles Law, and then having submitted to it, given that the blood of the Church's most faithful sons has been shed.... It will be thought that this has been in vain, that the blood of our martyrs has been fruitless....

h) *The certainty, founded on bitter and certain experience, that the persecutors will not fulfill the commitments made....*

i) The firmest conviction that many entertain that what the persecutors intend is to dishonor the cause defended by Catholics, creating the spectacle of a Church subject to a law that she herself condemned, and *to obtain the surrender of those who, in the sacred right of legitimate defense,* have confronted the tyrants by resisting with armed resistance.

j) From this it would follow, as a natural consequence, if this law were in force and obeyed by the clergy, that the persecutor, would know how to win the good will of some ecclesiastics, and with them it would then be possible to begin working effectively in favor of the schism....

k) The repugnance which all sincere believers experi-ence to see their clergy subject themselves to humiliation, of disgraceful registration in the municipal records, forced by a law which has cost the Catholics so much blood, and by tyrants whom the whole nation justly detests....

6) That, instead, we must bear witness...and that it is certain that...*the faithful do not want peace if it is to be obtained by provisional and deficient pacts*, and they even accept the possibility, truly groundless, that the Catholic faith will disappear and be extirpated in Mexico, if this is to be accomplished by tyrants who drown Catholics in blood and destroy the Mexican nationhood—all the more so since *the daily growth of our armed movement allows us to have solid hopes that the government will at least be severely chastened*....

7) That it is true that there are some unmistakable signs of discouragement, bewilderment, tiredness, resignation, but this is largely due to the disruption caused by fears of a poor settlement....

8) How well known is Your Holiness's firmness both for this and because the Holy See has categorically condemned the Calles Law and everything that can be interpreted by the faithful as compliance with that law; *any fear that the Mexican Church will be subject to certain chains, even if they are silken, must be discarded*, and it could never happen that the pacts concluded would appear as a transaction that would mean a defeat.... Our conscience commands us, in an urgent way, to bear witness to what this faithful and deeply believing people want and feel in the face of the possibility of an agreement based on the word of honor of the persecutors.

9) That, given all that has been said, we ask with all respect to Your Holiness, whom we acknowledge as wearing the Fisherman's Ring, with sentiments of the deepest gratitude in our souls, and may our Father and protector deign to remember, at the moment of truth, this testimony that we render to him. We pray to Heaven that God our Lord will preserve the life of Your Holiness for many years, and we ask Him for the Apostolic Blessing. Mexico City, May 31, 1928.[8]

The negotiations, which had been carried out quietly for fear of the combatants, were interrupted in 1928 — as we said — as a result of the assassination of the newly elected Obregón. The young Catholic José León Toral, who acted alone in the tyrannicide, brought everything back to square one.

---

[8] Meyer, *La Cristiada*, 2:323–28.

It was only with Emilio Portes Gil that the negotiations continued. It is worth emphasizing that, for the latter, the religious conflict did not have as its main protagonist the Church's hierarchy, but *the people*, as he said only a few years later, in 1930:

> When I took charge of the Ministry of the Interior on August 28, 1928, in my first agreement with President Calles, I told him that, in my opinion, the fundamental problem that urgently needed to be studied and resolved was the conflict... *not against the leaders of the Church per se, but against a very large sector of the people.*[9]

That is what he claimed.

On the part of the clergy, the struggle had been long and the wait enormous. Although, as we shall see, there were those who opposed an unequal settlement, the great majority of the bishops were already in favor of ending the religious war at the beginning of 1929. To this end, Mgr. Ruiz y Flores, Archbishop of Morelia, was appointed Apostolic Delegate with Mgr. Pascual Díaz as secretary. Rome was beginning to speak.[10] On the other hand, the American ambassador Morrow was the hidden protagonist.

For the government in 1929, negotiations seemed inevitable: General Gorostieta and Degollado Guízar, two generals of the Cristero army, were about to take Guadalajara. At the same time, the Escobarista rebellion emerged, mainly branching out in the regions of Veracruz, Sonora, and Durango. This made the government suspect, and rightly, an alliance between the Cristeros and the insurgent military forces of Escobar.[11] As Rius Facius correctly notes:

> Escobar's rebellion threatened the stability of the Government. The Cristeros were consolidating their positions and the economic wear and tear on the regime put the economic interests of Wall Street in Mexico at serious risk. Calles and

---

[9] Emilio Portes Gil, *Autobiografía de la Revolución Mexicana* (Instituto Mexicano de Cultura, 1964), 574, emphasis ours.

[10] See Mutolo, *Gli "arreglos" tra l'episcopato e il governo*, 96.

[11] "Our Center in Mexico City," Gorostieta communicated, "when informing me of all the above, notified me, for the knowledge of the National Guard and my approval, of a pact that, before starting the movement, the head of the new movement, General Gonzalo Escobar, made with our directors. This pact is basically reducible to two conditions: Solemn commitment, on the part of the new movement, to grant all the freedoms that we have been demanding, in a very particular way the freedom of conscience and education; and the full recognition of the National Guard, with all the ranks granted or to be granted by the head of the Guard." Rius Facius, *México Cristero*, 2:443.

his camp understood that it was time to turn back in order to save themselves.[12]

On June 12 and 13, 1929, the bishops met directly with President Portes Gil. As no agreement was reached, Morrow himself drafted a *memorandum* that was eventually signed by both parties. This document, let us repeat, had to be reviewed by Rome first. After the dispatch (on June 20) the Holy See sent a confusing document in which it did not give a concrete answer but an explanation of what the Vatican expected from the negotiations: peaceful solution, general amnesty, return of property, and new relations between Church and State. The answer was very generic, and time was pressing. *The idea was to find a solution at all costs.* Portes Gil said he did not have the power to repeal the laws enacted by Congress, but the bishops were satisfied with the minimum. The following shorthand version of the words of Mgr. Pascual Díaz before Portes Gil shows this. He said to Mgr. Ruiz y Flores at that time:

> "He (Portes Gil) cannot make any reform to the current laws, but he can influence things so that these are not applied in a sectarian spirit and that some tolerance is allowed in the exercise of our religious duties. To discuss again what has been discussed so much would be to put ourselves at the beginning of the road and not reach any agreement. In this regard, I asked the President to be lenient and to allow us to open the churches so that our faithful can exercise their religious rights...." (To this Portes Gil replied): "You may resume worship whenever you wish on the sole condition that its exercise is strictly in accordance with the legal regulations in force..."[13]

According to the bishops "the Vatican wanted appeasement.... It was inclined to a policy of accommodation, of tacit arrangement, which would have left the offending texts intact, but would have allowed, by not entering into the realm of principles, to hope that they would not in fact be applied."[14] The settlement would become an "unsettlement," as we shall see. Abide by laws that would be "enforced," benevolently... Other people would pay the price.

---

[12] Rius Facius, 2:455. A special mention should be made of the Chilean diplomat Miguel Cruchaga Tocornal (Santiago, May 4, 1869–Santiago, May 3, 1949), who played a fundamental role in the arrangements. His intervention, as well as the details of the actions of Frs. Walsh and Burke, has been treated by Meyer in his *La Cruzada por México.*

[13] Emilio Portes Gil, *Autobiografía*, 575–77, emphasis ours.

[14] "He regretted that the Mexican clergy, divided and combative, instead of seeking a *de facto accommodation* with the public authorities, remained in open hostility and obstinately had no relationship with the government" (Meyer, *La*

*MODUS VIVENDI* OR *MODUS MORIENDI?*

The conditions for peace were in place: the actions of the United States and the talks concluded. Thus, on June 21, 1929, the declarations of both parties were released at almost the same time. According to the typed version of López Beltrán:

> I have had talks with Archbishop Ruiz y Flores and Bishop Pascual Díaz. These talks took place as a result of the public statements made by Archbishop Ruiz y Flores on May 2 and the statements made by me on May 8.
>
> Archbishop Ruiz y Flores and Bishop Díaz told me that the Mexican bishops believed that the Constitution and the laws, especially the provision requiring the registration of ministers and granting the states the right to determine the number of priests, threaten the identity of the Church by giving the State control of its spiritual affairs.
>
> They assure me that the Mexican bishops are animated by a sincere patriotism and that they have a desire to resume public worship if this can be done in accordance with their loyalty to the Mexican Republic and their consciences. They declared that this could be done if the Church could enjoy freedom, *within the law*, to live and exercise its spiritual functions.
>
> I gladly take this opportunity to declare publicly, with complete clarity, that it is not the intention of the Constitution, nor of the laws, nor of the Government of the Republic, to destroy the identity of the Catholic Church, or of any other, or to interfere in any way in its spiritual functions. In accordance with the oath I took when I assumed office in the Provisional Government of Mexico, to comply with and enforce the Constitution of the Republic and the laws that emanate from it, my purpose has always been to honestly comply with that oath and to see that the laws are applied without sectarian tendencies and without any prejudice. The administration under my charge is willing to hear from any person, whether a dignitary of a Church or simply from a private individual, the complaints he may have regarding the injustices committed through improper application of the laws.

---

*Cristiada*, 2:237–38, emphasis ours). "All the members of the curia (were inclined) to appeasement" (ibid., 241). Perhaps that is why the change of allegiance, from 1926 onwards, was from González y Valencia (president of the Episcopal Committee) to Monsignor Pascual Díaz y Barreto, as Mutolo declares (*Gli "arreglos" tra l'episcopato e il governo*, 42): "Díaz meets twice with the pope and twice with Gasparri (1927), while the Episcopal Commission does not know what they are actually talking about. What is certain is that the Vatican's position changed sharply because González and the Commission were removed from Rome."

With reference to certain articles of the law, which have been misunderstood, I also take this opportunity to declare:

1. That the article of the law that determines the registration of ministers does not mean that the Government can register those who have not been appointed by the hierarchical superior of the respective religious creed, or in accordance with the rules of that creed.

2. Regarding religious education, the Constitution and laws in force strictly prohibit its teaching in primary and higher schools, whether official or private, but this does not prevent ministers of any religion from imparting their doctrines to older people or their children who come for that purpose.

3. That both the Constitution and the laws of the country guarantee to every inhabitant of the Republic the right of petition, and in virtue of this, the members of any Church may apply to the corresponding authorities for the reform, repeal, or issuance of any law.

National Palace, June 21, 1929.
The President of the Republic, E. PORTES GIL.[15]

Portes Gil's statements were complemented by the following ones signed by the Archbishop of Morelia, Leopoldo Ruiz y Flores, but which, according to López Beltrán, American Ambassador Morrow himself wrote, in his own hand and probably in English,[16] without heading, title or epigraph:

Bishop Díaz and I have had several conferences with the President of the Republic and their results are evident in the statements he issued today.

I am pleased to say that all the talks have been marked by a spirit of mutual goodwill and respect. As a consequence of these declarations made by the President, the Mexican clergy will resume religious services in accordance with the existing laws.

---

[15] López Beltrán, *La persecución religiosa en México*, 525–26. Before signing, President Emilio Portes Gil had asked that the Archbishop of Guadalajara, Francisco Orozco y Jiménez, the Archbishop of Durango, José María González y Valencia, and the Archbishop of Huejutla, José de Jesús Manríquez y Zárate, remain in exile *indefinitely* (Monsignor Orozco y Jiménez was always on the side of the Cristeros, supporting them spiritually and within the national territory, never having abandoned his diocese, nor did the bishop of Colima, Amador Velasco y Peña). The request was meekly accepted (see ibid.).

[16] The text was written in English and then translated, according to Degollado Guízar himself (*Memorias*, 275).

It is my hope that the resumption of religious services
will lead the Mexican people, animated by a spirit of good
will, to cooperate in all moral efforts for the benefit of all
those in the land of our ancestors.

Mexico City, June 21, 1929.
LEOPOLDO RUIZ y FLORES,
Archbishop of Morelia, and Apostolic Delegate.[17]

Immediately after, the churches were reopened. With this, the conflict "was over," according to the bishops, and the discharge of troops
became imperative. If the churches were opened, then why fight?

The Cristeros began to leave their guns at the feet of their opponents. There was talk of disarmament, not "surrender." In response
to the imprisonment suffered by some Catholic combatants, immediate release was requested. Strictly speaking, very few Cristeros were
detained, since the practice had been to shoot or hang captives, not
to keep them as prisoners. On the other hand, many Catholics who
had not participated in the armed struggle but who had given political or civic support were confined to the prison at the Islas Marías.

Although terms had been agreed, the government gave a glimpse
of what the "compliance" with the agreement would be like. Only
at the beginning was confiscated property — and only a minimum —
returned to the Church. In some states of the Mexican Republic, far
from stopping, persecution increased in the following years: Veracruz, Tabasco, and Chiapas were known for the cruelty with which
the clergy and laity, now defenseless, continued to be mistreated. In
twenty-one states of the Republic, the regulatory laws of Article 130
were restructured, making the situation even worse. In Oaxaca, in
1934, only one priest was allowed for every sixty thousand inhabitants — that is to say, out of one hundred and sixty-seven priests in the
state, only eighteen could have authorization to exercise the ministry.
Something similar happened in Michoacán, where out of six hundred
and twenty priests only thirty-three were authorized to exercise their
ministry. By the end of that same year, only 501 priests were legally
found in the entire country and about 3,500 were illegal.

Laws against religious education remained in force because the
state maintained a monopoly on education. In October 1934, "socialist education" was introduced, and the teaching provided by the

---

[17] López Beltrán, *La persecución religiosa en México*, 527. Such documents, as the
author correctly observes (530), were not official because the Church did not
have the legal status for that purpose!

state became so contrary to the Church that the bishops issued a collective pastoral letter (1935) warning the faithful that they were sinning gravely if they brought their children to public schools, and that absolution would be denied to them until they withdrew their children from them. We ask: what kind of "arrangement" was this? As Meyer rightly states: "The *modus vivendi* soon became a sinister *modus moriendi*, endured as a trial worse than the war itself and carried like a cross, an incomprehensible mystery to which they submitted for love of the pope and Jesus, Christ the King. All the old Cristeros say: More have died after the 'settlements' than during the war."[18] This statement—which, incidentally is widely held to be true—is minimized by Meyer, for whom "it does not correspond to an arithmetical truth, but to a subjective truth: the leaders fell especially after the war, and these murders were felt much more harshly than a death, natural and justified, when faced with the enemy."[19] Some estimate more than five hundred Cristero leaders were assassinated after the terms were agreed upon.[20]

Just to provide a few examples, we list the following:

- The Cristero general José María Gutiérrez, who had been granted amnesty and had disbanded his troops, was assassinated at point-blank range on December 8, 1929, for stating that he would rise up again if religious freedom were not respected.

- On February 14 of that same year, forty-one Cristeros who had been given amnesty were killed in Martín de Bolaños (Jalisco).

- Among priests, on April 20, 1930, the parish priest of Cañadas, Jalisco, Fr. José Lezama was lynched, and, while celebrating Mass, at the rancheria of Tabernas, Michoacán, Father Epifanio Madrigal was murdered along with six other faithful.[21]

- On July 1, 1929, a week after the settlements, Father Aristeo Pedroza, general of the Cristeros, was shot by orders received from the capital.[22]

---

[18] Meyer, *La Cristiada*, 1:336–37.
[19] Meyer, *La Cristiada*, 3:265.
[20] *Razón y Fe*, February 1936, 116–22, quoted by González Navarro, *Masones y cristeros en Jalisco*, 68.
[21] See Rius Facius, *México Cristero*, 2:500.
[22] See Meyer, *La Cristiada*, 2:340. He was shot between sunrise and midnight, in retaliation for the recklessness of one of his soldiers who fired first at a group of soldiers encountered along the way.

• Despite the promise of amnesty, executions followed one after another. "When someone presented the document stating that he had surrendered voluntarily and they gave him guarantees, they put the document on his chest and pierced it with bullets," according to Navarrete.

Most of the state legislatures undertook to amend laws again and again, worsening in each "correction," the laws passed before 1929 regulating the exercise of public worship.[23]

In his 1931 work *Documents for the History of Religious Persecution in Mexico*, Mgr. Lara y Torres said:

> As the so-called Cristeros, who had taken up arms to defend the rights of the Church and of the Catholics, were left without any protection, by virtue of the fact that nothing had been stipulated in their favor in the Accords of 1929, many of those who did not perish on the battlefields have been murdered by more or less hidden hands of the Government.... In the region of Jalisco, as I have been assured, about *four hundred Cristeros have been murdered*.... The government's hostility towards Catholic zeal is increasing.... We were told that the churches and adjoining buildings would be returned to the Catholic priests...as soon as the services were opened.... They have been returned to Catholic priests, but not as property or in recognition of the right of the Church, but as a loan.[24]

Additionally, those who had doubts about whether or not they should lay down their arms were subjected to enormous moral pressure from the clergy. There were priests who said "that it was now a mortal sin to continue feeding the Cristeros"[25] who remained armed.

In an interview with Mgr. Díaz, the Catholic general in charge of the Cristeros,[26] Jesús Degollado Guízar, vainly asked for guarantees:

---

[23] "Here are some data taken from the official newspapers of the states: Aguascalientes issued a new law in 1934, Campeche in 1934, Coahuila in 1934 and '36, Colima in 1932, '33, and '34, Chiapas in 1929, '32, '33, and '34, Chihuahua in 1931, '34, and '36, the Federal District in 1931, Durango in 1932 and '34, Guanajuato, Guerrero, Jalisco, and Michoacán in 1932, Hidalgo, Oaxaca, Puebla and Sinaloa in 1934, Mexico in 1932 and '34, Nayarit in 1934 and '36, Querétaro in 1933 and '36, Veracruz in 1931, Yucatán in 1931 and '32, Zacatecas in 1933, '34, and '35." F. Navarrete, *La masonería*, 177.

[24] "Memorial on the present situation of the Catholics of Mexico, respectfully sent to our Most Holy Father Pius XI by the Bishop of Tacámbaro," dated November 1, 1931, Mexico City. Quoted by López Beltrán, *La persecución religiosa en México*, 574–76.

[25] Rius Facius, *México Cristero*, 2:492.

[26] He took the place of General Gorostieta after the latter's death.

The Cristeros... suffered the worst test of the entire war, *a peace that delivered them bound hand and foot....* Throughout the war, the bishops and Rome, with rare exceptions, had refused to take sides openly with them.... The general in charge, Jesús Degollado, marched to the capital to ensure that the combatants were not forgotten, and Mgr. Díaz spoke harshly to him: "*I do not know nor am I interested in knowing what conditions you are going to be left in.* We have already spoken to the President of the Republic, the *Holy See has already authorized everything,* we have already agreed with what was published. *When we spoke with the President about your specific case, we did not come to any conclusion.* The only thing I have to tell you is that you must lay down your arms, because right now the situation has changed completely, and the Catholic people would now see you as rebels against the ecclesiastical authorities and they themselves would cooperate with the government to fight you."[27]

But it was not only the clergy who were asked to guarantee the combatants. Degollado Guízar also entrusted one of his lieutenants, Luis Beltrán, with the delicate mission of delivering to the president his conditions to carry out the discharge. As delivered, the letter requested:

1) Full guarantees of lives and interests for all civilians, who in any way have helped the movement to defend religious freedom.

2) Absolute freedom for all religious prisoners, whether civilians or members of the National Guard.

3) Dismissal of the lawsuits initiated against Catholics on the occasion of the religious question.

4) Repatriation of exiles for the same reason.

5) Delivery of twenty-five pesos per rifle to the soldiers of the National Guard who surrender their arms, giving their horses to those who need them.

6) The chiefs and officers will be allowed to retain their pistols, with the respective license to carry arms and safe-conducts, and a cash allowance at the discretion of the Heads of Operations.

7) That the necessary facilities be given so that the work can be carried out.

8) That the discharge of the troops of the National Guard be before the chiefs of Operations.[28]

---

[27] Meyer, *La Cristiada*, 2:371, emphasis ours.
[28] Jesús Degollado Guízar, "Report submitted to the vice-president of the National League for the Defense of Religious Liberty, Miguel Palomar y Vizcarra,

Rius Facius added, not without irony, that faced with this request, "Portes Gil had no qualms about accepting these conditions knowing that he would not comply with them: to do this he counted on the validity of the persecutory laws and the force of anarchy sown in the Catholic ranks with the submission signed by Monsignors Díaz and Ruiz y Flores!"[29]

What happened seems to have been prophesied by General Gorostieta who, in view of the imminent settlements, went so far as to say in a dialogue:

> Look, Santiago Dueñas, I don't want to be a prophet, but I am sure that if any of our ringleaders escapes with their lives, in the event that we hand over our arms to the Government, it could be considered a miracle. That does not matter to those who play high politics, even if they are very distinguished characters of the Clergy. After all, after the honeymoon that will cost our people so dearly, we would become a constant danger to some and a living accusation to others. And the tension of relations between the Clergy and the Government is going to return — do not doubt it for a moment. The hour of disappointment for the Bishops will come soon.[30]

His worries were not minor. The hunt for Cristeros can be read in the first person, as the priest Heriberto Navarrete, one of Gorostieta's lieutenants, later recounted, speaking about the "discharge" of the troops:

> We distributed the money that was in the box according to the seniority and rank of each one, and on July 19, 1929, we delivered the weapons and horses to Colonel Vizcaíno Hueso in Tepatitlán. Once back in Guadalajara, I presented myself to General Figueroa asking him to grant me a license to carry a firearm, and on that occasion he showed me his friendly sympathy with a piece of advice that perhaps was the cause of my fate being different from that of so many comrades-in-arms who later fell to the henchman's treacherous blow. When I entered the General's office, Silvano Barba González was in conference with him. We knew each other. He left as I was talking to the General.
>
> "General, I should be grateful if you would give me a license to carry a pistol. You know very well the reasons I have for asking you."

---

on November 21, 1953," LNDLR Archive, quoted by Rius Facius, *México Cristero*, 2:493–94.
[29] Rius Facius, 2:495.
[30] Navarrete, *Por Dios y por la Patria*, 231.

"Do you plan to stay and live on your land?"

"That's right, General. I was in my fourth year of Engineering when this campaign began, which we are ending. I plan to get my degree and work in my profession."

"But... Sir!... You are naive. I'm going to offer you my friendly advice. I understand of course that if you insist, I have not the slightest objection to granting you the license you ask for. But it would be a grave mistake on your part to stay in Guadalajara. No, my friend, go far away. I am grateful to you.... But because of that, I would regret that what will undoubtedly happen to many should happen to you without being able to prevent it. No, my friend Navarrete, do not stay here. They would kill you soon. They would assassinate you treacherously. It would be of no use to be armed. I am the representative of the Federal authority in Jalisco, of the country's military power. I assure you on my honor that you have nothing to fear from this side. But these local politicians will always believe they are earning favor with the Central Government by committing such atrocities. They will also satisfy their desire for revenge — don't forget that you gave them more than one serious headache. Some of them hate you very much."[31]

How did the settlements come about? Were the bishops not aware of what they were signing? Didn't they realize what would happen? This is not a rhetorical question, but an almost existential one. One never ceases to be surprised when reading these details closely. What guaranteed that the "Settlements" would be observed?

This question was asked, a few years later, of one of the agents of the settlements, Father Edmund Walsh (SJ), as Rius Facius recounts: "After some time, Mgr. Orozco y Jiménez met in Rome[32] accompanied by Father Ramón Martínez Silva, S.J., chaplain of the National Confederation of Catholic Students of Mexico, with Father Edmund Walsh, S.J., whose decisive influence had been felt in the conclusion of the *modus vivendi*. The archbishop, somewhat annoyed, said to him, addressing his companion: "Ask him, Father Ramon, ask Father Walsh what the guarantee of the settlements was!" "And Father Walsh replied, even more annoyed: 'Morrow...! But Morrow died on us.'"[33]

---

[31] Navarrete, 258–59.
[32] He had been asked by Portes Gil to leave the country.
[33] See Luis Calderón Vega, *Cuba 88. Memorias de la UNEC* (Fimax Publicistas, 1959), quoted in Rius Facius, *México Cristero*, 2:503–4. Indeed, Morrow would die shortly after the arrangements, in 1931.

The Church would remain "as free as a prostitute inside a brothel," in the words of Antonio Estrada. This led some Cristeros to rise up again in what was called "*La Segunda*" (Cristiada), a subject which we will not discuss.[34] We will only say that this second time the ecclesiastical hierarchy opposed the uprising much more tenaciously, asserting the pope's position in the encyclical *Acerba animi*,[35] in which violence was condemned. Soldiers were forbidden to fight and priests were forbidden to assist them. To this end, they threatened not to administer the sacraments to them even in danger of death,[36] something that would make an impact on a people as Catholic as the Mexicans.

## RESPONSIBLE PARTIES (1): THE UNITED STATES

"Poor Mexico: so far from God and so close to the United States," said Don Porfirio Díaz...

The influence of the United States[37] in Mexican history is immense, as we have said. Religious liberty advocates understood this well,

---

[34] As Meyer recounts, "practically all the leaders who had again taken up arms succumbed, and it must not be overlooked that the tenacity with which they waged a hopeless war, against all powers and dominations, resembled a quest for death. Antonio Estrada, discussing this 'Segunda,' chooses the title of *Rescoldo*, the embers that remains in the badly extinguished hearth and that refuse to die. Between *rescoldo* and *raskol* there is no logical relationship, but those indomitable men, who refused to submit to Caesar and the Church because they have given their word to Christ the King and to the Virgin of Guadalupe and they don't want the Church *to be free like a prostitute in a brothel*, may remind one of the Old Believers of Russia. And so it was that a bloody war resumed in the mountains, decimating experts and leaders of agrarian committees, accompanied by dangerous strikes against the federal forces. In a country like this, still without peace, battered and obstinate, victim of a swarm of local politicians and a terrible economic crisis, these rebels represented a dangerous unrest. A few thousand men—7,500 in 1935, 2,000 in 1939, remain unyielding in their mountains and declare that they will never submit until the government has abandoned all persecution against the Church" (Meyer, *La Cristiada*, 1:368.). A good film by the film director Matías Meyer (Jean's son) gives an account of this almost forgotten episode: *The Last Cristeros* (2012). Although it has not been widely disseminated, it has already won several awards outside Mexico for recounting the last days of the second Cristiada. It can be viewed online.
[35] See Meyer, *La Cristiada*, 1:369.
[36] See Meyer, 1:371.
[37] The recent work carried out since the opening of the archives of the Vatican Secretariat of State is of immense value: see Alfonso Alcalá Alvarado, "Los fondos del ASV [Archivo Secreto Vaticano] sobre la reanudación de cultos en la República Mexicana (1929)," *Anuario de historia de la Iglesia* 16 (2007): 391–93; idem, "Los acuerdos del 21 de junio de 1929 según el Archivo Secreto Vaticano: Documentos," *Efemérides Mexicana* 26, no. 78 (2008): 413–39; idem, "Gestación y realización de los Arreglos," *Libro anual de la Sociedad Mexicana de Historia Eclesiástica* (Minos iii Milenio Editores, 2011), 215–73.

which is why one of their leaders said that "Yankee imperialism is for us — and for all Mexicans who yearn for their fatherland's salvation — something that is in itself evil, and as evil it must be vigorously fought. History shows that almost all of the national ills that afflict our country are due to U.S. imperialism."[38] The proximity of the United States was not going to come cheap for a nation that, according to poet Rubén Darío, still spoke Spanish and prayed to Jesus Christ.

Not only would the United States not help the Cristero leadership (despite certain promises that Capistrán Garza made on their behalf[39]) but it would play a decisive role in the "settlements." Nor could it be otherwise in an environment where, only a few years before the enactment of the Calles Law, in 1924 American Protestants were trying by every means to spread Protestantism in that Catholic and Hispanic country. One of these religious leaders declared in a letter to Calles:

> Knowing that the President persecutes Catholics, I want to go to Mexico to establish a branch office [of the American Protestant Lodge] and teach the people Protestantism. If the president succeeds in preventing the spread of Catholicism, the country will become one of the first in the world.[40]

On the one hand, the persecution by Calles; on the other, the interest of important groups of United States leaders in de-Catholicizing Mexico. Even within the American Catholic hierarchy, there was a certain indifference to Mexican Catholics. Regarding the latter, the paragraph we transcribe below gives an idea of the suffering endured at the hands of co-religionists:

> Once the convenience and possibility of obtaining help from those exiled by Calles' regime had been discarded, and letters of introduction in their possession listed above, Capistrán Garza and his companions began their tour — which promised to be fruitful, given all that they expected from the Yankee Catholics — visiting the diocese of Corpus Christi, Texas.
>
> They were received by the bishop, who, after listening to René's long explanation, translated by Gaxiola, and receiving the request for financial aid for the defense of the Church

---

[38] Palomar y Vizcarra, "Memorándum relativo a la influencia de los EEUU sobre México en materia religiosa," manuscript, *21* pp., *LNDR, 14,* quoted in Meyer, *La Cristiada*, 1:63–64.

[39] See Meyer, *La Cristiada*, 1:74.

[40] Quoted in Meyer, *La Cristiada*, 2:136. Carranza had favored Protestant proselytization and the Obregón government followed the same policy, facilitating the work of American Protestant missionaries.

in Mexico, answered that he would send his reply to the hotel. The brave young men were stunned to receive it in a telegram that read: *"Nothing doing. They do not like Mexican people in this diocese..."* From Corpus Christi they went to Galveston. The same presentation, the same request, the meticulous examination of credentials and the immediate response by the bishop, contained in *a ten-dollar bill* that he took from his wallet and handed to Capistrán Garza, ending the interview. *That was all the help of the Diocese of Galveston for the defense of the Church in Mexico.*

In contrast, what a significant outpouring of dollars went to the Freemasonry of the American Union for fomenting anti-Christian revolutions in Mexico! *Houston, Dallas, and Little Rock did not give better results: twenty, thirty, fifty dollars, which were not enough to cover the expenses of the tour itself.* With their bodies battered, but with their spirits intact, without fainting before such notable failures, René pawning a pistol and Luis his gold watch, a gift from his father, they arrived, with a broken car, in St. Louis, Missouri, where they received a thousand dollars that, from his own pocket, were given to them by Mr. Jenaro Núñez Prida to continue their fruitless tour.

"The interview with the archbishop of St. Louis had special characteristics," a witness to that journey later recounted.... "After René had once again explained with redoubled heat the legal situation of the Church in Mexico and the practical situation of the Mexican Catholics, His Excellency was indignant, and banging on his desk said that if this happened in the United States, the government that dared to do so would be crushed by the American Catholics, who would know how to assert their rights. A magnificent start that for a moment awakened hopes of beginning to solve the problem, since the only thing the Mexican people asked for were elements to fight against the tyrant, and had given ample proof of having courage and decisiveness. But the flash of hope soon dissipated: *a hundred-dollar bill*, insufficient to equip a one-man war, was the practical result of such moral fortitude."

East Saint Louis, Indianapolis, Dayton, Columbus, Pittsburgh, Altoona, Harrisburg — all these episcopal sees were visited with disastrous results: none of those most illustrious gentlemen had the generosity even of the archbishop of St. Louis, Missouri.[41]

No aid for armed warfare, then.

---

[41] Rius Facius, *México Cristero*, 2:110–11, emphasis ours.

By mid-1929 the situation was far from easy: "The Escobarista rebellion threatened the stability of the government. The Cristeros were consolidating their positions and the economic wear and tear of the regime put Wall Street's economic interests in Mexico at serious risk. Calles and his group understood that it was time to turn back in order to save themselves."[42] This is how the veteran "acejotaemero," Antonio Rius Facius, recounted the beginning of the settlements. It was the government, according to this former Catholic militant, that was more concerned with "Settlements" than the Cristero side.

The United States, as we said, was interested in the settlements because in that way, Mexican oil could continue to be exploited. It is true that the oil-producing areas were not affected by the war, but the outbreak of a civil war is not always favorable to economic interests.[43] It was not for nothing that it had supported Carranza against Huerta (1914–1915). His position was not indifferent to the extent that when Meyer said that never an "insurrectionary movement has had ranged against it, in Mexico, an army as strong as the one set up by General Amaro, in spite of all its defects, nor a government so firmly supported by the United States (financial, police and military aid, and political support)."[44] Thus it was an unequal struggle. It was David's fight against Goliath. "It's as clear as day," explained Mutolo,

> that those who took the initiative for the resumption of wor-
> ship, and those who were most determined to have talks about
> settlements with Portes Gil, were the U. S. bankers and capi-
> talists, because they saw that the religious conflict had reduced
> Mexico to a state in which they could not continue their plans
> of imperialism, could not continue to hoard the riches of
> Mexican soil; they saw that Mexico's chaotic situation (today's
> is still more chaotic) did not allow them to found the Branch
> of the Bank of New York to further extend their financial
> domination, to further take over the republic's trade and wrap
> the tentacles of expansionism more tightly around Mexico.[45]

Behind (or in front of) the United States there were broad economic interests driving the hasty conclusion of the settlements. Dwight
Morrow, appointed U. S. ambassador to Mexico and partner of the

---

[42] Rius Facius, 2:455.
[43] "In Mexico, no political party has sufficient vigor by itself to dominate; its security and its strength demand the assistance of an alien power..." Meyer, *La Cristiada*, 2:174.
[44] Meyer, *La Cristiada*, 3:259.
[45] Mutolo, *Gli "arreglos" tra l'episcopato e il governo*, 109.

J. P. Morgan bank (the creator of the Federal Reserve), would be in charge of this.[46] Less ideological than Calles (naturally), he wanted practical measures that would not hinder the extraction of oil. The interests of the United States were clear and despite having an apostolic delegate in his own country, Morrow always preferred to influence the Mexican government to negotiate the settlements with the bishops and not with the pope directly. It was important to move without delay. To this end, "Morrow made Calles and Portes Gil give up their intention to reach a direct understanding with the pope, and took the necessary steps to *trick the Mexican bishops who resided in Washington and were ignorant of what was happening in Mexico.*"[47]

The memoranda of the settlements for both parties was carefully written and studied by Morrow who (as a pragmatist) wanted to find "a *modus vivendi* for getting along well with the Mexicans.... The United States could gain no advantage from the Mexican difficulties, and all its interest was in pacification," as Meyer points out.[48] Hence the Catholic magazine *The Commonwealth*, published in New York, on May 22, 1929, said:

> Let us be forgiven for the image he presents to us: in this we see a stage in the background, and an actor in it, but *the most important character* in the representation *is almost hidden*. He is, at the same time, the entrepreneur, director, and prompter. *And he's called Morrow.*[49]

On the part of the Catholic Church, from January 1928, the American priest John Burke would act as a "true Roman agent," according to Ortoll.[50] Meyer, for his part, affirms that Rome had understood

---

[46] "In early 1927, Lamont, Dwight Morrow, and other Morgan and Co. agents met on several occasions with their Mexican colleagues, Pañi, Manuel C. Téllez, A. L. Negrete, Montes de Oca, and Agustín Legorreta (several of whom performed the same good offices between Rome and the government). Members of 'the revolutionary family' were able to present the point of view of the American bankers to Calles. Morrow and Lamont also helped establish official contacts between the government, U.S. oil companies, and the State Department. Oilmen and bankers were involved in the source of all the difficulties, and Morrow, Morgan's agent, at the time, insisted on the need to give primacy to actions over theories." Morrow to Lamont, April 12, 1927, in Morrow Papers, Amherst College Library, quoted in Meyer, *La Cristiada*, 2:315.
[47] Rius Facius, *México Cristero*, 2:458.
[48] Meyer, *La Cristiada*, 2:316.
[49] Rius Facius, *México Cristero*, 2:476, emphasis ours. It was not for nothing that the rumor of a possible attack on the ambassador had been circulating: see Alcalá Alvarado, *Gestación y realización*, 219.
[50] See, for Burke's relevance, the article by Servando Ortoll, "John Burke, la

the value of Morrow's attitude and, at the prompting of some American Catholics, allowed Fr. Burke...to go to Havana, where he spoke with Morrow and the prelates Mora and del Río and Tritschler. After Morrow had presented his plans to him, Fr. J. J. Burke asked the bishops for permission to enter into negotiations with Calles, to which the elderly archbishop replied that only the *United States was in possession of the key to the problem.* This was in January 1928.[51]

After a first attempt failed due to a newspaper leak, negotiations continued:

In accordance with the plan, Fr. Burke sent a letter to Calles, who had agreed to receive and reply to it. *Morrow controlled the drafting of both letters.* On March 29, Burke wrote:

"From people whom I have good reasons to believe are well informed, I have learned that you never intended to destroy the integrity of the Church, nor to cause obstacles to its spiritual functions, but that the purpose of the Constitution and the Mexican laws, as well as your desire to make them effective, have been and are preventing ecclesiastics from intervening in political struggles, while leaving them free, at the same time, to devote themselves to the good of souls. The Mexican bishops believed that the Constitution and laws, especially those requiring the registration of priests and those attributing to the states the right to fix the number of priests, applied in a spirit of antagonism, would threaten the identity of the Church, giving the State the power to oversee spiritual affairs. I am convinced that the Mexican bishops are animated by sincere patriotism and yearn for lasting peace. I am also convinced that they wish to resume public worship if this can be done in accordance with their loyalty to the Mexican Republic and their consciences. I believe that this could be done if they were assured of a tolerance within the Law that would allow the Church to exist and exercise its spiritual activities freely. This means that they would leave the settlement of the other pending issues to the Mexican people, acting legally, through their duly constituted authorities.

If you think you can, in accordance with your constitutional duties, make a declaration that it is not in the intention of the Constitution and the laws, nor in your own, to destroy

---

insurrección cristera y las relaciones diplomáticas entre México y los Estados Unidos," *Nueva Antropología* 45 (1994): 9–20.

[51] Meyer, *La Cristiada,* 2:318–19.

the identity of the Church, and that, in order to avoid an
excessive enforcement of the laws, the government would be
willing to deal periodically with the head of the Church of
Mexico, duly authorized, I am certain that no insurmountable obstacle would remain to prevent the Mexican clergy
from immediately resuming their spiritual functions. If you
believe in the desirability of such an agreement, I would be
very pleased to be able to go to Mexico to discuss with you,
confidentially, practical measures...."

Calles replied: "Informed of the desires that the Mexican
bishops have to resume public worship (which is essential
for the government, since this would put an end to the
Cristero war), I take this opportunity to state clearly, as I
have done on other occasions, that it is not the purpose of
either the Constitution or the laws, nor of myself, to destroy
the identity of any Church, nor to interfere in any way in
its spiritual functions."[52]

Similar statements were made by Portes Gil at the request of the
prelates, who were acting—in the words of Meyer—under obedience
to the Apostolic Nuncio in the USA, Mgr. Pietro Fumasoni Biondi[53]
(in the absence of one in Mexico). On May 2, 1929, Morrow sent an
American journalist to make a report on Portes Gil, in order to have
statements that would allow the negotiations to continue.

Portes Gil responded to the questionnaire presented to him,
without hiding his contempt for the Church and those who
defended it.... "On the part of the government of Mexico
there is no inconvenience for the Catholic Church to resume
its worship whenever it wishes, with the assurance that no
authority will harass it, as long as the representatives of the
Church itself are subject to the laws that govern the matter of

---

[52] Meyer, 2:319-20, emphasis ours.
[53] Here is an example: on April 15, 1928, Calles, at the request of Ambassador
Morrow, made a gesture of goodwill known as the "mea culpa of Celaya." That day,
during an official ceremony, in the presence of Generals Obregón and Calles, Secretary Puig Casauranc, under pretended fealty to the Virgin of Guadalupe, mother
of Mexican identity, issued a frank invitation to the bishops. "Morrow immediately
asked the State Department to suggest to the apostolic nuncio in Washington a
show of goodwill. The nuncio called Bishop Díaz, who agreed to welcome 'the
evident proof of the desire expressed by General Calles to restore to the Mexican
Catholic people their hope and their right to freely practice their religion.' These
statements provoked such anger among the League members and such attacks on
their part *against Monsignor Díaz, who was only obeying orders*, that Monsignor de
la Mora and Monsignor Armora (of Tamaulipas) deemed it appropriate to convey
them with indignation to the bishop of Tabasco." Meyer, 2:321, emphasis ours.

worship, comply with all that they prevent and show respect for the legally constituted authorities." And although it may seem grotesque, it was these statements that were taken by Mgr. Fumasoni Biondi, apostolic delegate in Washington, undoubtedly influenced by the U. S. State Department, as a cordial invitation to reach an agreement, and urgently called Mgr. Leopoldo Ruiz y Flores, who had just arrived from Rome, to order him to "make a statement in response to President Emilio Portes Gil." On May 2, 1929, Archbishop Leopoldo Ruiz y Flores made the following statements to the American press: "The religious conflict in Mexico was not motivated by any cause that cannot be corrected by men of good will. As a proof of goodwill, the words of President Portes Gil are of great importance. The Church and her ministers are prepared to cooperate with him in every just and moral effort for the advancement of the Mexican people ...." Portes Gil delivered new statements to the metropolitan press. In them he made no reference to possible changes in the legislation.[54]

To summarize: the American influence through the ambassador appointed for this purpose was all-encompassing. This, added to the function of the apostolic delegate in the United States and the intermediary of the bishops who received his orders to settle, made the unequal and difficult diplomatic campaign a tangled web, to the likes of which only diplomats are accustomed. Be that as it may, the influence of the northern country was more than decisive for the achievement of the agreement on "pacification."

RESPONSIBLE PARTIES (2): THE BISHOPS

Ambassador Dwight Whitney Morrow, though a Protestant, had various Catholic friends. In early 1928, it was through them that he managed to get in touch with Father John J. Burke, secretary of the National Catholic Welfare Conference of the US Bishops in Washington. As the United States ambassador to Mexico, Morrow knew he had a particular role when he was appointed: to pacify the neighboring country. This is what motivated him to arrange a meeting between the aforementioned priest and Calles, in which he also participated, with the aim of reaching a preliminary agreement.

President Calles himself chose the day and time of the possible meeting: Good Friday of 1928 in San Juan de Ulúa, a secluded spot near the port of Veracruz. In that interview, Calles presented himself

---

[54] Rius Facius, *México Cristero*, 2:473–75, emphasis ours.

as inflexible in the face of Father Burke's claims who, misinformed
by the ideas of Morrow and Ruiz y Flores, believed that the issue
was political rather than religious. A few days later, on May 28, 1928,
the Feast of the Ascension, Mgr. Ruiz y Flores (recently appointed
president of the Mexican Bishops Committee) and Father Burke
had "a conference with Calles in Chapultepec and they found him,
thanks to certain influences, mellower and offering, in essence, the
same thing that Portes Gil later granted in June 1929."[55]

After this meeting, Ruiz y Flores left for Rome by order of the
apostolic delegate in Washington; there he informed the pope about
the successful efforts that were being made. They were not the only
ones: Mgr. Pascual Díaz, who "as a bishop and as a citizen condemned
rebellion, whatever its cause,"[56] was also negotiating with Obregón.[57]

We should also bear in mind, as Alcalá Alvarado points out,[58] the
observations Mgr. Francisco Banegas Galván (1867–1932) sent in to
Rome in April of that year. The bishop of Querétaro since 1919, he
was undoubtedly one of the most illustrious members of the Mexican
Episcopate of his time and author of several works on Mexican history.

His report, dated April 23, 1929, and sent to the Holy See, was
entitled: "Considerations on the State of the Religious Question."
He started off with a description of the *state of the Catholics*. Banegas
pointed out to Pius XI that during the years of fighting, not only
had the war worsened considerably, but also above all morale among
Catholics had also suffered greatly. The prelate lamented that many
Catholics in Mexico considered murder, kidnapping to obtain money
for the campaign, and attacks on people and passenger trains licit,
and denounced the publication of pamphlets that defended the doctrine of tyrannicide glorifying José de León Toral, General Obregón's
assassin. Even among the clergy, he said, with the exception of a few
bishops, there were those who thought and expressed themselves in
this way. Banegas also denounced the corruption of the Faith and

---

[55] Rius Facius, 2:418.
[56] Rius Facius, 2:225.
[57] As Mutolo correctly observes (*Gli "arreglos" tra l'episcopato e il governo*, 38), the bishops in charge of "fixing" were the ones who had the most influence in the Vatican: "These are the two bishops who most influence the Vatican. With their trips to Rome, first Díaz in 1927 and then Ruiz in 1928, they manage to ensure that the Vatican increasingly follows their line. All this is demonstrated by the removal of the Episcopal Commission residing in Rome, which has ideas that conflict with those of Ruiz and Díaz."
[58] Alcalá Alvarado, *Gestación y realización*, 215, 223, 229.

even the spread of socialist and theosophist errors among Catholics, saying that it had spread to the peasants and townspeople who were previously pious and sane. The bishop concluded with this wise and prudent reflection: "I believe that there must be souls who have been purified in this tribulation, and that if it were not so, God would not have allowed it. But would it be lawful for us not to seek the remedy for the evils we are seeing, on the pretext that God permits them for his greater glory?"

Regarding the *active resistance or armed movement*, these were his observations: he had been there for more than two years and had been unable to leave the mountainous areas of Jalisco, Colima, Zacatecas, Guanajuato, and part of Querétaro despite the fact that his men had fought with generosity and courage to the point of heroism. The help they could receive was very little and every day it would be less. They were fighting against a well-armed army supported by the United States government.

It was true, he said, that during the military conflict, those armed by the League had achieved some victories, but this was because they probably received arms and ammunition from the rebel soldiers, or because the Government had withdrawn its troops, or because it had sent improvised troops of farmers and an unskilled general against the League. In short, prudently speaking, nothing should be expected from the armed resistance. In addition, he said, assuming the elections and assuming the best in them for the Cristeros, that is, that José Vasconcelos, or some other more favorable candidate was elected. Would the current Legislature declare that election valid?

In *conclusion*, it would be necessary to seek, from the President or from his successor, *the greatest possible freedom* and re-establishment of public worship and the public administration of the sacraments. There was a chance of a reconciliation, since the opinion of the necessity of a settlement had spread, not only among the liberals but also among the revolutionaries. For this rapprochement to take place, however, a fairly long period of relative tranquility was necessary, as could easily be seen, since if tempers were continually excited, animosities would fester and, far from coming closer, they would drift away, such that, if God did not remedy it, worse things would come for religion and society.

To achieve a peace agreement, a certain tranquility was necessary, which could only be achieved if the bishops and clergy refrained from helping the armed movement (which by the time they had already done), but appeared to be unconnected with it. It was not necessary to condemn the armed movement, it was only necessary to stand aside and also convince the League to cease its provocative propaganda. By publicly condemning the attacks and maintaining calm, everything could be solved. This opinion was endorsed in its entirety by Mgr. Leopoldo Ruiz, who a few days later endorsed Banegas' statements. Both were certain that to carry out the directives, it was essential for the bishops to be united in their approach before reaching a *modus vivendi* and that, in order to ensure the unity necessary for the Catholic restoration of Mexico, the presence of an Apostolic Delegate with full powers to lead and guide the bishops was absolutely necessary.

So much for the position of Archbishop Banegas, which, in practice, was the one that carried the day in subsequent events.

Returning to the negotiations, they were never held in public nor were they entirely transparent. When they became known through the press, they provoked enormous unease in some bishops, the League, and those who had taken up arms, as shown by the following paragraph where Mgr. Manríquez y Zárate wrote to the secretary of the Episcopal Subcommittee:

> The latest news in the press about the religious negotiations has filled me with anguish. I know that Archbishop Ruiz has gone to Rome precisely *to incline the Holy Father to a settlement of the religious question*, more favorable to our enemies than to the interests of the Church.... I also ask myself: Who has appointed Bishop Ruiz as the bishops' representative to the Vatican?[59]

However, the same newspapers listed Monsignors Ruiz y Flores and Fumasoni Biondi as the pope's "official" negotiators, in May 1929:

> The newspaper *Excélsior*...on May 14, 1929, published this cable: Washington, May 13.—The settlement of the religious question in Mexico during the summer of this year is judged to be very probable in Washington's diplomatic circles.... Orders from the Vatican are expected to arrive overnight for Archbishop Leopoldo Ruiz y Flores to return to Mexico City to confer with the provisional president, Emilio Portes Gil, and arrange a meeting between the pope's personal envoy and representatives of the Mexican government.... Morrow is determined that the negotiations will be brought to a successful conclusion and he has used the

---

[59] Rius Facius, *México Cristero*, 2:419, emphasis ours.

State Department's influence over the Mexican government to secure a compromise. Mgr. Fumasoni Biondi, apostolic delegate in the United States, may have been given the necessary instructions by the Vatican to allow the preparation of an agreement with the government of Portes Gil.[60]

Faced with such controversy, Ruiz y Flores was compelled to seek confirmation of his authority to take charge of the negotiations. To this end, on May 13, 1929, since he was still the president of the Episcopal Committee, he sent a short telegraph to some Mexican bishops: "Higher authority requests that you telegraph me if you vote in favor of accepting the conference agreement."[61] This amounted to a kind of moral pressure to be accepted as the supreme negotiator. Just three days later, on May 16, Mgr. Pedro Fumasoni Biondi arrived in Washington from Rome with the appointment of Mgr. Ruiz y Flores as apostolic delegate *ad referendum* (that is, provisionally and subject to others' agreement). According to Rius Facius, his mission was "solely to confer and inform the Holy See of the results of his efforts."[62] The die was cast: the bishops would seek a "lasting" peace on the pope's orders, influenced by the nuncio in the US, and pressured by Ambassador Morrow. But the protagonists, the great protagonists of the fray, were left out: they were the soldiers, the Cristeros who had left home, mother, father, family, estate, wealth.... *They counted for nothing,* and the negotiators of surrender did not even want to meet them,[63] as Ruiz y Flores said: "We decided not to receive anyone, not even the bishops, which caused grumbling and resentments."[64] The very harsh letter that General Gorostieta sent as a missive to the Mexican bishops at that time is quite understandable and must be quoted:

---

[60] Rius Facius, 2:476–77.
[61] Rius Facius, 2:477.
[62] Ibid.
[63] Heriberto Navarrete recounts (*Por Dios y por la Patria*, 250): "We arrived in Mexico. I spoke with Don Rafael Ceniceros y Villarreal, and with several high ranking members of the League. There was bewilderment, and rightly so. The ideas are very clear, but the situation, in particular, is too complex. I tried in various ways to make personal contact with His Excellency Ruiz y Flores, but I failed in my attempt. I was told that the Archbishop intended not to receive anyone to discuss the problem of the arrangements or anything connected with it, until the period of preparation of the negotiations had passed. I had to keep the original letters I brought because I couldn't even deliver Pedroza's personal message."
[64] Meyer, *La Cristiada*, 2:338.

254          The Cristero Counterrevolution

Since our struggle began, the national press, and even the
foreign press, has not ceased to deal periodically with possible
peace settlements between the so-called government and
some distinguished member of the Mexican Episcopate, to
end the religious problem. Whenever such news has appeared,
men in the struggle have felt a shiver of death invade them, a
thousand times worse than all the dangers they have decided
to face, worse, much worse than all the bitterness they have
had to endure. Every time the press tells us of a bishop who
could be a parliamentarian with Calles' regime, we feel it as
a slap in the face, all the more painful because it comes from
someone we could expect to give a consolation, a word of
encouragement in our struggle; encouragement and consolation that, with one honorable exception, we have received
from no one.... That news has always been like a bucket of
ice water poured over our warm enthusiasm.... Now that
those of us who lead in the field need moral support from
the governing bodies, especially the spiritual ones, the press
is once again spreading the rumor of possible talks between
the current President and Archbishop Ruiz y Flores....

I do not know what is true in this matter, but since the
National Guard is an institution interested in it, I want once
and for all, and through your worthy offices, to convey the
feelings of those of us who are fighting in the field so that it
reaches the knowledge of the Mexican Episcopate, and also
so that you may be aided in taking the necessary measures
to ensure that when it reaches Rome *we obtain from our Holy
Vicar a remedy for our ills. That remedy is none other than obtain-
ing the appointment of a nuncio or of a primate who comes to bring
an end to the existing chaos and who will unify the political-social
work of our bishops*, who are independent princes.

Those of us who struggle in the field believe that the
bishops, when entering into talks with the government, can
only [legitimately] present themselves *by approving the attitude
assumed certainly by more than four million Mexicans, and from
whose attitude the National Guard emerged, which for now has
more than twenty thousand armed men* and as many others
unarmed, who can surely be legally regarded as belligerents....

If the bishops, in dealing with the government, disapprove
of our attitude, if they do not take into account the National
Guard and try to solve the conflict regardless of our desires,
and without heeding the outcry of the enormous multitude
that has all its interests and ideals at stake in the struggle;
if our dead are forgotten, if our thousands of widows and
orphans are not taken into consideration, then *we will angrily*

*raise our voice and in a new message to the civilized world we
will reject such an attitude as unworthy and as treasonous, and
we will prove our assertion.*

I will personally bring charges against those who now
appear as possible mediators.... The bishops, who have been
far from the country for whatever reason, have lived these
years disconnected from national life, ignorant of the transfor-
mations that this period of bitter struggle has brought upon
the people, and therefore incapable of representing them in
an act of such importance.... *It is the people themselves who
need representation, it is the popular will that must be consulted,
it is the populace's feeling that must be taken into consideration:*
this very poor people of ours who are fighting in their own
country against a band of bastards who shield themselves
with a mountain of weapons of destruction and torture.

*It is not truly the bishops who can justly claim that represen-
tative role. If they had lived among the faithful, if they had felt
themselves united with their compatriots under the constant threat
of death for merely confessing their faith, if they had shared, like
good shepherds, the fate of their sheep, if they had even adopted
a firm, decisive, and forthright attitude in every case, by this time
they would truly be the most worthy representatives of our people.*
But this was not the case, because it should not have been
or because they did not want it to be so....

What we lack in material strength we do not ask of the
Episcopate, we will obtain it by our own efforts. *We do
ask the Episcopate for the moral strength* that would make us
unstoppable and that is in their hands to give to us, just by
unifying their principles and guiding our people to fulfill
a duty, advising them to *adopt a dignified and virile attitude
proper to Christians and not to slaves....*

I believe it is my duty to declare emphatically and categorically that the main problem that we, the leaders of this
movement, have had to face is not that of supplies. *The main
problem has been and continues to be to avoid the harmful and
fatal impact on the spirit of the people caused by the constant
actions of our bishops and the more direct and misguided actions
of some priests and clergy,* following the guidelines laid down
by their prelates. We would have had abundant supplies and
manpower if, instead of five states of the Republic, thirty or
more dioceses responded to the cry of death raised by the
fatherland. The tyrant's much vaunted power...would have
shattered into pieces at the first blow of a sledgehammer,
perhaps if it had been possible, for the first and only time
in the history of our national martyrdom, for the Princes of

our Church to agree simply to declare that: *Defense is lawful and, in some cases, obligatory....*

Let the bishops be patient, let them not despair, for the day will come when we can proudly call them together with our priests to come again among us to carry out their sacred mission, then indeed in a country of free people. *A whole army of the dead bids us to do so!*[65]

These are tremendous truths, spoken without mincing words. Gorostieta hit the nail on the head, in a letter written not with ink but with blood—blood that was spilled two weeks later in a confrontation that smelled of betrayal[66] and that honorably cost him his life, perhaps because he did not realize, as his lieutenant Navarrete said, that "in Mexico the bishops enjoy a quasi-infallibility among the great majority of believers."[67]

However, it was not Gorostieta alone who would cry foul. Once the settlements were finalized, the League went so far as to ask for the death of those who had betrayed the fighters. In an open letter to the prelates, readers were asked: "We beg the people who read this to pray an Our Father and a Hail Mary to the Heart of Christ the King so that the Holy Father may order the retirement of Messrs. Leopoldo Ruiz y Flores and Pascual Díaz y Barreto." In other leaflets the people were asked to obtain the liberation of the Mexican Church

---

[65] Enrique Gorostieta, "Carta a los prelados sobre los arreglos del 16 de Mayo de 1929," quoted in Meyer, *La Cristiada*, 1:316-18, emphasis ours. The letter is harshly criticized by Rius Facius, *México Cristero*, 2:458-61. Gorostieta's indignation was fierce (see Navarrete, *Por Dios y por la Patria*, 229). "Look, Major, I'm not going to argue with the priests, but I want you to understand our situation. If the bishops manage to end our movement, know that we will have missed the only opportunity we had in our hands to restore order and establish a regime of law in Mexico. It's not just that. It is possible that by a concession of the Government, which follows orders from the Americans, worship may be resumed. But it is naive to believe that opening the churches would resolve the problem of freedom in the country. There is no freedom of education, of the press, of worship, of election, of association, etc., etc. I am fighting to gain *all* freedoms! Property rights are systematically violated, justice is mocked, and we Mexicans are at the mercy of a group of bandits who get rich at the cost of the hard work of a large majority of honest people, and they mock every tradition, no matter how respectable. And when we already had a good beginning of impetus to throw that scoundrel out of power, a transitory, fallacious alliance with them is about to suffocate and render useless our effort. If this were not a monumental blunder, I would call it a swindle" (Navarrete, 230).
[66] Some pointed to Navarrete himself as the one who betrayed him, because the future Jesuit had escaped three similar ambushes. We have not found anything to support such a hypothesis.
[67] Navarrete, *Por Dios y por la Patria*, 168.

through the intercession of St. Jude Thaddeus, advocate of desperate cases, *for the departure or death of the prelates themselves.*[68] Indeed, as some said with the bravura of the Mexican rancher: "If the padres turn against us, we shoot the padres."[69]

The fighters had not been taken into account, not even when desperate pleas called for it, as was the case of Father Aristeo Pedroza. On June 11, 1929, he wrote in a letter to Ruiz y Flores: "Allow the people to continue the struggle and do not hand over an entire portion of your flock to a senseless slaughter. Remember that you declared three years ago that armed defense against Calles' tyranny was licit. Do not deliver your sheep to the executioner's blade."[70]

Many of the laity felt betrayed by the settlements, and the wound would not be easy to heal, especially when they saw confirmation that the settlements would never be respected by the government. A couple of years after the "peace," in 1932, a group wrote to Mgr. Ruiz y Flores:

> Is Your Excellency a representative of the Holy Father or of the tyranny dominant in our country?... Do the Mexican bishops not protest against the frequent murders of priests and Catholic faithful because His Holiness told them not to?... Does Your Excellency worry more about the attacks that the people justly direct at the tyrants than about the offenses that the tyrants commit against the Catholics, the Church, the Blessed Virgin, and Christ our Lord?... Has His Holiness ordered that Your Excellency and the Archbishop of Mexico become the most faithful defenders of the revolution and the prevailing tyranny, and not only prevent Mexican Catholics from attacking them but also try to force them to cooperate with them?... Have you received instructions from His Holiness that, when you report to the Holy Father on the Mexican situation, you should fail to be truthful? Has the Supreme Pontiff ordered some Mexican prelates to deny the sacraments to Mexican citizens who, by force of arms, defend their NATURAL RIGHTS and, instead, authorized the celebration of religious ceremonies in the homes of persecutors?... Why were the words spoken in 1926 in favor of armed defense "not valid for the present moment?"[71]

---

[68] Meyer, *La Cristiada*, 1:331–32.

[69] According to Navarrate (*Por Dios y por la Patria*, 231), he heard them from a Cristero.

[70] Meyer, *La Cristiada*, 2:338.

[71] Open letter to His Excellency the Apostolic Delegate D. L. Ruiz y Flores, signed José Gutiérrez, R. C. Ontiveros, M. de los Ríos. Recto and verso, undated (1932), AAA, quoted in Meyer, *La Cristiada*, 1:332–33. Capitals are in the original text.

The sorrow in the souls of the Cristeros after the settlements, believing their bishops, left the laity perplexed, even shedding tears of pain and helplessness. To obey the hierarchy against one's will, against one's conscience... To obey when one knew that they were probably being deceived... To obey, when they could have resisted...

With his heart in his hand, this is how one Cristero leader described the discharge of his troops after the accords and out of obedience to the clergy:

> Finally, on August 12, Fr. Encarnación Cabral convinced the leaders of Zacatecas to end their wait, because, "otherwise, the unfortunate news of bad Catholics will be spread and the bishops will be harmed by manifest rebellion." At the same time, Degollado's circular arrived ordering the discharge (and not the surrender) of the National Guard: "Did we sleep that night? I doubt it. I remember that in the early hours of the morning a voice whispered in my ear: "Don't be sorry, my friend, this is God's will. Christ the King no longer wants you to defend His cause..." And Acevedo explained to Captain Sebastián Arroyo:
>
> "But... Sir, even though it may seem like madness, our duty is stated in that piece of paper, we must obey and let Christ our King and the Virgin Mary of Guadalupe have this great sacrifice for the good of their cause and as reparation for the sins of the fatherland. We must be wary of any insubordination. There is nothing more to do."
>
> Doubt began to torture those hearts that were once strong and accustomed to suffering... The hope of being free or of dying for the cause of Christ had encouraged and sustained them in the struggle... Now... It was August 15, 1929. The last day to reach the Hacienda of San José de Sauceda...in front of General Anacleto López... A short time later he saw the troops that arrived immediately... *The women of the village were crying. "No, no, little brothers, what are you going to do, come and prostrate yourself before these unworthy men? No, the Blessed Virgin would not want that."* And they kept crying... I sent a sergeant to order dismounting. The sergeant ordered in a deep voice: "Get ready to dismount, dismount." And the movement was executed with such precision that it amazed me and even more so the soldiers, who expressed their astonishment at our progress.
>
> What followed was routine: men unsaddling horses, delivery of horses, receipt of safe-conducts, etc.
>
> An event of great significance took place on this day. López, grieving that those men had nothing to eat, bought a

bull that he had slaughtered and turned into half-kilo rations. But...there was no one to claim their ration. When they were ordered to pass through the place to pick it up, they all pretended not to hear, and withdrew with dignity, and then came into my presence, hat in hand, and said in a tone more or less veiled by emotion and with a fortitude that was clearly forced: "General, is there anything else you need?"

I couldn't respond to my men and just made a hand signal for them to go on their way...

With their blankets on their shoulders, those who had them, and as if it were a bunch of schoolchildren going out for recess, those soldiers, already hardened in pain and accustomed to the harsh laws of war, set off at a pace commensurate with their strength in the direction of their homes...

"It was the only day — said the Cristero leader Aurelio Acevedo — that *I wanted to die*. A day as beautiful as if I'd entered hell."[72]

Not only were the settlements not fulfilled, but rather than being a *modus vivendi* they ended up being a *modus moriendi*. This was so true that not even Ruiz y Flores himself would dare to call them "*arreglos*" (settlements) just two months later. The same prelate wrote in August 1929, "The settlements — if they can be called that — were those published by the press."[73] In these "settlements," as we saw at the beginning, "no mention, other than a slight journalist's conjecture, was made about the fate that the Cristeros would meet as a result of the infamous settlements."[74]

When reading what happened next, one can't help but wonder why. Were the bishops aware of what they were doing? Was the pope? The combatants kept asking themselves this question. And they had an answer. One of them, the future Father Heriberto Navarrete, declared, "The men at arms, as far as I could tell, were pushed into surrender by a political alliance (perhaps necessary, perhaps advantageous for the country — God knows). However, its authors obviously could not have been unaware that we were affected, of the impact of their attitude and decision."[75] The aforementioned Mgr. Lara y Torres went so far as to exclaim in perplexity:

---

[72] Meyer, *La Cristiada*, 1:327–28, emphasis ours.
[73] Meyer, *La Cristiada*, 2:372.
[74] Navarrete, *Por Dios y por la Patria*, 249.
[75] Navarrete, 256. There are even some among the supporters of the Cristeros who agree with the "arrangements." One of them, who cannot be branded as a

Does this mean that we have taken the wrong path? Why then did they rush into the suspension of worship and why did we sacrifice or allow so many people to be sacrificed? This is not the time for diplomacy. *It is better to let the ashes of our heroic Church be consumed than to sully it with an ineffective and disgraceful armistice.* And to think that in the meantime our children, in overwhelming numbers, proudly raise their heads and oppose the humiliation of the prelates! It is necessary that the two or three most radical of us that remain apply ourselves strongly and raise the banner of our brave Catholics so that they do not believe that the entire Episcopate is abandoning them.[76]

There were others who without hesitation began to speak of outright apostasy led by the Mexican episcopate. Meyer, who does not give unnecessary praise, says:

Most Cristeros had the appalling impression of living in a truly schismatic Church, convinced as they were that their bishops had knowingly lied to the pope. As of June 1929, what was impossible to accept in 1926 — the very thing that had caused the suspension of worship and then the war — was now acceptable? And they said, "I can't believe this. Is it possible that the bishops have broken their word?... *Why did the priests and the pope do this to us?*" the elderly still asked in 1969, with tears in their eyes, and distinguishing between God and his priests, preserving a faith that an educated man would lose for far less.[77]

---

communist or pro-government, Salvador Abascal, affirmed that "if the armed struggle continued, increasingly disadvantageous for the Cristeros... much less than the least freedom would be achieved. Therefore it was necessary and urgent at least to resume Divine Worship." Salvador Abascal, *Lázaro Cárdenas: presidente comunista* (Tradición, 1988), 36. "Every day many lives continued to be sacrificed, many more than would be lost later *despite the Settlements.* It is true that Gorostieta did not want to give in, and then Degollado Guízar, who would succeed him in the supreme command, but it is clear that they were very wrong, blinded by their own heroic spirit" (ibid., 42, italics in the original).
[76] Sáenz, *La nave y las tempestades*, 348. Mgr. Lara y Torres would be suspended by the Vatican. His statements continued to be politically incorrect.
[77] Meyer, *La Cristiada*, 1:351, emphasis ours. On the part of the priests, some were not far behind, as was the case of Fr. Agustín Gutiérrez, who published a book entitled *What Are We?* (1933) without ecclesiastical permission, which was therefore removed from circulation by order of the Archbishop of Guadalajara. In it, Father Gutierrez presents the case of a general apostasy by the episcopate and harshly criticizes Pope Pius XI on the matter of the Settlements. See Juan González Morfín, "Un libro incómodo: ¿Qué somos?," *Boletín Eclesiástico de la Diócesis de Guadalajara* 11 (2011).

Let us now go higher still—namely, to the difficult problem of the Roman attitude to the settlements, and to the question of papal responsibility.

## RESPONSIBLE PARTIES (3): ROME

*Alea iacta est*—the die is cast, Caesar would have said. The settlements ("if they can be called settlements") were made. At this point the historian cannot (must not) fail to ask himself what was the degree of responsibility that lay with the highest hierarch of the Church.[78]

If the testimonies of the Cristeros are to be believed, the vast majority thought they were obeying the pope when they laid down their arms before their adversaries. For context, it must be remembered that a little more than half a century earlier the dogma of *papal infallibility* had been declared, and it was not always well understood by some Catholics (even in our days, too, it must be said). This dogma maintains that Peter's successor cannot err when speaking as supreme pontiff and teacher of all Christians (not as a private teacher) in matters of faith or morals, when intending and making it clear he intends to teach a dogma binding on all. However, quite a few believed (and continue to believe) that the pope is infallible in all other areas, including that of political prudence, the realm of the contingent. We are not going to expand on this point, but simply say that for Catholic theology it is just as erroneous to think that the Supreme Pontiff is wrong when he teaches authoritatively on faith and morals as it is to think that he is never wrong when he speaks or acts in other areas.

It is on this historical basis that responses regarding responsibility for the settlements divide opinion in two directions: either the fault was that of the bishops who, exceeding their authority, arranged a misguided compromise—or the fault lies with Pius XI and his entourage.

The tragedy of the Cristeros was part of a series of decisions and positions aimed at peace, and more particularly, at dissolving the possible union between *Catholicism* and *nationalism*. To name just a few examples: the condemnation of Charles Maurras's Action Française (1926), the opposition in Poland to the nationalist movement led by Cardinal Adam Sapieha, the dismantling in Canada of Henri Bourassa's nationalist movement, and the support (at least initially) of the Spanish Republic of 1931.[79]

---

[78] For an updated version, see the work of Juan González Morfín, *El conflicto religioso en México y Pío XI* (Minos-Tercer Milenio, 2009).

[79] On this subject, see the book by Philippe Prévost, *La condamnation de l'Action*

Above, we have seen, albeit briefly, the role of the Mexican hierarchy. We will now try to analyze the Vatican's involvement in the settlements, offering our view of the facts at the end.

As we said, the Cristeros were *convinced that they were obeying the pope* by laying down their weapons. This is what General Degollado Guízar said, in a very harsh proclamation that became well-known after the "pacification":

> Long live Christ the King!
>
> Comrades in struggle:
>
> In a painful and tragic moment, when the undefeated organizer of the National Guard, Major General Enrique Gorostieta, fell heroically under the enemy's bullets, I had to receive from his hands the flag that he, with so much courage, had raised to lead us to victory. I resolutely accepted the position offered to me, though it was beyond my strength, but then I was very far from thinking that I would have to face the most serious of problems: that of the cessation of hostilities, that of the termination of the fighting. It is very likely that if I had known that such a decision had to be made by me, I would not have resolved to put myself in charge of the National Guard. But, thank God, I am a man of faith, and I have never shirked responsibilities when I have been burdened with positions or honors that I have neither sought nor desired. That is why, as soon as I learned from the press that His Excellency the Apostolic Delegate and Portes Gil had concluded a *sort of armistice* in the religious conflict, with complete resolve I confronted the conundrum in which that deed placed the Supreme Command of the National Guard, the solution of which was to lead me to a sacrifice perhaps more bitter than that of my own life. Immediately, I commissioned a person to investigate the state of the problem with those in charge. But perceiving that a solution was urgently needed and that it was essential for me to be close to where the negotiations were to take place, without hesitation of any kind, I went to the capital city, and there I worked, through trusted persons unrelated to the struggle, to bring about an end to the hostilities.
>
> In arriving at this resolution, I have adopted the considerations that the National League for the Defense of Religious Liberty adduces in its manifesto of July 12 of this year, declaring that the time has come for the military

---

*Française 1926–1939. Autopsie d'une crise politico-religieuse* (Libraire Canadienne, 2008), 690.

action to cease. But as a soldier, as a man taught by the hard experience of a relentless struggle that we have waged for nearly three years, I must invoke other reasons, which our compatriots must know, and which effectively support the resolution adopted.

Our resistance has been a fact whose magnitude cannot yet be understood by those who have not lived through it. In Mexico (say those who always take pleasure in disparaging us), in the last three years heroism has become commonplace. We know well, comrades, that although we have had to give repeated and constant proofs of bravery and tenacious perseverance to endure for a very long time bitter suffering, our conscience has been sustained not only by the courage and selflessness we combatants have shown each other, but, in a special way, by the cooperation that the inhabitants of the regions where we have fought have given us tirelessly and with boundless self-sacrifice and in an astonishing manner, thousands and thousands of people from many parts of the country. This effort, this help, this cooperation, partly explains the reason for our resistance against an enemy endowed with all kinds of supplies and sustained by the gold and power of the richest nation on earth. And this effort, this help, that cooperation, was given by people of all classes and conditions, but especially by the humble people, truly Catholic, who have always longed to enjoy the supernatural benefits that the priest bestows in the exercise of his ministry. The rigid application of a sectarian law sought to stifle consciences, and these Catholics stood proudly, longing for sacrifice, demanding what the Christian soul asks for with unspeakable anguish.

*His Holiness the Pope*, through His Excellency the Apostolic Delegate, has ordered for reasons we do not know, but which, *as Catholics, we abide by*, that without repealing the laws, worship should be resumed, and that the priests, placing themselves in a certain way under their protection, should begin to exercise his ministry publicly. At that moment, our situation, comrades, has changed.

The cooperation indispensable for the struggle, it is true, has not ceased, but it has suffered a severe setback, and the priest, on returning to the place where he exercised his ministry, on reoccupying his church, has been left standing before us in an extremely difficult and delicate position. Given the immediate action of our opponents, and knowing that our troops would also be nearby, it would be impossible for him to remain neutral in the conflict: if he were to condemn our actions, he would then be condemning the very best members of his flock and thus have to suffer untold difficulties for the exercise of his sacred duties. This would not bring him any more trust from our adversaries, except if he became a villainous betrayer of those who fought to win the freedom — although somewhat diminished — which he now enjoys. If, on the other hand, he were to declare himself in our favor, by that fact alone, in addition to seeing himself in grave danger of perishing as a victim of our enemies, he would be left with the impossibility of exercising his ministry among the non-combatant population. Hence that same peaceful population, which had formerly been our most effective support, was divided, wanting, on the one hand, the struggle to continue, and the other, that it should cease. From there, as an inevitable consequence, came division among those who, only a short time before, had been united in their support for us. From there, eventually, came denunciations, discords between people who profess the same faith and are inspired by the same ideals. Therefore, the most abundant and secure source of supplies was cut off.

Patriotism, the very love we profess for the holy cause for which we have fought relentlessly, demanded of us, although it tore our souls, to see that the war ceased at once. In fact, the initial arrangement agreed between His Excellency the Apostolic Delegate and Portes Gil has taken from us the noblest, the most holy thing, which was on our flag, from the moment the Church declared that, for the time being, it was resigned to what it had obtained, and that it hoped to arrive by other means to regain the freedoms it needs and to which it has a legitimate right. Consequently, the National Guard has assumed all responsibility for the conflict, but this responsibility cannot be attributable to it since last June 21st: the current situation has neither been created nor desired by it.

I am certain that some of my comrades, perhaps the most battle-hardened, will think that fear and self-interest have driven me to the decision I have made. I swear before God that they are mistaken if they think so: although I can neither disregard nor should I disregard the judgment of men, I declare that I adhere to the judgment of God, and before Him, I am sure that I have performed not only a praiseworthy deed, but a heroic one, something as bitter and painful as the sacrifice of something which is flesh of my flesh and bone of my bones.

We must, comrades, humbly accept the inevitable decrees of Providence: it is true that we have not achieved complete

victory, but as Christians, we have a much richer inner satisfaction for the soul: the fulfillment of duty and the offering to the Church and Christ of the most precious of our
sacrifices, seeing our ideals broken before the world, but
harboring, yes, by God!, the supernatural conviction, which
our faith maintains and nourishes, that in the end, Christ the
King will reign in Mexico, not halfway, but as an absolute
Sovereign, over souls.

As men, we also have another satisfaction that our opponents will never be able to take away from us: the National
Guard is disappearing, not defeated by our enemies, but in
reality, abandoned by those who should have been the first
to receive the precious fruits of their sacrifices and self-denial.

"Hail, Christ, those of us who, for you, go to humiliation,
exile, perhaps an inglorious death, victims of our enemies,
with the most fervent of our loves, we salute you, and, once
more, we acclaim you King of our fatherland!"

Long live Christ the King! Long live Our Lady of Guadalupe!

Mexico, August 1929.
God, Country, and Freedom
Jesús Degollado Guízar, Soldier of Christ the King[80]

"And without surrendering"—Rius Facius adds—"the Cristeros
abandoned the war, convinced that they were thereby fulfilling a
desire of his holiness Pius XI."[81]

It was Ruiz y Flores himself, one of the two bishops in charge
of the conciliation, who corroborated the quoted text, arguing that
not only did they act at the pope's request, but that the Mexican
faithful believed it to be so. This self-defense was not without reason
because there were many who, after the settlements, denounced the
two bishops for *betraying* the pope.[82] This was the case, for example,
with Father Leopoldo Gálvez, who opened fire in a letter to the
Mexican bishops:

> To the venerable and august His Holiness Pius XI, our com-
> mon Father, who has been badly informed about the religious
> situation in Mexico: we have suffered an outrageous scandal,
> nor has it yet ended or will it be ended. Prelates *acceptable to*

---

[80] Degollado Guízar, *Memorias*, 270–73, emphasis ours.
[81] Ruiz y Flores, *Lo que sé del conflicto religioso*, quoted in Rius Facius, *México Cristero*, 2:497.
[82] There was even talk of "Masonic plot" to kill the Cristero army, as a parish priest of Tapalpa said: see Meyer, *La Cristiada*, 1:335.

*Lucifer!* The evil lay... in not having taken into account at all
the country's ordinary priests and the poor and self-sacrificing
Catholic Mexican people. *They* [the prelates] *misinformed*
the Holy Father of our circumstances and future, surely. He
was always deceived, always tricked. I don't know how their
Excellencies could bear to do it. Prelates contracted to hand
over, without any consideration whatsoever, poor children
into the hands of godless executioners and oppressors, with
their hands tied... This act takes on greater and greater
significance, given the nobility, status, and sacred character
of those who participated in it. Because there is no doubt
about it: *the Catholic people and clergy of Mexico were betrayed.*
In the end, the episcopate robbed us of the dear hopes and
faith that we placed in them, so that the Church might be
enslaved. And since not all of them were man enough to take
up arms in the name of God, God humbled us until we were
forced to accept the yoke. Is it not *vile treason* and ingratitude
against that saddened and suffering people, to supposedly ally
themselves with their tyrannizers and executioners? For God's
sake, bishops, don't say it so obviously, no, for God's sake!

The Sunday bulletin of Morelia, dated May 16, 1926, however, published these words by Mgr. Ruiz: "Conscience does
not allow us to accept such conditions" and so we do not
sin by not submitting to "such conditions." But are we not
sinning *now*, by submitting to the same government? That is
my question. One thing cannot be at the same time bad and
good, as is the case here. Was it not the episcopate that one
day resolved quite rightly "not to yield an inch of ground and
not to enter into dishonorable transactions and to stand firm
until complete religious freedom is achieved?" And we see
precisely the opposite: the defenders were forced to surrender
to the government and renounce all the promises and oaths
they had made. If three years ago it was not just to submit,
why is it now? Not even the Catholic people of Mexico, nor
I, a simple priest, deserved to be sold as slaves.... What has
been granted, then, "for the good of the Mexican people" and
"the peace of the Church"? This is not acceptable.[83]

---

[83] Open letter from Father Leopoldo Gálvez (quoted in Meyer, *La Cristiada,*
1:339–41, emphasis ours). "While Rome removed those who could hinder its
policy, beginning with its most passionate servants, the ultramontanes, it defended
the supporters of its policy, who were to find themselves, later, after the failure
of the *modus vivendi*, victims of the attacks of the rabid ultramontanes. These
latter, rather than recognizing that the final decision had been Roman, and that
it was nothing more than logically crowning a policy that had been followed with

The first question that emerges from the documents is this: did the bishops have the authority to make the arrangement? The answer is affirmative. As we noted above: at the end of May 1929, Pius XI had declared Ruiz y Flores apostolic delegate with the aim of settling the painful issue. Ambassador Morrow, with whom he was to discuss matters, thought the same.[84]

But didn't the bishops overstep their boundaries? Did Ruiz y Flores perhaps go beyond his powers? We believe that he did not. Rome's idea was to end the conflict. The pope could have chosen other prelates for the task (there were many to choose from), but he chose the most conciliatory ones, those who had never been in favor of the Cristeros.[85]

Already at the beginning of 1926, three years before the "settlements," Mgr. Ruiz y Flores, being the Archbishop of Morelia, had accepted the de facto suspension of the anti-religion legislation with no more guarantee than the words of the local authorities, which had earned him praise from the Freemasons, as "a truly wise and holy bishop."[86]

The "betrayal" is, in our opinion and Meyer's,[87] one of the many misconceptions because, after the settlements, the myth of the betrayal of the two prelates was propagated. They were said to have deceived the pope about the nature of the settlements, forcing his hand through a real breach

---

tenacity for ten years, *preferred to believe that all the evil came from their personal enemies*, Bishop Ruiz y Flores and Bishop Pascual Díaz, whom *they accused of having deceived Rome*. Rome had, however, appointed Bishop Ruiz as apostolic delegate and Bishop Díaz as archbishop of Mexico and later as papal count." Meyer, *La Cristiada*, 2:346, emphasis ours.

[84] See Meyer, 2:339–40.

[85] The latest investigations since the opening of the Vatican archives are of the same opinion; see Alfonso Alcalá Alvarado, "Gestación y realización," 267.

[86] Spectator, *Los cristeros del volcán de Colima*, 1:69.

[87] The belief originated in the good faith of the Mexican people and from a certain fear of "criticizing" the prudential decisions of the Pope. Added to this, there is the letter from the Catholic leader Palomar y Vizcarra who almost forty years later wrote to Cardinal Tisserant: "When the institutional freedom of the Church was about to be achieved ... the conformist or defeatist tendency prevailed, thanks to the support of the U.S. government, and with the intervention of that same government which was a presence in the capital.... Mgr. Ruiz ... in the company of ... Mgr. Díaz ... pretended to celebrate with Portes Gil ... 'arrangements' without legal or canonical form of any kind, determining that worship would be resumed in accordance with the laws in force.... Even if one feels repugnance, one must remember that the Pope, the noble Pope, was the victim of a deception." Quoted in Meyer, *La Cristiada*, 1:333–34.

of trust.... An explanation had to be found for the papal decision to bring an end to the fighting, at the time when the Cristeros felt stronger than ever.[88]

The Cristeros laid down their arms, said Rius Facius, "convinced that they were thereby fulfilling the desire of His Holiness Pius XI."[89] They "obeyed, their hearts filled with sorrow, convinced that the pope had been deceived, and in the untimely death of the two negotiating archbishops some saw the punishment of heaven, others the effects of remorse."[90] Today (2016), when the Vatican Secret Archives for this period have been opened and classified in an orderly manner, Roman responsibility seems indisputable. As Stephen Andes points out, the Vatican's approach at the time was "pragmatic":

> Under Gasparri, one can see the fusion of the legal with the pragmatic.... A concordat should always be the goal between the Vatican and the [Mexican] state.... He understood that the Holy See and the apostolic nuncios would have to negotiate to achieve that goal, and sometimes that would mean that Rome would have to accept small treaties, that is, settlements or the *modus vivendi*, what was pragmatic.[91]

Among the enormous number of quotations that could be gleaned from the study of the Vatican Secret Archives, we will include here, by way of illustration, some that scholars in the field have brought to our attention:

> The challenges of the difficult negotiations of the Apostolic Delegate with the Mexican government were known and guided by Cardinals Pietro Gasparri and Eugenio Pacelli and by Mgr. Giuseppe Pizzardo, *under the supervision and authority of Pope Pius XI.*[92]

The Holy See was informed in detail of what was happening:

> On May 12 [1929] the situation reached a critical point and the U.S. embassy unexpectedly contacted Father John Burke

---

[88] Meyer, *La Cristiada*, 1:333-34. It was, apparently, Cardinal Boggiani, former Apostolic Delegate in Mexico, who spread the idea that the pope had been "deceived on the question of the arrangements in Mexico." Mutolo, *Gli "arreglos" tra l'episcopato e il governo*, 122.

[89] Ruiz y Flores, *Lo que sé del conflicto religioso*, quoted by Rius Facius, *México Cristero*, 2:497.

[90] Meyer, *La Cristiada*, 1:351.

[91] Stephen J. C. Andes, "El Vaticano y la identidad religiosa en el México posrevolucionario, 1920-1940," *Estudios* 95 (2010): 85-86.

[92] Alcalá Alvarado, "Los fondos del ASV sobre la reanudación de cultos," 392.

and Mgr. Leopoldo Ruiz y Flores, announcing the possibility of a meeting with Calles and Obregón. On May 17, this conference became a reality, and in a coded message dated May 18, the apostolic delegate of the United States, Mgr. Pietro Fumasoni Biondi, *asked the Vatican Secretary of State, Cardinal Pietro Gasparri*, for his authorization for Mgr. Ruiz to go to Rome once he returned from the United States. On May 21, Cardinal Gasparri indicated that if there was no progress, the visit of Ruiz and Flores would not be necessary and that the report of the United States delegate would suffice.[93]

Even those who were delegates for the negotiations in a subsidiary capacity followed the express directives of the pope, as was the case of Fr. Burke. When recounting one of his interviews with Ambassador Morrow, he wrote:

> Again I pressed the point that a conference with the priests [and Calles] could result in detailed negotiations .... Assuming that all this was accomplished, the action of the priests would have to receive *the approval of the Holy See*; this would now be a matter for the Church in Mexico and *such action would be determined by none other than the head of the institutional Church, the Holy Father.*[94]

The same results emerged from the negotiations of Fr. Burke himself with Calles:

> Father Burke, Morrow's guest, *with pontifical authority*, was going to meet with President Calles to settle the religion question.[95] [The interview had to be suspended due to leaks to the press, so] *the Holy See, fully informed of the situation*, sent a telegram via Secretary of State Pietro Gasparri to the apostolic delegate of the United States, both to deny

---

[93] Message from Cardinal Gasparri, Vatican Secretary of State, to the Apostolic Delegate of the United States, Fumasoni-Biondi, May 21, 1928. ASV, Affari Ecclesiatica Straordinari, México, periodo IV-11, Pos. 521, fasc. 228 (we follow here the excellent work in the consultation of the ASV of Yves Bernardo Roger Solis Nicot, "El fin de la intransigencia de los obispos y arzobispos mexicanos" en *Caminhos*, Programa de Pós-Graduação Stricto Sensu em Ciências da Religião (PUC, Goiâs), January-June 2015, vol. 13, no. 1, p. 123.

[94] Second interview between John Burke and Dwight Morrow, Sevilla Biltmore, Havana, Cuba, January 18, 1928 at 3:30. ASV, Affari Ecclesiatica Straordinari, México, periodo IV-11, Pos. 521, fasc. 228 (Solis Nicot, 115).

[95] Record of Fr. Burke's trip and interview with President Calles. Plea to Report No. 760-b of the Apostolic Delegate Sent to Rome on May 10, 1928. ASV, Affari Ecclesiatica Straordinari, México, periodo IV-11, Pos 521, fasc. 228 (Solis Nicot, 116).

that John Burke was sent by the Holy See and to assure the
Mexican bishops that *no decision of the pope would be made
without first consulting them.*[96]

In other words, Rome was always in charge of the settlements and
decided what to do and what not to do.

Fumasoni Biondi...was in charge of religious affairs in
Mexico. The apostolic delegate then replied that no door
should be closed to achieve this end and affirmed that *the
Holy Father was eager to bring about a solution to the conflict in
a peaceful manner* and that his heart was with the Mexican
people and that every opportunity should be seized to find
a way that would allow the bishops to return with dignity.[97]

Shortly after the "settlements," Ruiz y Flores, as we said, had to
defend himself against accusations by saying that

no Catholic can condemn what His Holiness Pius XI
approved.... Once the pope has decided that a path of a
compromise should be followed, as far as conscience permits,
it is not licit for any Catholic to rebel and set himself up as
a judge of the Supreme Authority: because obedience to the
Supreme Pontiff is not limited to dogmas but extends to all
disciplinary and administrative matters.... I myself loyally
sent to the Holy See reports from various prelates and priests
during the years of the conflict to this effect, and I know
of the cables that various groups sent to the Holy Father,
asking him not to give in on anything, not to trust certain
people, and not to allow himself to be deceived. Moreover,
I have not failed to communicate to the Holy See faithful
copies of the letters, articles, and pamphlets that, in any way,
have criticized the settlements. But those who held to this
opinion had to be asked to submit to the pope's final decision
once he had made it.... From the moment the pope made
his decision, no Catholic, priest, or bishop is permitted to
publicly censure what has been agreed upon or to denigrate
before the faithful those who in any way represented the
pope. The door is open for them to send to the Holy Father

---

[96] Telegram of May 5, 1928 from Cardinal Gasparri to the Apostolic Delegate
of the United States, Monsignor Fumasoni Biondi. ASV, Affari Ecclesiatica
Straordinari, México, periodo IV-II, Pos 521, fasc. 228 (Solis Nicot, 117).
[97] Report on Fr. Burke's trip and interview with President Calles. Plea to Report
No. 760-b of the Apostolic Delegate sent to Rome on May 10, 1928. ASV,
Affari Ecclesiatica Straordinari, México, periodo IV-II, Pos 521, fasc. 228 (Solis
Nicot, 119).

any accusations and complaints that may contribute to the scandal and discord that has been caused in recent days, a year and some months after the settlements.[98]

Ruiz y Flores had full powers to act on behalf of Rome — so much so that the great agent of the settlements, Morrow, when drafting the *memorandum* that was to be signed by both parties, was surprised that it was sent to Rome before the signing to corroborate that what had been agreed was best. The response to the telegraph message came on July 20, 1929. According to Meyer:

1) The pope wanted a peaceful and secular solution;

2) complete amnesty for bishops, priests, and faithful;

3) restitution of property, churches, houses of the priests and of the bishops and seminaries;

4) unrestricted relations between the Vatican and the Mexican Church.[99]

*Roma locuta, causa finita*, as the saying goes. But the government did not respect the terms of the agreement.

With the passage of time, Rius Facius, more than eighty years after the Cristiada, did not speak of *treason* but rather of the government *taking advantage* of the bishops who had papal faculties. In an interview, the great historian of the ACJM said:

Journalist: *In spite of the years that have passed, do you think that there was a "betrayal" on the part of the ecclesiastical hierarchy in having signed the settlements of June 1929?*

R.F.: "Betrayal" is too strong a word to describe what happened. In reality, it was a different view of the conflict. Seen sixty or seventy years later, we see that it was not the bishops who took advantage of the situation, but the politicians who realized that the cause was already lost...

Journalist: *Like whom?*

R.F.: Like Emilio Portes Gil, and all those others. When they saw that Vasconcelos had stirred up discontent, it was not convenient for them to continue this conflict because a new movement led by Vasconcelos might be relaunched, and it would have ended the regime. Portes Gil, Calles, and all of them saw that very clearly. So with great malice they

---

[98] Mutolo, *Gli "arreglos" tra l'episcopato e il governo*, 130–31.
[99] Meyer, *La Cristiada*, 2:339.

were able to deceive the bishops with clever trickery; they were of course already very upset, because after three years of Mass not being said or ministry exercised, vocations had been lost, influence had been lost, money had been lost, and all that had to be restored: that there was a rift between one part of the Episcopate and another, that is clear. This represented an opportunity for the revolutionary politicians led by Dwight Morrow, U.S. ambassador to Mexico.[100]

To support our thesis about papal responsibility, the episode of March 16, 1927, comes to mind: on the morning of that day, two individuals sent by Álvaro Obregón appeared at the episcopal palace in Mexico City and proposed to Mgr. Ruiz an *extra legem* arrangement, that is, outside Roman jurisdiction. The proposal was that the clergy should resume public worship and that, in a few months, the Constitution would be reformed. Ruiz left the following words in the Curia Archive:

> We did not for a moment depart from our course of action, making him see that the suspension of worship was not only due to the decree but to the legislation in general and its aim of subjugating the Church and that we could not give partial or total, definitive or provisional settlements without the approval of the Holy See.[101]

After that and a feeble attempt to "fix" matters behind the scenes and behind the back of the Holy See, Miguel de la Mora, writing to González y Valencia, told him that Mgr. Ruiz had received a warning from the Vatican.

THE FUNDAMENTAL BASIS WAS THAT THE BISHOPS COULD NOT RESOLVE ANYTHING AND THAT EVERYTHING, ABSO-LUTELY EVERYTHING, WOULD BE SUBJECT TO THE DECI-SIONS OF THE HOLY SEE AND THAT BEFORE ANYTHING COULD BE CONSIDERED RESOLVED, THE HOLY SEE WOULD HAVE TO BE CONSULTED.[102]

---

[100] *Un hombre con historia. Charla sin café con Rius Facius*. Interview by Luis Humberto Espinosa Díaz, no date (2005–2006?), at http://cristeros.uag.mx/public_charla.htm.

[101] Letter from Mgr. Leopoldo Ruiz y Flores to Mgr. Pascual Díaz, 16-III-1927, in Archivo de la Curia del Arzobispado de México, Correspondencia Pascual Díaz 1926–1936, drawer 191, 3, 9, no. 2, 1928, Document 5, quoted by González Morfín, *Murieron por sus creencias*, 94, and by Mutolo, *Gli "arreglos" tra l'episcopato e il governo*, 73.

[102] See Archivos Misioneros Josefinos Roma, en *Fuentes inéditas,* doc. 75, in Mutolo, *Gli "arreglos" tra l'episcopato e il governo*, 73; capitals in the original.

As Archbishop Manríquez said:

> We must not forget that in the end we are simply in the hands of God and in those of the pope: Mgr. Ruiz is nothing more than the pope's mere instrument, who will have to carry out his orders and adjust all his actions to the Supreme Pontiff, who will have the last word."[103]

We believe that responsibility for prudential action should be assigned to the main cause. From the start, Rome had given instructions to Mgr. Ruiz y Flores to solve the conflict once and for all. For further evidence, in a message from August 1926, and just as the first uprisings were beginning, Cardinal Gasparri, the Vatican Secretary of State, had been informed of a possible premature settlement, to which he replied by telegram to Ruiz y Flores: "Newspapers announce settlements that do not comply with the instructions given by the Holy See. We await information."[104] Whatever was done, the Holy See was always behind it, as Meyer harshly states:

> This peace, good or bad, was made by Rome, willed by Rome, for pastoral reasons set forth in *Acerba animi*, and because the Vatican believed in the possibility of the *modus vivendi* .... The decision was Roman and so was the level of information .... Rome therefore wanted peace, and believed in the possibility of winning in the long term by making short-term concessions. The entire Vatican policy of Pius XI, at that time, went in this direction and was based on centuries of experience of conflict with the modern state.... The papacy was willing to make very great concessions, and this is the reason why it accepted a *modus vivendi* incomprehensible to Mexican Catholics.... Under these conditions, Bishop Ruiz y Flores and Bishop Díaz cannot be accused of having deceived the pope, of having forced his hand, of having signed settlements that exceeded the pontifical instructions. If they can be accused of having sinned out of excess optimism, even out of rashness, in accepting verbal guarantees, the Vatican incurs the same guilt, since it prepared them to accept everything their conscience allowed them to accept.[105]

---

[103] Mutolo, 98. While we can understand that, as Mutolo says, "no one can prove with a public and authentic document that the Pope approved the *arreglos*," the appointment of the delegates who approved it came from the pontiff.

[104] Meyer, *La Cristiada*, 2:296.

[105] Meyer, 2:376–77, emphasis ours. Almost fifty years later, Meyer held the same view, as he told us by correspondence: "La responsabilidad es vaticana." Letter in our files, dated August 3, 2011. A year later, Pius XI would regret what

Mgr. Manríquez y Zárate, the bishop of Huejutla exiled in Rome, in an interview only two months after the "settlements," wrote to Miguel Palomar y Vizcarra on October 24, 1929:

> Today, the feast of St. Raphael the Archangel, I was received by His Holiness the Pope, and with such demonstrations of affection, which were truly a consolation to my spirit, embittered by so many setbacks... One thing must be borne in mind by all Mexicans: that if His Holiness has made any mistake in this practical matter, *it is due to many, many individuals* determined to impose their point of view triumphantly against all odds... and the pope, overcome by his immense charity towards Mexico, wanted to test the suggestion of these scheming gentlemen in the hope of thereby obtaining the freedom of the Mexican Church.[106]

After this interview, Manríquez y Zárate wrote a speech that he intended to give in Louvain and that reached the hands of the Mexicans. The controversial speech said in its key sections:

> The Mexican people... know perfectly well that the pope is the vicar of Christ on earth.... The enemies of Jesus Christ were extremely cunning in going to Rome to break through the impenetrable wall of armed resistance. They saw that the people would surrender their arms at the first sign from the Vicar of Jesus Christ, and so *they cunningly and skillfully approached certain prelates excessively inclined to conciliation,* making a thousand offers for the future, but not really taking away a single comma of the monstrous laws that mortally wound the Holy Church and strangle the most sacred rights of man and society.[107]

In short, Calles had won, at least momentarily: "The Cristeros laid down their arms because the Church wanted it that way—and the government had not relented on anything."[108] Just two years earlier, the Holy Father had said that "resuming worship without the modification of the laws would unleash a scandal on the part of the clergy and the faithful" but that, in any case, "the Holy See reserved the last word."[109]

---

happened, as Cardinal Boggiani recounted in 1930: "I myself have seen the Pope [Pius XI] weep when discussing the question of the Settlements in Mexico" (López Beltrán, *La persecución religiosa en México*, 517).

[106] Rius Facius, *México Cristero*, 2:521, emphasis ours.

[107] Quoted by Rius Facius, 2:523, emphasis ours. The speech was harshly criticized by Mgr. Ruiz, who labeled it as implausible coming from a Mexican prelate.

[108] Meyer, *La Cristiada*, 2:374.

[109] Mutolo, *Gli "arreglos" tra l'episcopato e il governo*, 77.

After the settlements, in September 1932 and in view of the possibility of a new armed uprising, the pontiff declared in the encyclical *Acerba animi* that it had been convenient to end the conflict that had ravaged Mexico for three long years. Pius XI himself explained that promises might not be kept:

> Although unfortunately, *we knew from experience that there was no certainty in trusting such promises, we nevertheless judged that we must consider whether it was appropriate or not to publicly continue the suspension of the sacred religious rites*.... It was certainly not Our intention either to approve the Mexican laws against Religion, nor to retract the claims made against them in such a way that we decreed that there was no longer any reason to resist and oppose these laws with all possible means. It was only this: that since the rulers of the Republic implied that they espoused different purposes, this seemed to require that those methods of resistance which might be injurious to the Christian people should be suspended, and that others should be adopted which were actually more opportune.[110]

Pius XI himself took responsibility for the decision, which, as Meyer says, "quickly forced him to prohibit any talk, writing, or thinking about the settlements."[111]

---

[110] Pius XI, *Acerba animi*, 29-XI-1932, AAS 24 (1932), 323–24.

[111] Meyer, *La Cristiada*, 1:330. Pius XI had given the order to avoid "any discussion of the *modus vivendi*, which does not mean the slavery of the Church to the government; on the contrary, the Church maintains all its protests." Carreño, *El Arzobispo de México Excmo. D. Pascual Díaz y el conflicto religioso*, 399.

*Those responsible for the Settlements (left to right): Fr. Edmund Walsh,
Archbishop Leopoldo Ruiz y Flores, Ambassador Miguel Cruchaga,
Bishop Pascual Díaz, Sergio Moret*

*Cristeros shot in cold blood in Zacatecas on July 6, 1929,
after the Settlements and the surrender of their weapons*

# CONCLUSION

T O CONTEMPLATE MEXICO OF THE 1920S is to be confronted with two worldviews or two cities, according to the old Augustinian sense: that of a secular state opposed to religion, and that of Christianity, that is, the philosophy of the Gospel (in the words of Leo XIII), which endeavored to permeate the social order. These images, which later become harsh reality, are at the heart of the subject we have studied, but they are not born of spontaneous generation or the force of fate; they are the product of a historical confrontation that arose, without going too far back in time, in the origins of the new Mexico, as we have seen.

Liberals against conservatives, socialists against Catholics, Catholic nationalists against corporatist fascists. Three pairings that, although not entirely interchangeable, always have a common appearance, an analogous way of being. Thus, since the times of uprising and independence, Catholic and Hispanic Mexico has been opposed to liberal and non-religious (and irreligious) Mexico: the worldview of an Iturbide against that of a Morelos, and that of an Alamán against that of a Juárez, or, in other words, on the one hand clinging to Spain and what it had done as "a novel achievement," in the words of José María Pemán, or, on the other, seeking new horizons under the liberal wing and the material patronage of its neighbors to the north. Mexico, "so far from God and so close to the United States" as Porfirio Díaz put it, would not emerge unscathed from this internal struggle.

With the Constitution of 1917, the famous Constitution of Querétaro, the liberal and most radical wing began an ascent towards socialism that culminated in a persecution of the Catholic Church as never seen before in Latin America. It was a struggle for power that sought to subjugate Christianity to the point of making it official in order to bring it under its control. Its protagonists were the nation's president, Plutarco Elías Calles, and the ordinary Catholic, Mexican people, whose Faith was threatened. Peaceful confrontation, first, and armed struggle later, would turn the central strip of Mexico into a cultural, religious, and military battlefield that would last for three years.

On the part of the ecclesiastical hierarchy, however, the answer was not always clear or consistent. There were undoubtedly commendable and even heroic cases, but the hierarchy was not the principal protagonist of the conflict. The great participant was the Mexican people, the Catholic laity who would not renounce their beliefs, their churches, and their independence. From it would emerge the cry for blood, as Joaquín Blanco Gil said. Faced with the passivity or defeatism of some prelates, it was simple peasants, women, men of the various professions, even children who would fight for freedom — for "all freedoms," as General Gorostieta said. To this end, the organization of Catholic groups that arose at the beginning of the century was crucial. The ACJM, The League, People's Union, Women's Brigades, etc., were in the trenches safeguarding the unity of the faithful. Everything served to defend their interests: boycotts, petitions through the collection of signatures, demonstrations and, when there was no other way, the bayonet. It was, as Calles said, "the Congress or arms," and when peaceful and legal approaches were not heeded, Mexican Catholicism was almost forced to oppose evil militantly.

It was the Catholic population that rose up and fought for the Church without depending on its hierarchy. The combatants (there were fifty thousand who took up arms, not counting those who acted as logistical support), although in a very few cases they took chaplains to the battlefield, depended only on Christian morality, as we have seen. As for dogmatics, they followed the teachings of the Church, but with regard to prudential decision-making, they knew that they were in the realm of the contingent and that, therefore, they had to fight following the dictates of their conscience. However, they did not neglect moral consultations at the critical moment of rising up in arms. The Church's history and the opinion of serious moral theologians gave them reasoning on behalf of defending with arms what words could not achieve.

Morale in times of war did not change the soul of the Cristero who, by all accounts, not only fought well but conducted a war worthy of medieval times, and without forgetting that it was brothers who faced each other: brothers, children of the same God.

The war was waged at the expense of the Mexican people, and it was only at the express request of the Church's hierarchy that, in the end, without surrendering, Catholic laity would yield to their opponents. It is a period that is difficult to recount and even more difficult to understand. Why did those who had thrown themselves into war almost automatically then lay down their arms at the request of the Church? Why did the pope and the Mexican bishops ask for this supreme sacrifice of intelligence and will? The questions exceed the scope of our work and, for a man who does not understand what the Faith of the Mexican people is, perhaps there is no solution. The answer, it seems to us, is to be sought in the gesture that Hernán Cortés made five hundred years ago when, kneeling in front of twelve ragged Franciscans, he showed the Aztecs that the priest is above the conqueror and that the life of the Faith is above earthly life. Devotion to the pope and his ministers made Mexico a country of blood-drenched altars, as Bishop Francis C. Kelley wrote, making the *modus vivendi* or "settlements" a *modus moriendi*.

How was this peace reached? We believe there were two main factors. We must take into account, both in the development of the conflict and in its formal culmination, the political and economic interests of the United States, the great promoter and author of the "settlements." And while the Roman *divide et impera* may have served for a time, permanent revolutionary unrest was not the intention of the "brothers from the north," nor of the Morgan Bank, nor of Freemasonry, as we saw. Peace was needed. In addition, however, there were religious motives. The hierarchy feared that prolonged suspension of worship would undermine the evangelizing work of several centuries. Without confession, without preaching, and without Christian morality, Mexico would be lost, they said. In addition, Vatican policy at the time saw a definite danger in the growing independence of the Catholic laity from the hierarchy, which further motivated the decision to end the conflict.

The Mexican people, then, after offering their lives, now gave the offering of their will through a prudential, contingent, and political decision. There were two paths to follow: either disobey those who had not expressly condemned the use of arms, or religiously obey the ineluctable decrees of Providence with consent of the will. It was the second path that was chosen by that great nation, by that marvelous people who, as Degollado Guízar said, had the "supernatural conviction that, in the end, Christ the King would reign in Mexico."

# CHRONOLOGY OF
# IMPORTANT EVENTS
# (1911–1937)

**1911**
May 21    *Treaty of Ciudad Juárez*: Porfirio Díaz agrees to leave the country.

November 6    Francisco I. Madero assumes the Presidency of Mexico.

**1913**
February 19    After a coup d'état against Francisco I. Madero, Victoriano Huerta assumes the presidency of Mexico. Three days later, Madero is murdered.

**1914**
July 15    Huerta resigns presidency.

**1915**
October 19    The United States recognizes the Carranza government.

**1917**
February 5    The new Constitution is promulgated in Querétaro.

April 26    Collective Pastoral of the Mexican Episcopate denouncing the anti-Church laws of the Constitution.

**1920**
May 21    Carranza assassinated.

June 1    General Adolfo de la Huerta declared Interim President.

December 1    Álvaro Obregón assumes presidency (until November 30, 1924).

**1923**
January 12    Obregón decrees the expulsion of the Apostolic Delegate.

December 7    The "Delahuertista" rebellion led by Adolfo de la Huerta begins.

**1924**
March 10    Once the rebellion is put down, Adolfo de la Huerta flees the country.

December 1    Plutarco E. Calles assumes presidency (until November 30, 1928).

**1925**
February 21    Attempted schism by the "Mexican Catholic Apostolic Church."

March 14    The National League for the Defense of Religious Liberty is founded.

**1926**

January        Calles urges all legislatures to enforce Article 130 of
               the Constitution. In addition, extraordinary powers are
               granted to modify the Penal Code.

February 2     Pope Pius XI issues the Apostolic Letter *Paterna Sane*,
               to the Mexican episcopate, in which he addresses the
               prevailing persecution. The letter calls on the Mexican
               people to pray and take action.

February 4     The Archbishop of Mexico José Mora y del Río declares
               that the demands remain for reform of the Constitution.

March          All remaining foreign nationals serving as priests are expelled.

July 2         Publication of the "Calles Law," approved on June 14.

July 14        The *League* initiates an economic boycott to put pressure
               on the government.

July 25        In a collective Pastoral letter, Mexican bishops suspend
               all acts of public worship once the Calles Law comes
               into effect.

August 1       The Calles Law comes into force and, therefore, acts of
               worship involving a sacred minister are suspended.

August 22      Armed uprisings in the state of Zacatecas and, immediately
               after, in Jalisco, Michoacán, and Guanajuato.

September      The Chamber of Representatives rejects three petitions
               to revoke the Calles Law, one of them with more than
               two million signatures.

November 18    Pope Pius XI in his encyclical *Iniquis afflictisque* denounces
               the sad condition into which Mexican Catholics had
               been placed.

December       The *League* calls for armed defense.

**1927**

January        In response to the League's call, uprisings increase.

July           General Enrique Gorostieta Velarde is hired by the *League*
               to organize the groups of insurgents.

**1928**

July 1         Obregón is re-elected President. He takes office on
               December 1.

July 17        General Obregón is assassinated by José León Toral.

September 9    Another petition with two million signatures is presented
               to the Chamber of Representatives to reconsider the
               Calles Law.

December 1     Emilio Portes Gil replaces Calles in the Presidency. The
               self-proclaimed "Supreme Leader of the Revolution,"
               Calles becomes de facto ruler during the "Maximato"
               period, decisively influencing the destiny of the country.

**1929**

*March 3*    Led by generals of the Obregón group, a rebellion breaks out in which a large part of the army participates.

*April 10*    The government of Portes Gil defeats the "Escobarista" rebellion, led by General Gonzalo Escobar.

*April*    Religious persecution intensifies. Hundreds of Catholics are interned at the prison in Islas Marías.

*June 5*    Bishops Leopoldo Ruiz y Flores and Pascual Díaz travel to Mexico, seeking an agreement with the government on a *modus vivendi to* allow the resumption of worship.

*June 21*    The agreement between the government and the hierarchy, known as "settlements," are made public.

**1932**

*September 2*    President Pascual Ortiz Rubio resigns.

*September 3*    Abelardo L. Rodríguez replaces President Ortiz Rubio.

*September 29*    Pope Pius XI publishes his encyclical *Acerba animi*, lamenting the government's failure to honor the *modus vivendi*.

**1934**

*December 1*    Lázaro Cárdenas assumes presidency until November 1940.

**1935**

*April 1*    Following a proclamation by General Lauro Rocha to resume armed defense, the second Cristero uprising began. "La Segunda" had little success.

**1936**

*April 9*    General Calles leaves for exile, thus ending the "Maximato."

**1937**

*March 28*    Pope XI publishes his third encyclical on the condition of the Church in Mexico: *Firmissimam constantiam*.

# BIBLIOGRAPHY

## 1. CLASSIC AND RENOWNED WORKS

Acevedo, Aurelio, ed. *David I–VIII*. Estudios y Publicaciones Económicas y Sociales. First edition facsimile. No publisher, 2000.

Cardoso, Joaquín. *Los mártires mexicanos. El martirologio católico de nuestros días*. Buena Prensa, 1958.

Carreño, Alberto María. *El Arzobispo de México Exmo. Sr. D. Pascual Díaz y el conflicto religioso*. Victoria, 1943².

Degollado Guízar, Jesús. *Memorias de Jesús Degollado Guízar, último general en jefe del Ejército Cristero*. JUS, 1957.

González Navarro, Moisés. *Masones y Cristeros en Jalisco*. El colegio de México, 2000.

Meyer, Jean. *La Cristiada a la distancia*. Siglo veintiuno editores, 2004.

———. *La Cristiada*. Three volumes. Siglo veintiuno editores, 1974.

Navarrete, Heriberto. *Los cristeros eran así*. JUS, 1968.

———. *Por Dios y por la Patria. Memorias de mi participación en la Defensa de la Libertad de Conciencia y Culto, durante la Persecución Religiosa en México de 1926 a 1929*. Tradición, 1980.

Olivera Sedano, Alicia. *Aspectos del conflicto religioso de 1926 a 1929, Sus antecedentes y sus consecuencias*. SEP-Cien de México, 1987.

Reguer, Consuelo. *Dios y mi derecho*. Four volumes. JUS, 1997.

Rius Facius, Antonio. *La juventud católica y la Revolución Mejicana*. JUS, 1963.

———. *México cristero*. Two volumes. APC, 2002.

———. *Un joven sin historia*. Editorial Tradición, 1973.

## 2. SECONDARY WORKS

Belgodere, Francisco and Guillermo M. Havers. *Obispos mexicanos del siglo XX*. Libros Católicos, 1994.

Blanco Ribera, Carlos. *Mi contribución a la Epopeya Cristera*. APC, 2002.

García Gutiérrez, Jesús. *La lucha de Estado contra la Iglesia*. Tradición, 1979.

González Flores, Anacleto. *El plebiscito de los mártires*. ACJM, 1961.

González Morfín, Juan. *El conflicto religioso en México y Pío XI*. Minos Tercer Milenio, 2009.

———. *La guerra cristera y su licitud moral*. Porrúa y Universidad Panamericana, 2009.

González, Fernando M. *Matar y morir por Cristo Rey. Aspectos de la cristiada*. UNAM, 2011.

Gutierrez Gutiérrez, José G. *Mis recuerdos de la Guerra Cristera*. Guadalajara [no publisher], 1975.

Hernández, Silviano. *En la ruta de los mártires cristeros*. APC, 2006.

Kelley, Francis Clement. *México. El País de los Altares Ensangrentados*. Folia universitaria, 2003.

Lara y Torres, Leopoldo. *Documentos para la Historia de la persecución religiosa en México.* JUS, 1954.
López Beltrán, Lauro. *La persecución religiosa en México.* Tradición, 1991.
Mauri, Tiberiano M. *Derramaron su sangre por Cristo.* Ediciones Xaverianas, 1998.
Meyer, Jean. *La cruzada por México. Los católicos de Estados Unidos y la cuestión religiosa en México.* Tusquets, 2008.
———. *La Cristiada* [in images]. FCE-Clío, 2007.
———. *Las naciones frente al conflicto religioso en México.* Tusquets, 2010.
Meyer, Jean, Enrique Krauze, and Cayetano Reyes. *Historia de la Revolución Mexicana 1924-1928, Estado y sociedad en Calles.* El Colegio de México, 2002.
Mutolo, Andrea. *Gli "arreglos" tra l'episcopato e il governo nel conflitto religioso del Messico (21 giugno 1929). Come risultano dagli archivi messicani.* Editrice Pontificia Università Gregoriana, 2003.
Olimón Nolasco, Manuel. *Paz a medias, El modus vivendi entre la Iglesia y el Estado y su crisis (1929-1931).* IMDOSOC, 2008.
Ortega, Margarito. *Un párroco. Semblanza biográfica del Siervo de Dios, Sr. Cura Cristóbal Magallanes.* Guadalajara [no publisher], 1966.
Parsons, Wilfrid. *Mexican Martyrdom.* TAN Books, 1987.
Pereyra, Carlos. *México Falsificado.* Two volumes. Folia universitaria, 2003.
Spectator. *Los Cristeros del Volcán de Colima.* JUS, 1961.
Valdés Sánchez, Ramiro. *Testamento Espiritual de los Beatos Mártires Mexicanos, Sacerdotes Diocesanos de Guadalajara.* Comisión Diocesana de Causas de Canonización [Guadalajara], 1999.
Valdés Sánchez, Ramiro and Guillermo M. Havers. *Tuyo es el Reino.* Libros Católicos, 1992.

3. RELATED WORKS
Abascal, Salvador. *Mis recuerdos. Sinarquismo y Colonia María Auxiliadora.* Tradición, 1980.
Aguilar Camín, Héctor and Lorenzo Meyer. *A la sombra de la Revolución Mexicana.* Cal y Arena, 19904.
Alamán, Lucas. *Disertaciones.* Three volumes. JUS, 1969.
———. *Historia de México.* Three volumes. JUS, 1990.
Ball, Ann. *¡Viva Cristo Rey! Beato Miguel Agustín Pro Juarez, SJ.* New Hope Publications, 2003.
Barquín y Ruiz, Andrés. *José de Jesús Manríquez y Zárate, gran defensor de la Iglesia.* Red-Mex, 1942.
———. *José María González y Valencia, Arzobispo de Durango.* JUS, 1967.
Blanco Gil, Joaquín. *El clamor de la sangre.* Rex-Mex, 1947.
Bravo Ugarte, José. *Compendio de Historia de México, hasta 1964.* JUS, 1968.
Bulnes, Francisco. *Los grandes problemas de México.* Editorial Nacional, 1952.
Camacho Mercado, Eduardo. *Reforma eclesial y catolicismo social en Totatiche y el Cañón de Bolaños (1876-1926).* CIESAS, 2012.

Cárdenas Noriega, Joaquín. *Reflexiones y Consideraciones sobre la Historia de México.* Folia universitaria, 2003.

Cardoso, Joaquín. *Los mártires mexicanos. El martirologio católico de nuestros días.* Buena Prensa, 1958.

Castillo Murillo, David B. *La extrema derecha del conservadurismo mexicano: El caso de Salvador Abascal y Salvador Borrego.* Universidad Autónoma Metropolitana, 2012.

De la Peña, Luis J. *La legislación mexicana en relación con la Iglesia.* Universidad de Navarra, 1965.

De Maistre, Joseph. *Consideraciones sobre Francia.* Dictio, 1980.

Díaz Araujo, Enrique. *La Epopeya Cristera,* IVE Press, 2013.

Disandro, Carlos. *Las fuentes de la cultura.* La hostería volante, 1965.

Dragón, Antonio. *El Padre Pro.* Editorial Vasca, 1934.

Dumont, Jean. *El amanecer de los derechos del hombre: la controversia de Valladolid.* Encuentro, 1997.

Estrada, Antonio. *Rescoldo. Los últimos recuerdos.* JUS, 1988.

Fábregas Puig, Andrés. *La formación histórica de una región: Los Altos de Jalisco.* Ciesas, 1986.

Gibaja y Patrón, Antonio. *Revoluciones sociales de México.* Three volumes. Tradición, 1973.

González Fernández, Fidel. "Los 28 mártires mexicanos." *Ecclesia* 15 (2001): 7–122.

———. *Sangre y corazón de un pueblo. Historia de la persecución anticatólica en México y sus mártires.* Two volumes. Arzobispado de Guadalajara, 2008.

González Morfín, Juan. *El conflicto religioso en México y Pío XI.* Minos Tercer Milenio, 2009.

Gram, Jorge. *La Guerra Sintética.* APC, 2003.

Hernández Quesada, Alfredo. *A salto de mata. Voces de la Cristiada.* Secretaría de Cultura Gobierno del Estado de Jalisco, 1999.

Hernández, Silviano. *El Catorce. La muerte de Victoriano Ramírez.* APC, 2005.

Krauze, Enrique. *Álvaro Obregón.* FCE, 1987.

———. *Plutarco E. Calles, Reformador desde el origen.* FCE, 1987.

Lara Martínez, José Manuel. *Jesús Méndez Montoya. Primer beato michoacano.* Morelia [no publisher], 1997.

López Ortega, Juan Antonio, ed. *Las naciones extranjeras y la persecución religiosa.* No publisher, 1944.

López Ramos, Juan Arturo. *Oaxaca: cuna y destino de la Civilización Americana.* Fundación Cultural Fernández Pichardo, 2010.

Meyer, Jean. *El conflicto religioso en Oaxaca 1926-1929.* CIDE, 2005.

Moctezuma, Aquiles. *El conflicto religioso de 1926, sus orígenes, su desarrollo, su solución.* No publisher, 1929.

Munguía, Clemente de Jesús. *En Defensa de la Soberanía. Derechos y libertades de la Iglesia.* Tradición, 1973.

Navarrete, Félix and Eduardo Pallares, eds. *La persecución religiosa en México desde el punto de vista jurídico.* No publisher, no date.

Peón, Cristóbal. "La situación religiosa en México y su legalidad." *Razón y Fe* 27 (1927): 285–300.

Pereña Vicente, Luciano, ed. *Teoría de la guerra en Francisco Suárez*. Volume 2. CSIC, 1954.

Pereyra, Carlos. *Breve Historia de América*. Zig-Zag, 19462.

Portes Gil, Emilio. *Autobiografía de la Revolución Mexicana*. Instituto Mexicano de Cultura, 1964.

Prévost, Philippe. *La condamnation de l'Action Française 1926–1939. Autopsie d'une crise politico-religieuse*. Libraire Canadienne, 2008.

Ramírez Torres, Rafael. *Miguel Agustín Pro*. Tradición, 1976.

Reynoso de Alba, Soledad. *La Actuación de la Mujer en la Cristiada*. APC, 2005.

Rivero del Val, Luis. *Entre las patas de los caballos*. JUS, 1953.

Romano Gómez, Miguel. *Titanes de la Evangelización*. Arquidiócesis de Guadalajara, 2012.

Sáenz, Alfredo. *Anacleto González Flores y la Epopeya Cristera*. APC, 2002.

———. *La ascensión y la marcha*. Gladius, 1999.

———. *La nave y las tempestades. La gesta de los cristeros*. Gladius, 2012.

Sandoval Godoy, Luis. *San Cristóbal Magallanes*. Guadalajara [no publisher], 2000.

Schlarman, Joseph H. L. *México tierra de volcanes*. Porrúa, 1973.

Silva de Castro, Emilio. *La Virgen María de Guadalupe Reina de México y Emperatriz de las Américas*. APC, 2003.

Valdés Sánchez, Agustín. *La Cristiada en Villa Guerrero y los pueblos de la comarca*. Guadalajara [no publisher], 1997.

Vasconcelos, José. *Breve Historia de México*. Cultura Hispánica, 1952.

Ycaza Tigerino, Julio. *Las formas políticas. México o la revolución*. Folia universitaria, 2003.

Zalce y Rodríguez, Luis. *Apuntes para la historia de la masonería en México*. Talleres Tipográficos de la Penitenciaría del Distrito Federal, 1950.


## 4. ARTICLES

Alcalá Alvarado, Alfonso. "Los fondos del ASV sobre la reanudación de cultos en la República Mexicana (1929)." *Crónicas*, Anuario de Historia de la Iglesia 16 (2007): 391–93.

Andes, Stephen J. C. "El Vaticano y la identidad religiosa en el México posrevolucionario, 1920–1940." *Estudios* 95 (2010): 65–97.

Espinosa Díaz, Luis Humberto. "Un hombre con historia. Charla sin café con Antonio Rius Facius." Interview. http://cristeros.uag.mx/public_charla.htm.

Frahm, Sara A. "La Cruz y el compás, compromiso y conflicto." *Secuencia* 22 (1992): 67–102.

García Dávalos, Luis A. "Jean Meyer, *La Cruzada por México. Los católicos de Estados Unidos y la cuestión religiosa en México*, Tusquets/Océano, 2008." Review, in *Estudios de Historia Moderna y Contemporánea de México* 26 (2008): 283–84.

González Morfín, Juan. "El Archivo Secreto Vaticano: una ventana a la historia de México." *Boletín Eclesiástico de la Diócesis de Guadalajara* 10 (2011).
———. "*L'Osservatore Romano* y la guerra cristera." *Boletín Eclesiástico de la Diócesis de Guadalajara* 7 (2011).
———. "Un libro incómodo: ¿Qué somos?" *Boletín Eclesiástico de la Diócesis de Guadalajara* 11 (2011): 29–42.
González Schmal, Raúl. "Un amparo insólito y el conflicto religioso de 1926–1927." In *El juicio de Amparo a 160 años de la primera sentencia*, ed. Manuel González Oropeza and Eduardo Ferrer Mac-Gregor, 559–86. Universidad Nacional Autónoma de México, 2011.
Gutiérrez Hernández, Alejandro. "La masonería mexicana, un caso de estudio pendiente para la historia." In *El anticlericalismo en México*, ed. Franco Savarino and Andrea Mutolo, 227–51. Cámara de Diputados-Porrúa-ITESM, 2008.
Meyer, Jean. "El anticlerical revolucionario. 1910–1940. Un ensayo de empatía histórica." In *Las formas y las políticas del dominio agrario*, ed. Ricardo Ávila Palafox, Carlos Martínez Assad, Jean Meyer, 284–304. Universidad de Guadalajara, 1992.
Olivera Ravasi, Javier. "Desobediencia debida: Justificación doctrinal del alzamiento cristero. México (1926–1929)." *Revista de Historia americana y argentina* 47 (2012).
Ortoll, Servando. "John Burke, la insurrección cristera y las relaciones diplomáticas entre México y los Estados Unidos." *Nueva Antropología* 45 (1994): 9–20.
Solis Nicot, Yves Bernardo Roger. "El fin de la intransigencia de los obispos y arzobispos mexicanos." *Caminhos*, Programa de Pós-Graduação Stricto Sensu em Ciências da Religião (PUC, Goiâs), January/June 2015, vol. 13, no. 1.
Urías Horcasitas, Beatriz. "De moral y regeneración: el programa de 'ingeniería social' posrevolucionario a través de las revistas masónicas, 1939–1945." *Cuicuilco* 32 (2004): 87–119.
Vázquez Samadeni, María Eugenia. "Masonería, papeles públicos y cultura política en el primer México independiente, 1821–1828." *Estudios de Historia Moderna y Contemporánea de México* 28 (2009): 35–83.

## 5. MAGISTERIUM, FATHERS, AND DOCTORS

Augustine of Hippo. *Contra Faustum*. Edited by Joseph Zycha. *Corpus Scriptorum Ecclesiasticorum Latinorum* (CSEL) 25. Vienna, 1866.
———. *De civitate Dei*. Edited by Bernardus Dombart and Alphonsus Kalb. *Corpus Christianorum, Series Latina* 47 and 48. Brepols, 2014.
———. *Epistulae*. Edited by Alois Goldbacher. CSEL 44, 57, and 58. Vienna, 1911.
———. *In Heptateuchum*. Edited by Ioannes Fraipont. CCSL Brepols, 1953, 33, 1–465.
Ambrose of Milan. *De officiis*. Edited by Mauritius Testard. CCSL 15. Brepols, 1953.

Athanasius of Alexandria. *Epist. ad Amunem monachum.* In *Patrologia Graeca,*
ed. J. P. Migne. Volume 26. Paris, 1857–1866.

Benedict XV. *De gravi mexicanae Ecclesiae statu.* 25-X-1914. AAS 6 (1914), 543.

———. *Exploratum vobis.* 15-VI-1917. AAS 9 (1917), 376–77.

Gasparri, Pietro. *Litterae circulares de rei catholicae iniqua condicione in Mexico.*
AAS 18 (1929), 326–27.

Leo XIII, *Diuturnum illud.* 29-6-1881. AAS 14 (1881), 3–14.

———. *Libertas praestantissimum.* 20-6-1888. AAS 20 (1887), 593–613.

———. *Quod apostolici muneris.* 28-12-1878. AAS 11 (1878), 372–79.

Pius XI. *Acerba animi.* 29-XI-1932, AAS 24 (1932), 323–24.

———. *Chirographus ad Card. Pompili.* Holy Saturday, 1926. AAS 18 (1926),
181–82.

———. *Consistorial allocution.* 14-XII-1925. AAS 17 (1925), 642.

———. *Firmissimam constantiam.* 28-3-1937. AAS (1937), 189–211.

———. *Iniquis afflictisque.* 18-XI-1926. AAS 18 (1926), 465–77.

———. *Paterna sane.* 2-11-1926. AAS 18 (1926), 175.

Thomas Aquinas. *Summa theologiae.* BAC, 1956.

# INDEX OF NAMES

www.ingramcontent.com/pod-product-compliance
Lightning Source LLC
Chambersburg PA
CBHW030909120626
46554CB00001B/74